# NEXT-GENERATION LEADERSHIP

Also by William J. Byron, S.J.


*Toward Stewardship* (1975)

*The Causes of World Hunger* (editor, 1982)

*Quadrangle Considerations* (1989)

*Take Your Diploma and Run!* (1992)

*Take Courage: Psalms of Support and Encouragement* (editor, 1995)

*Finding Work without Losing Heart* (1995)

*The 365 Days of Christmas* (1996)

*Answers from Within* (1998; revised 2010)

*Jesuit Saturdays* (2000; revised 2008)

*The Power of Principles* (2006)

*A Book of Quiet Prayer* (2006)

*Words at the Wedding* (2007)

*Individuarian Observations* (2007)

*Praying with and for Others* (2008)

*Faith-Based Reflections on American Life* (2010)

# NEXT-GENERATION LEADERSHIP

## A TOOLKIT FOR THOSE IN THEIR TEENS, TWENTIES, AND THIRTIES, WHO WANT TO BE SUCCESSFUL LEADERS

WILLIAM J. BYRON, S.J.

WITH AN APPENDIX
ON
PRINCIPLES OF IGNATIAN LEADERSHIP

University of Scranton Press
Scranton and London

**Library of Congress Cataloging-in-Publication Data**


Byron, William J., 1927-
  Next-generation leadership : a toolkit for those in their teens, twenties,
and thirties, who want to be successful leaders / William J. Byron ; with an
appendix on principles of Ignatian leadership.
      p. cm.
  Includes bibliographical references (p.        ) and index.
  ISBN 978-1-58966-221-6 (pbk.)
  1. Leadership--Religious aspects--Catholic Church. 2.  Catholic youth--
Religious life.  I. Title.
  BX2355.B97 2010
  253.088'282--dc22

                                                                  2010019150

Distribution:
University of Scranton Press
Chicago Distribution Center
11030 S. Langley
Chicago, IL  60628

**PRINTED IN THE UNITED STATES OF AMERICA**

FOR


RAY BAUMHART AND JIM CARTER


JESUIT LEADERS

WITH WHOM I'VE WORKED

IN FAITH AND FRIENDSHIP

OVER THE YEARS

# CONTENTS

# INTRODUCTION

This is a book for young men and women on their way to the top in organizational life—in business and the not-for-profit sector.

I wish I could say it *provides* them with the tools they will need, but at the very least, it identifies the tools and suggests how they might be acquired. This book presumes our future leaders to be persons of integrity, honesty, intelligence, creativity, and character. It is obvious, therefore, that some major assumptions underlie this project. First, I assume that there are young men and women out there who are willing to read a book like this and who want to prepare themselves for leadership responsibilities. Second, I'm assuming that family, education, religion, and other forces are at work in the lives of the young, shaping their intellects, cultivating their characters, and encouraging growth of integrity, honesty, and creativity in their developing minds. Both are untested assumptions.

Moreover, I am giving future leaders, especially teens and twenty-somethings, an opportunity to set themselves apart right now by committing themselves to serious interaction with the printed page. Lead by reading is good advice. It is never too late to begin to cultivate a habit of lifelong reading. All ages can join the forward march to leadership right here. But only if they commit themselves to taking time to read.

My publisher is betting that the numbers are there, even in this age of youthful migration away from page and print toward image and sound. That bet may be hedged by the hope that parents will see in these pages information (and inspiration) that their offspring need. The elders will, it is hoped, buy the book and put it in the hands of the young for their as-yet-unrecognized good.

Moreover, others in mid-life and mid-career, who harbor a deep-down desire to lead, will find hope in this book along with advice on how to convert the assets they know they have into leadership opportunities they

1

know they can handle. The word is getting around that leaders are grown, not manufactured or mass-produced. Their obedience to the laws of growth renders them open to and appreciative of words in print. They will come to see that with this book in hand, leadership becomes something within reach.

But by specifically including the teens, I'm taking note of a vestibule category that comes before those we tend to call *young adults*. That term refers to those who are in their twenties and thirties. Technically speaking, however, there is in the "young adult" category a spread—over two generations. One is called "Generation X" (born between 1964 and 1981); the other is known as "Generation Y" or the "Millennials" (born between 1982 and 2001, the first year of the new millennium). Without getting lost in the X-Y-Z demographic designations, this book looks to these young adults as the "next generation" of leaders in organizational life. It also serves to remind them that a whole new world of opportunity is opening up for them. They can take it or leave it. It is an opportunity to serve by leading, to find meaning and purpose in their lives.

My personal belief in the basic goodness of the young people I've met in recent years in high school, college, and university classrooms; summer camps, the world of part-time jobs, and volunteer community service; as well as in early stages of adult careers, convince me that young adults of integrity and honesty are there in ample supply. I'm also convinced that their intellects and characters are on growth paths that will lead to abundant potential for effective leadership.

We, as a society, just have to make sure that we talk to them about leadership and encourage them to keep developing their potential for it. Leadership is both art and craft. It has to be seen before it can be practiced; it has to be understood before it can be applied. The challenge this book hopes to meet is getting the attention of potential leaders, the young and not so young, but especially the young.

For their part, all that the young have to do is put themselves in front of the mirror, look themselves in the eye, smile, and say, "We are the leaders we've been waiting for," and then get to work on building a better world. But if they are going to lead effectively, they will need the toolkit that is described in these pages.

So I write first about the nature of leadership, then follow with a chapter that offers introductions to a few great leaders. Chapter three is devoted to a discussion of attitudes associated with effective leadership. Without a positive attitude (that's why a smile is important when you look at yourself in the mirror!) grounded in hope, effective leadership simply will not happen.

I assemble the tools of leadership in chapters four through eleven. The tools can be classified under the following labels: listen, speak, write, read, think, remember, decide, and effect change. Each of these tools must be carefully designed (that will be the objective of the chapters whose titles bear those labels) and then entrusted to willing hands that, I hope, will prove to be, in later years, the hands of an ethical leader and a servant leader. The final two chapters—one on the ethical leader, the other on the servant leader—offer the reader a picture of the leader he or she can become. Those who read the whole book carefully and internalize the principles it describes will be ready to lead.

No one can predict the future, but anyone can choose the future he or she would like to have. And those who take the contents of this book with them into an unknown future, will be equipped to face the challenges that await those who want to make a leadership mark in any area of organizational life—all the way to the top.

Be forewarned, however, that "the top" is not the uppermost point on a pyramid. As both the imagery and advice to be found in subsequent chapters will suggest, there is a servant dimension in contemporary organizational leadership. Those who understand it will lead effectively. Those who ignore it will not succeed. *Primus inter pares* (first among equals) is one way of thinking about it; co-laboration (working together) is another. Think horizontally, not vertically, when you locate yourself in the organization. And always think about what you can do to help.

It is not by accident that servant leadership is the theme of the final chapter of this book. Nor is the appendix to this book an idle afterthought. It is a compendium of Ignatian principles of leadership, the secrets, if you will, of the leadership style of Ignatius of Loyola, founder of the Jesuit Order, who committed his life to One who "did not come to be served, but to serve and to give his life as a ransom for many" (Matthew 20:28). The countercultural principles of Ignatian leadership can be keys to success in the secular city. This book will show the way.

Now that we've set our course, let's get going!

# CHAPTER ONE

## LEADERSHIP EXPLAINED

The purpose of this book is to make young potential leaders better equipped to meet the challenges of leadership. Not every challenge admits of a technical solution; some require emotional adjustments, culture shifts, and realignment of values. This book can remind older readers—middle managers, would-be leaders, and parental "elders" who will be putting it in the hands of their offspring—of the intricacies, nuances, tools, and strategies of effective leadership.

John W. Gardner was President Lyndon B. Johnson's secretary of health, education, and welfare—heading a federal agency now known as the Department of Health and Human Services. Mr. Gardner held many leadership positions; he was founder of Common Cause, co-founder of Independent Sector, and president of the Carnegie Corporation and the Carnegie Foundation for the Advancement of Teaching. His excellent book, *On Leadership*, makes a point about young people with leadership potential that I want to highlight here because I'm writing primarily for the young.

Most of the leadership literature ignores the young. Yet there is nowhere else to look, but to the young, if this nation is going to find future leaders for the world of work—for business, government, education, military, and social service. Listen, then, to Mr. Gardner: "Young potential leaders who have been schooled to believe that all elements of a problem are rational and technical, reducible to words and numbers, are ill-equipped to move into an area [leadership] where intuition and empathy are powerful aids to problem solving."[1]

John Gardner's mention of "intuition and empathy" points to a possible bridge between the young, with their undeveloped intuitive and empathetic potential, and their more experienced elders, whose potential for

5

intuition and capacity for empathy will have increased with the passage of the years. (It would thrill me to know that older and younger readers might choose to work their separate ways through this book together!)

The world moves on words and numbers, without which no one can lead, but progress—forward motion—depends not only on rational and technical prowess, but also on intuitive decision making and empathetic persuasion on the part of leaders who can connect with those who are willing to be led. Intuition, which fosters adaptation, goes beyond technical expertise; it draws on life experience and wisdom on the way to making business decisions. Most young people don't have enough life experience to put intuition to work for them in business.

Neither intuition nor empathy is part of the secondary school or collegiate curriculum. The young will not find them there, if they are still in school, and will not remember having seen them there if they are now out of school and in the world of work. Nor can these qualities be acquired in requisite amounts through extracurricular leadership experiences that are available as part of formal education.

But they can be acquired, and this book will help show the way.

## DESCRIPTIONS AND DEFINITIONS

I have a pen-and-pencil holder on my desk (I regret to say I can't remember what organization gave it to me as a token of appreciation for a speech I gave) that has "The Essence of Leadership" inscribed on its side. Here are the words: "A true leader has the confidence to stand alone, the courage to make tough decisions, and the compassion to listen to the needs of others. He or she does not set out to be a leader, but becomes one by the quality of his or her actions and the integrity of his or her intent. In the end, leaders are much like eagles . . . they don't flock, you find them one at a time." There is no attribution of authorship. My effort to track that down led me to the Website of the Institute of Association Management (iofam@secretariat.org.uk) where slides, including one with the quotation I cited, were posted from a presentation by Susan Sarfati, the association's president and CEO. The quotation was accompanied by a statement that the source of these wise words is anonymous.

Let the reader note in that inscription, as this exploration begins, the words *confidence, courage, decisions, listen, actions, integrity,* and *intent*. I plant them here as seeds; you will find them sprouting up throughout this book.

Leadership can more easily be described than defined. It is worth the effort, however, here at the outset, to attempt a definition. I'll approach that task by rounding up a few definitions that are already in print, and then I'll offer a working definition of my own.

You'll need a working definition to accompany you not only through all the chapters of this book, but through the rest of your life! You're welcome, of course, to fashion one of your own that might improve on the definitions you'll find in this chapter. You decide.

Here's how James MacGregor Burns defines the term in his land-mark book *Leadership*:[2] "Leadership is leaders inducing followers to act for certain goals that represent the values and the motivations—the wants and needs, the aspirations and expectations—of both leaders and followers. And the genius of leadership lies in the manner in which leaders see and act on their own and their followers' values and motivations."

You can all too easily dismiss this definition as stating the obvious: leadership is what leaders do. But that would be a mistake. Note that the verb *inducing*, as employed by Burns, is essential to leadership. And not to be ignored is the importance of "the values and motivations" not only of the leader but of those whom the leader would lead. Their motivations and values must be known; they have to be heard. Listening is an important leadership tool. Both old and young have to learn to listen.

Burns focuses on the "manner in which leaders see and act." That says something about the importance of leadership style. And his definition includes "the aspirations and expectations" of both the leader and those to be led. This suggests that no understanding of leadership will be complete without inclusion of the notion of hope. Moreover, mention is made of the "wants and needs" of those to be led. It would not be wise to think of lead-ership without due regard for the self-interested wants and needs of those who might be persuaded to follow.

John Gardner writes, "Leadership is the process of persuasion or example by which an individual (or leadership team) induces a group to pursue objectives held by the leader or shared by the leader and his or her followers."[3] Notice that he uses the verb *induces*. Gardner is at pains to point out that leadership must not be confused with status ("In large cor-porations and government agencies, the top-ranking person may simply be bureaucrat number one."), or with power ("Many people with power are without leadership gifts. Their power derives from money, or from the ca-pacity to inflict harm, or from control of some piece of institutional ma-chinery, or from access to the media."), or with official authority ("[This] is simply legitimized power. Meter maids have it; the person who audits your tax return has it.").[4] Gardner also includes the notion of "example" in his definition of leadership.

I'm a bit partial to John Gardner because he touched my life directly and had significant influence on my career. I was chatting with him one afternoon in 1987 while we were waiting for the mayor of Washington to arrive for the dedication of a residential facility Stanford University had just opened to serve as a Washington, D.C. campus. Mr. Gardner inquired, "How long have you been in your present position (I was then president of The Catholic University of America)." "Five years," I replied. "Well," he said, "you ought to be planning your next move." "But, John, I'll be turning 60 in just a couple of months." "Right," he said, "you ought to be laying out a plan for the next twenty years." The next twenty?

He, fifteen years my senior, had done just that. He was then a professor of public service in the Stanford Business School. I reflected on his suggestion and decided to cap my CUA presidency at ten years, five years later when I would turn 65, and then move across town to Georgetown, where the dean of the business school had generously invited me to teach and offered me the title of "Distinguished Professor of the Practice of Ethics." I began teaching an applied business ethics course called "Social Responsibilities of Business" to Georgetown seniors, and I waded into a new career of writing and research. I had been influenced by Mr. Gardner's leadership.

## WILLINGLY

James M. Kouzes and Barry Z. Posner define a leader simply as "someone whose direction you would willingly follow."[5] Those several words say a lot. *Direction* implies that the leader has some standing, some authority; *willingly* implies that the leader's ideas are both intelligent and appealing, otherwise the follower would remain unmoved. In the preface to their book *The Leadership Challenge*, Kouzes and Posner use several words to explain their purpose in writing that can serve as a working definition of leadership. They say they want to help readers develop their capacity "to guide others to places they have never been before."[6] That opens up the idea of leadership to exploration and discovery; it introduces the possibility of risk.

Decades ago, Dwight D. Eisenhower explained that, "the President does not lead by hitting people over the head. Any damn fool can do that.

. . . Leadership is by persuasion, education, and patience. It is long, slow, tough work."[7] Eisenhower often said that leadership is "the art of getting someone else to do something you want done because he wants to do it."

Laura D'Andrea Tyson, who chaired the Council of Economic Advisers in the Clinton Administration, defines leadership as "recognizing a crisis, addressing its challenges, and setting new directions while remaining true to one's values."[8] Note the presence of crisis in the context of leadership. That notion will receive closer attention later in this book.

The term *centered leadership* was coined by researchers at the world-famous management consulting firm McKinsey & Company. It emerged from a research project conducted by McKinsey with a view to helping women become more confident and effective business leaders. The centered leadership model is "about having a well of physical, intellectual, emotional, and spiritual strength that drives personal achievement and, in turn, inspires others to follow."[9] There are five interrelated dimensions to this model: "*meaning*, or finding your strengths and putting them to work in the service of an inspiring purpose; *managing energy*, or knowing where your energy comes from, where it goes, and what you can do to manage it; *positive framing*, or adopting a more constructive way to view your world, expand your horizons, and gain the resilience to move ahead even when bad things happen; *connecting*, or identifying who can help you grow, building stronger relationships, and increasing your sense of belonging; and *engaging*, or finding your voice, becoming self-reliant and confident by accepting opportunities and the inherent risks they bring, and collaborating with others.[10]

Make a note of those five—especially if you are a female on the way to assuming leadership responsibilities—and tailor them to fit your personality and style: (1) finding your strength; (2) managing your energy; (3) adopting a positive view of the world; (4) connecting within a network; and (5) finding your self-reliant voice as you engage in collaborative efforts. Women are enrolling in business schools in increasing numbers, but business schools, as I observe them, are insufficiently attentive to the task of training women for leadership.

Chris Lowney speaks of "whole-person leadership" in his book comparing the "best practices" that were initiated in the sixteenth century by Ignatius of Loyola, founder of the Jesuit order, with the management practices in place today in the secular business world.[11] Lowery writes the following:

What often passes for leadership today is a shallow substitution of technique for substance. Jesuits eschewed a flashy leadership style to focus instead on engendering four unique values that created leadership substance: (1) self-awareness, (2) ingenuity, (3) love, (4) heroism. In other words, Jesuits equipped their recruits to succeed by molding them into leaders who (1) understood their strengths, weaknesses, values, and worldview; (2) confidently innovated and adapted to embrace a changing world; (3) engaged others with a positive, loving attitude; and (4) energized themselves and others through heroic ambitions. Moreover, Jesuits trained every recruit to lead, convinced that all leadership begins with self-leadership.[12]

As a Jesuit, I can easily relate to the quartet of qualities that Lowney selects to both describe and define leadership in the Jesuit tradition. Elements from that tradition will find their way into these pages, particularly into chapter ten where the reader is introduced to the very unfamiliar style of Jesuit decision making.

Another very helpful way of defining, or at least describing leadership comes from Robert Greenleaf—"going out ahead to show the way."[13] There is an echo here of the biblical description of leadership found in Exodus (13:21) where God led the Israelites out of Egypt: "The Lord preceded them, in the daytime by means of a column of cloud to show them the way, and at night by means of a column of fire to give them light."

The notion of showing others the way, whether from biblical or secular authors, can serve as a reminder that all of us are leaders, at least we can be, if we lift our heads a bit above the crowd and show others how to achieve a result that they may not previously have recognized as being within their reach. Robert Greenleaf further describes leaders as "bearers of responsibility," and sprinkles that notion throughout a chapter on leadership education in his famous book *Servant Leadership*.[14]

Let me dwell for a moment on the often expressed notion that we are all leaders. To a certain and not unimportant extent, this is true. The expression provides a necessary corrective to the command-and-control, somebody-has-to-be-in-charge understanding of leadership. But if everyone is in charge, can we clearly identify a locus of leadership? Can we locate the decision point? Will we know when and where to move? In any given situation—whether it be a crisis or just a good time for change—if everyone is a leader, is leadership in fact there? It can be; but where?

In my view, the way out of this thicket lies in a distinction between taking charge and exerting influence. The term *influencer* is unfamiliar, perhaps misleading, and surely awkward. The term *leader* is so much more familiar, easier on the ear, and smoother on the tongue. Let me suggest, therefore, that you think of the leader as an influencer who has been shaped by countless other influences and influencers. Together, leader and led constitute *a rising tide of influence* or *a prevailing influential wind* because of which change occurs, progress happens. Leaders do indeed influence others, but there is more to leadership than influence.

One, several, or a relatively few are out there on the point, but all are responsible for the leadership that has taken place. This is the meaning I attach to the saying, "We are all leaders." (We are. But I guess I would want to add, ". . . some, more than others.")

## THE ART OF INDUCING OTHERS TO FOLLOW

I think of *followership* as the ultimate test of leadership. That seems fairly obvious. If you are going to lead, someone has to follow. Hence, my personal definition of leadership is "the art of inducing others to follow." A variant on that would be, "the art of inducing change," because change is really the name of the leadership game.[15]

Leadership is, from any point of view and by any measure, an art, the art of inducing others to follow. Leaders have to maximize their power to persuade; without persuasion, leadership simply does not happen.

Leadership is, moreover, modeled behavior. The leader shows others the way and they can see the way because they see it in the leader. To be a leader is to be leading by example. Followers follow what they see in their leader. Any organization can be thought of as a big machine; all its moveable parts are people. The leadership challenge is to get those people moving! Persuasion releases the brake and ignites forward progress.

Leadership is not a science (although there are indeed theories of leadership), nor is it a craft (although leaders "make" things happen by "carving out" solutions, "hammering down" loose ends, and "fixing" broken policies). Just as politics is often called "the art of the possible," leadership is the art of getting things done willingly (if not always cheerfully) through the coordinated efforts of others.

Why not think of the leader as an artist, if leadership is, in fact, an art? I think we should. And the image of an artist can serve as a helpful corrective to the king-of-the-hill, leader-as-hero image that many uncritically assume to be an accurate portrayal of real leadership.[16]

William ("Speedy") Morris, a successful high school and college coach who holds a place of honor in the Philadelphia Big-Five Basketball Hall of Fame, once remarked to me that "stars shine, but teams win." I share that wisdom with students who tend to think exclusively of the leader-as-hero and forget about the importance of leadership coalitions and groups—what we typically call the "leadership team"—in moving an organization forward.

The leader is a *dux*, not a *rex*, not a ruler. Language comparisons are helpful in clarifying these concepts. Leaders induce others to act. The English verb *induce* comes from the Latin *duco, ducere* (to lead) whence spring many words that relate in one way or another to leadership: *duke, duct, educate, induct, introduce, abduct, conduct, produce.* As I said, a leader is a *dux*, not a *rex*. The leader is not a king (although a good king can be a good leader), nor a ruler (holding others under the thumb), and certainly not a dictator (keeping others under the heel).

Recall that the willingness dimension of followership is an essential component of effective leadership. Eisenhower had it exactly right when he said that the president doesn't lead by hitting people over the head. Moreover, Eisenhower believed that leadership can be learned. Stephen Ambrose quotes him as saying, "The one quality that can be developed by studious reflection and practice is the leadership of men. The idea is to get people to work together, not only because you tell them to do so and enforce your orders, but because they instinctively want to do it for you." A man need not be a "glad hander nor a salesman" to be successful as a leader, but "you must be devoted to duty, sincere, fair, and cheerful."[17]

## GOAL SETTING

The tasks of leadership are multiple and ever-changing. One of them, however, is always on the leader's mind, and that is goal setting. This is an essential part of leadership. You can't provide leadership unless you have a strong sense of where you want to go. Goals—long-term and short-term—bring people together, unify them, and motivate them; that's why goals are always on the leader's mind. Setting goals is a constant task of leadership. Articulating and communicating goals-to-be-achieved—near-term or out toward the horizon—is an ongoing leadership responsibility. Where are we going? How are we going to get there? Once there, what are we going to do? Moreover, there is a place for metrics in all this. Goals should be quantified. Progress toward them should be measurable.

In the first televised news conference of his presidency on February 9, 2009, President Barack Obama was trying to sell his urgently needed economic stimulus plan when a reporter raised a question about metrics. Here is the exchange[18] between Jake Tapper of ABC News and Mr. Obama.

QUESTION: Mr. President, the American people have seen hundreds of billions of dollars spent already, and still the economy continues to free-fall. Beyond avoiding the national catastrophe that you've warned about, once all the legs of your stool are in place, how can the American people gauge whether or not your programs are working? Can they . . . should they be looking at the metric of the stock market, home foreclosures, unemployment? What metric should they use? When? And how will they know if it's working, or whether or not we need to go to a plan B?

ANSWER: I think my initial measure of success is creating or saving four million jobs. That's bottom line number one, because if people are working, then they've got enough confidence to make purchases, to make investments. Businesses start seeing that consumers are out there with a little more confidence, and they start making investments, which means they start hiring workers. So, step number one, job creation.

Step number two: Are we seeing the credit markets operate effectively? I can't tell you how many businesses that I talk to that are successful businesses, but just can't get credit. Part of the problem in Elkhart [Indiana] that I heard about today was the fact that—this is the RV [recreational vehicle] capital of America—you've got a bunch of RV companies that have customers who want to purchase RVs, but even though their credit is good, they can't get the loan. Now, the businesses also can't get loans to make payments to their suppliers. But when they have consumers, consumers can't get the loans that they need. So normalizing the credit markets is, I think, step number two.

Step number three is going to be housing. Have we stabilized the housing market? Now, the federal government doesn't have complete control over that, but if our plan is effective, working with the Federal Reserve Bank, working with the FDIC [Federal Deposit Insurance Corporation], I think what we can do is stem the rate of foreclosure, and we can start stabilizing housing values over time.

And the most . . . the biggest measure of success is whether we stop contracting and shedding jobs, and we start growing again. Now, I don't have a crystal ball, and as I've said, this is an unprecedented crisis. But my hope is that after a difficult year—and this year is going to be a difficult year—that businesses start investing again, they start making decisions that, you know, in fact there's money to be made out there, customers or consumers start feeling that their jobs are stable and safe, and they start making purchases again. And if we get things right, then starting next year we can start seeing some significant improvement.

The President's response was not all that helpful. What, at the end of that lengthy reply, can we take to be the metrics, the quantifiable goals? To say that the initial measure of success is "to create or save four million jobs" (he dropped it to 3.5 million a week later), fails to distinguish jobs saved from jobs created and fails to give a number—to quantify a goal—for either. Moreover, what quantifiable measures will eventually show that the credit markets are operating effectively or ineffectively? And what indicators will show that those same credit markets are "normalized"? Finally, what measure will show that the housing market is "stabilized"?

As I mentioned earlier, setting goals is an essential function of leadership. Quantifying the goals sharpens communication about them. It also makes it easier for critics to react when goals are not met, but, by the same token, it virtually guarantees that praise or blame will be given when and where praise or blame is due.

Vision is the difference between leading and managing (we'll see more on this distinction in chapter two). Visionary leadership first involves seeing what just about everyone has seen (and what is seen, typically, will be a problem). Then, true vision produces something that no one else has yet seen—a workable solution. Next, the visionary leader translates his or her vision into a goal. It may be a goal without a specific goal line, but it is no goal at all if it is not the product of vision—the vision of the leader and of those to whom the leader listens. Note again the importance of listening as part of the leadership toolkit.

## LEADERSHIP STYLE

Whenever I ask students for examples of model leaders—imitable leaders that inspire them—I hear names from the world of sports: Vince

Lombardi, Joe Torre, Tony Dungy, Pat Summit, Phil Jackson, Joe Paterno. Military generals like Lee, Patton, and Eisenhower often make the list. Many will mention presidents—Abraham Lincoln, John F. Kennedy, Ronald Reagan, Barack Obama. Others look to Winston Churchill, Nelson Mandela, Mahatma Gandhi, Martin Luther King. One student, in a college seminar on leadership when I invited nominations for model leaders, mentioned Lucky Luciano. That young man bears watching!

Surprising to me when I first heard it (but I realize now that I should not have been surprised), a student mentioned his mother—a nurse in a hospital serving the urban poor. I later recalled that Abraham Lincoln famously eulogized his with these words: "All that I am or ever hope to be I owe to my angel Mother." It is not known for sure whether he was referring to Nancy Hanks, his birthmother who died when Lincoln was eight, or to his stepmother, Sarah Johnston, who taught him to read and encouraged him in many ways. My guess is that he was referring to Sarah Johnston.

Another student in my leadership seminar mentioned her father, who employed fifty people in a landscaping business she hoped to join after graduation. Still another mentioned his grandfather, a divisional chief of detectives in a large city, who, in retirement, drove this young man to elementary school every day for eight years and taught him "more during the ride to and from school than I ever learned in any classroom."

Ted Sorensen was just 24 years of age when he went to work for Senator John F. Kennedy in 1953. He worked at JFK's side for over ten years. In *Counselor: A Life at the Edge of History*,[19] Sorensen, who was special assistant to the president and best known, perhaps, as Kennedy's chief speechwriter, says,

> JFK was a wonderful boss. We never argued, quarreled, shouted, or swore at each other. He never bawled me out. He never asked me to lie to anyone. He never misled or lied to me. . . . When mistakes occurred, whether in his campaign or in his presidency, he never blamed me or anyone else on his staff, or disavowed me or others when under political or journalistic pressure. To the contrary, he always protected and defended us. When a speech of his on which I had worked went well, or a political task I had undertaken for him succeeded, he often telephoned me the next day with profuse thanks.[20]
>
> His only notable weakness as a boss was his reluctance— indeed, his inability—to fire anyone. Instead, he promoted them.[21]

Sorensen learned a lot about leadership style from his mentor. In his memoir, he offers some specifics: "What I learned from JFK was invaluable to me [later] as an international lawyer—to listen and learn from leaders of other countries, to be cautious on matters of war and peace until I knew the case for each side and all the facts and alternatives; to recognize that cultural differences can lie at the heart of political, policy, even legal disagreements; to be flexible, curious, friendly with all, and to keep my hopes high but my expectations low regarding the results that can be achieved and the amount of time they will require"[22]

We will be looking more closely at model leaders in the next chapter. The point of including the Sorensen observations on Kennedy here is simply to suggest the importance of future leaders learning, while they are young, about the nature of leadership from others, and noticing admirable and imitable leadership qualities in others. The young have to be conditioned to view leadership not as a position—a hierarchical rank—but as a person-in-action who speaks, writes, and does well the things that can move an organization forward.

The nature of leadership includes service. Chapter thirteen will emphasize this, but the notion of service must be factored into our understanding of the true nature of leadership here at the beginning of our journey of understanding.

I had never encountered the word *humbition* until I read *Mavericks at Work*,[23] a book whose subtitle promises to tell the reader "why the most original minds in business win." Speaking of the leadership of SEI Investments, a "back office" service company based in Oaks, Pennsylvania, the authors say, "At SEI, the most effective leaders exude a blend of humility and ambition—*humbition*—that relies on the power of persuasion rather than formal authority."[24] They quote an SEI executive who says, "We reject the idea that because people sit at the top of the organization, power resides with them and control comes down the line. Power is much more diffuse and dispersed in this organization. Power doesn't come from position, it comes from influence and the ability to engineer consensus—not in the Japanese sense of unanimity but in terms of the participation and support required to get things done."[25]

## THE GEOMETRY OF LEADERSHIP

It is useful to consider what I like to think of as the geometry of leadership. A top-of-the-pyramid perspective on leadership usually implies a king-of-the-hill attitude in the mind of the leader. Draw a triangle and picture yourself at the top; the horizontal line running from left to right below can support a wide base of potential followers. They may or may not be responsive to orders from above. If they are, you are exercising leadership. If not, you are whistling in the wind. And note, by the way, the possibility of impalement that is associated with a position at the top of the triangle!

It can be lonely at the top. The top can also be an out-of-touch, can-hardly-see-you, certainly-can't-hear-you perch that is usually accompanied by title and perks, but is largely ineffective as a power source or center of influence. Adopt instead a center-of-the-circle image of leadership. There you are—at the center, on a level plane—able to be seen and heard as you yourself see and hear, able to lift (encourage) and touch (pat on the back) because you are also one of the on-the-ground followers even though you carry the title of leader. Keep in mind the geometry of leadership as you work your way through these pages—indeed as you work your way to the top in any organization—understanding, as you go, that the top is really in the center and on common ground with your partners in the enterprise.

Few business schools stress the utility for leadership of a blend of humility and ambition. That's why *humbition* is a word worth adding to the would-be leader's vocabulary. Most films and novels about business overlook humility altogether in their portrayal of business leaders and in their depiction of the qualities of effective leadership. So I want to list those qualities here in the hope that they will, in the mind of the reader, add up to a working understanding of the nature of leadership.

## AN INVENTORY OF NECESSARY QUALITIES FOR EFFECTIVE LEADERSHIP

Qualities already mentioned in this book that help explain the nature of leadership are integrity, honesty, intelligence, creativity, character, service, and commitment. Here is how I understand each one of these:

*INTEGRITY*. For a useful and straightforward definition of integrity, let me turn to Stephen Carter, who writes, "When I refer to integrity, I have something very simple and very specific in mind. Integrity, as I will use the term, requires three steps: (1) *discerning* what is right and what is wrong; (2) *acting* on what you have discerned, even at personal cost; and (3) *saying openly* that you are acting on your understanding of right and wrong."[26]

Carter, a law professor at Yale, like some of the business practitioners with whom I have talked about integrity, expects "the integral leader to display the virtue of consistency," but acknowledges at the same time "how hard it can be to live a life of integrity so understood."[27] Consistency is certainly a dimension of integrity, but it has to be handled with care. It is not inconsistent to change your mind or revise a pre-announced policy in light of better information or new discoveries (despite the fact that your critics will accuse you of flip-flopping). It would be inconsistent to disrespect the dignity of one person over against another simply because the first person occupies a lower rung on the income scale or has less organizational responsibility. Generally speaking, I tend to think of integrity in terms of wholeness, solidity of character, honesty, trustworthiness, and responsibility. I expect consistency to accompany integrity unless integrity itself requires a departure from plan or a revision of a previously held opinion.

*HONESTY.* As I just indicated, honesty is associated with integrity. We all have a commonsense, practical, workable understanding of honesty; we easily recognize its presence or absence in ourselves and others. An "honest dollar," an "honest day's work," "honesty is the best policy"— these and other familiar expressions long ago worked their way into our consciousness, our understanding of honesty, and our view of the world.

As I write this, memory carries me back to my collegiate dramatics society's production of *Othello* and I can hear the voice of my friend, Tony Mamarella, in the title role of Othello addressing "honest Iago," as well as demanding to know whether Desdemona has remained "honest" in her relationship to him. The idea of honesty covers a lot of character terrain in life's journey. When Othello speaks of "honest" Iago, he is mistakenly judging the mendacious Iago to be open and sincere. When Othello asks his wife Desdemona if she is "honest," he is inquiring about her fidelity in marriage to him; he wonders about her chastity. He suspects, due to the pernicious promptings of "honest" Iago, that she has a sexual relationship with Cassio and is thus unfaithful—not honest.

*INTELLIGENCE.* Similarly, intelligence is a familiar term. Cynics speak of "military intelligence" as an oxymoron; this usually draws a chuckle along with an acknowledgment that intelligence can be underutilized, even misapplied. But ever since you were first tested for your IQ— Intelligence Quotient—you realized that intelligence was somehow related to the quality, speed, and strength of the mental machinery between your ears. No wonder we expect it in leaders. And it goes without saying that we expect our leaders to keep that mental machinery tuned up and running smoothly.

*CREATIVITY*. Business schools yield too much ground to the "creative arts" by failing, even in courses on entrepreneurship, to speak of creativity as a quality that will be expected of their graduates once they find their places in the world of work. Much of creative thinking is derivative thinking. This means that not all creative ideas will be original. The search for new ideas requires a familiarity with old ideas and with other organizations, industries, cultures, languages, art, and history. Avoid plagiarism, of course, but lift good ideas wherever you find them and apply them creatively, with all due respect to intellectual property rights, to solve new problems. Too often, those who stop reading, stop thinking. Sadly, those who stop mixing, mingling, and traveling, stop growing in the realm of imagination. Creative energy, like physical vitality, is essential to good leadership.

*CHARACTER*. I once heard a former athlete, in praising the character-building success of his high school rowing coach, say, "Reputation is what our peers think of us; character is what God and the angels know about us." But how do you develop character? God's grace will prepare the way. Coaches can help. So can parents and teachers. Books can make a difference. I'm not thinking of "how to" books, but good literature that portrays the best in human nature.

Models—exemplars—are crucial to the process. It has often been said that "values are caught, not taught." This means that you have to see values embodied in others (in what they say and do) and imagine their expression in yourself—in your choices, in your walking the walk, not just talking the talk. Nutritionists will remind you that you are what you eat. Psychologists might remark that you can become what you admire and decide to imitate. Character has to be built. Family values, religion, good education, positive peer pressure, and the exposure to good examples in life and literature can provide you with a set of plans for that building project.

*SERVICE*. "Don't be a bystander" were the words of advice the father of one of my young friends gave to him when he was finishing school and starting out on a career. That's good advice for any young man or woman moving into the world of work.

Every week or so, you will read a news account of how an "innocent bystander" was caught in gunfire or struck by an automobile. The point the father of my young friend was trying to make is that standing by, inactive and uninterested, when you might be making a positive contribution, is negligent—not innocent—behavior. Get involved. Reach out. Help. Serve. Service is an essential quality of leadership. As you will learn in Chapter thirteen, service is at the heart of a complete understanding of leadership.

*COMMITMENT*. This is another word for dedication. To be uncommitted is to be adrift and without purpose. That is surely not the stuff of leadership. Commitment provides focus. Commitment means a willingness to make and keep a promise. But it involves more than words spoken or reduced to print; it requires a pledge of self. The committed leader stands behind the promise or the contract. That's what it means to say that your word is your bond. When you say whatever you say to express your commitment, you literally put yourself on the line.

To gain an even fuller understanding of the nature of leadership, a consideration of the following additional qualities would be helpful.

*DECISIVENESS*. Everyone knows someone who just can't make up his or her mind. Popular songs have been written about this inability, as have more serious dramas and novels. Indecisiveness is good material for stories, but it is bad for anyone who wants to lead. The famous trial attorney Edward Bennett Williams often remarked that the two great culprits in the theft of time were regret and indecision. You lose more than time, however, when you cannot decide; you lose strategic advantage. To be decisive does not equate with being impulsive. Take time (just not too much time) and think it through (but not so far through that you find yourself coming out at the other end without having made up your mind), and then decide.

Procrastination comes from the two Latin words, *pro* and *crastina*, which simply say, "for tomorrow." Well, tomorrow may be too late. That's why the old saying reminds you not to put off until tomorrow what can be done today. Do it. Decide.

*COMPASSION*. Recall times when you may have experienced forgiveness, or when you knew, without doubt, that someone else really understood how you were feeling. At those moments, someone else was showing compassion toward you. To be compassionate means to be empathetic or sympathetic. The Latin word *passio* (see it there in *compassion*) and the Greek word *pathein* (there it is in *empathy*) are both related to the English word *suffer*. When you experienced compassion or empathy from another, that other person was, quite literally, suffering your suffering along with you. In effect, someone slipped inside your skin and felt what you were feeling. That's what leaders have to do in relating to those they want to lead.

*RESPECT FOR HUMAN DIGNITY*. No one can lead without having genuine respect for those who are waiting and willing to be led. And it is respect for the inherent dignity of these others as persons that comes into play here, not respect for their wealth, beauty, or whatever they have that is attractive. No, what motivates the good leader is respect for others as human beings of inestimable worth, not as human doings whose "doing" gained for them reputation and possessions.

*PERSISTENCE*. The leader has to stick it out—has to be there at the beginning, through the middle, right up to the end. That's what persistence means—being there. This is both concentration and courage. No let up, no break, no vacation until the job is done. The persistent leader can be a bit pesky, annoying, not easily put off, not necessarily a nuisance, but surely not one to fade away or avoid the fray. Just being there is to exercise a form of leadership.

*PERSEVERANCE*. This quality is a close cousin of persistence. One who perseveres has staying power. Perseverance is the explanation for more academic success than most students realize. Stay with it and the insight will come, the sought-after understanding will arrive. We all too glibly and often attribute "genius" to ordinary minds that have extraordinary staying power in the face of library challenges and laboratory problems.

To think you can lead, without demonstrating perseverance, is to fool yourself into believing that there is an autopilot ready to step in once your fade has folded into failure.

*STEADINESS*. There is something about steadiness that generates confidence. (Who will follow unless propelled by confidence?) Strength in steadiness is one way of viewing this leadership quality—a steady hand on the rudder, a firm grip on the wheel. "Steady as she goes," is a nautical expression that serves as good advice to mariners. "Slow and steady wins the race" applies in the very long run (but is not helpful, of course, for contestants in the 100-yard dash). Steadiness is surely needed in times of crisis. An unsteady leader is one who is simply not up to the job.

*VIGOR*. This quality needs no explanation. Anyone can tell whether the leader has a pulse, rings up high numbers on the vital-signs register, exudes energy. I ask my students to reflect on these words from Theodore Levitt, whose landmark 1960 *Harvard Business Review* article "Marketing Myopia" probably still holds the HBR record for reprints sold: "No organization can achieve greatness without a vigorous leader who is driven onward by his own pulsating *will to succeed*. He has to have a vision of grandeur, a vision that can produce eager followers in vast numbers. In business, the followers are the customers. To produce these customers, the entire corporation must be viewed as a customer-creating and customer-satisfying organism."[28] That "pulsating will to succeed" is a leadership characteristic needed in every organization; without it, not much is likely to happen.

You may by now be looking for the difference between a leader and an "all around wonderful person." The qualities I've listed do indeed describe a human being that most of us would regard as outstanding, wonderful. But such a person has to act in order to lead. Leadership action will be examined throughout the remainder of this book.

In retirement, the well-known automobile executive Lee Iacocca wrote a small book, *Where Have All the Leaders Gone?*[29] In it, he lists what he calls the Nine C's of leadership—his inventory of "the obvious qualities that every true leader should have."[30] And here they are:

- A leader has to show CURIOSITY.
- A leader has to be CREATIVE.
- A leader has to COMMUNICATE.
- A leader has to be a person of CHARACTER.
- A leader must have COURAGE.
- To be a leader you've got to have CONVICTION.
- A leader should have CHARISMA.
- A leader has to be COMPETENT.
- You can't be a leader if you don't have COMMON SENSE.

Iacocca caps his inventory with the comment that "the biggest C is CRISIS." This would be a tenth C. It identifies the crucial area where leadership stands or falls. We'll see more about crisis later in this book. Let me add here, however, that although Lee Iacocca is a business leader that many younger readers may know little about, he is a business legend who belongs to the top-of-the-pyramid class. Time spent learning more about him and his career (his association with the infamous Ford Pinto is a major negative, while his later role in negotiating a major federal bailout for Chrysler is a positive) is surely time well spent for tomorrow's leaders. Even though the world of business has changed, there is a place for the Iacocca brand of leadership energy in the business world today.

All of the above combines to flesh out the nature of the phenomenon we are considering in this book. There is some overlap, but not much. Added qualities may come to mind as you move through these pages; feel free to factor them into your own reflections. Your destination as you move through the subsequent chapters is, to repeat my definition of leadership, an understanding of "the art of inducing others to follow."

All will agree that the nature of leadership is both complex and completely human. And leadership itself, some will notice, is in dangerously short supply today in America—a condition that can be remedied if those in their teens , twenties, and thirties to whom I address this book are willing to take themselves and the chapters that follow seriously.

I certainly agree, and I hope my readers will too, with the priorities embodied in the "essence of leadership" inscription I mentioned at the beginning of this chapter: "A true leader has the confidence to stand alone, the courage to make tough decisions, and the compassion to listen to the needs of others. He or she does not set out to be a leader, but becomes one by the quality of his or her actions and the integrity of his or her intent. In the end, leaders are much like eagles . . . they don't flock, you find them one at a time."

## NOTES:

1. John W. Gardner, *On Leadership* (New York: Free Press, 1990), 14.
2. (New York: Harper & Row, 1978), 19.
3. Gardner, *On Leadership*, 1.
4. Ibid., 2–3.
5. "To Lead, Create a Shared Vision," *Harvard Business Review* (January 2009): 20.

6. (San Francisco: Jossey-Bass, fourth edition, 2007), xiii.

7. Quoted in Emmett John Hughes, *Ordeal of Power* (New York: Atheneum, 1963), 124.

8. "In Defense of Obamanomics," *Wall Street Journal* (March 9, 2009): A19.

9. *The McKinsey Quarterly: The Online Journal of McKinsey & Co.* (January 30, 2009): 2; http://www.mckinseyquarterly.com/article_print.aspx?L2=18&L3=31&ar=2193.

10. Ibid.

11. *Heroic Leadership: Best Practices from a 450-Year-Old Company that Changed the World* (Chicago, IL: Loyola Press, 2003).

12. Ibid., 9.

13. *Servant Leadership* (Mahwah, NJ: Paulist Press, 25th anniversary edition, 2002), 109.

14. Ibid., see especially 209–14.

15. Barbara Kellerman offers a helpful corrective to the "leadercentric" emphasis in contemporary leadership literature by showing how followers, as followers, have both the power and responsibility to exercise leadership. See her *Followership: How Followers Are Creating Change and Changing Leaders* (Boston: Harvard Business Press, 2008).

16. For a fuller discussion of the notion of leader as artist, see "Toward a More Adequate Myth: The Art of Leadership," chap. 9, in Sharon Daloz Parks, *Leadership Can Be Taught* (Boston: Harvard Business School Press, 2005), 201–30.

17. Stephen E. Ambrose, *The Supreme Commander: The War Years of General Dwight D. Eisenhower* (New York: Doubleday, 1970), 214.

18. See the official transcript available online from the White House Press Office at www.whitehouse.gov.

19. (New York: Harper Collins, 2008).

20. Ibid., 111.

21. Ibid., 114.

22. Ibid., 427.

23. By William C. Taylor and Polly LaBarre (New York: Harper Paperback, 2008).

24. Ibid., 240.

25. Ibid., 238.

26. *Integrity* (New York: Harper Perennial, 1996), 7. Carter acknowledges influence in forming this understanding from Martin Benjamin's book *Splitting the Difference: Compromise and Integrity in Ethics and Politics* (Lawrence: University Press of Kansas, 1990).

27. Ibid., 47.

28. (July–August, 1960): 56.

29. (New York: Scribner, 2007).

30. See Ibid., 6–10.

# CHAPTER TWO

## LOOKING AT LEADERS

There is much wisdom to be found in *The Leadership Challenge*,[1] a book by James M. Kouzes and Barry Z. Posner. They lay out "five practices of exemplary leadership" under the following headings: (1) Model the Way; (2) Inspire a Shared Vision; (3) Challenge the Process; (4) Enable Others to Act; and (5) Encourage the Heart. They also identify the four primary characteristics that we look for and admire in our leaders. We expect our leaders to be honest, forward-looking, inspiring, and competent.[2] And given the title of the present chapter, here is one more observation from Kouzes and Posner that deserves special attention: "When we look at leaders, we see that they're associated with transformation, large and small. Leader's don't have to change history, but they do have to change 'business as usual.'"[3] This is not to suggest that there will never be times when the leader must resist change, or cope with change that is not of his or her own doing. Not every "change agent" is a leader, but few if any leaders will never have to initiate change.

You have to "model the way" if you want to lead. You cannot simply give orders, directions, or commands; you have to embody within yourself the way—understanding "the way" to mean both path and style—that you want your followers to take. This chapter showcases a variety of leaders. It invites you to look at leaders—some well-known, others relatively obscure—who have succeeded in inducing others to act. They succeeded in getting others to follow willingly once "the way" was laid out—that is to say, once the way was exemplified in the person of the leader. Unless you first model the way, you cannot lead.

"Leadership is not a gene and it's not an inheritance," say Kouzes and Posner. "Leadership is an identifiable set of skills and abilities that are available to all of us."[4] It follows, then, that if you want to become a leader, it would be wise to take a look at successful leaders and see what it is in their leadership style that you might make your own. Adopt a model leader. Imitate his or her leadership style so that you eventually can model the way for others. Or take a few imitable qualities from one model leader and other qualities from another for an amalgam of imitable characteristics that can help you become a better leader.

Take a moment now to reflect on the difference between being a manager and being a leader. In chapter one, you saw that vision is pivotal to the distinction. You may decide that separating leaders from managers is a distinction without a difference, but don't come to that conclusion too hastily. There is indeed a certain amount of overlap between the two functions. Leaders sometimes manage; managers sometimes lead. But true leadership, as we examined it in chapter one, involves a dimension and includes hard-to-define characteristics that lie outside the management orbit. That's why it is important now to take a few moments to compare the two notions; it is also why it will be important to be mindful that there is a distinction—however difficult to pin down—as you make your way through this book. Ponder this comparison:[5]

Leaders, Not Managers
The manager administers.
The leader innovates.
The manager is a copy.
The leader is an original.
The manager maintains.
The leader develops.
The manager focuses on systems and structures.
The leader focuses on people.
The manager relies on control.
The leader inspires trust.
The manager has a short-range view.
The leader has a long-range perspective.
The manager asks how and when.
The leader asks what and why.
The manager keeps an eye always on the bottom line
The leader keeps an eye on the horizon.
The manager imitates.
The leader originates.
The manager accepts the status quo.

The leader challenges it.
The manager is the classic good soldier.
The leader is his or her own person.
The manager does things right.
The leader does the right thing.

Do you agree or disagree with any of these assertions? Can you add a few of your own? As you scribble through and around these notions, you will find yourself sharpening your awareness of the special qualities that only leaders possess. Have you begun to notice that management seems to deal a lot with process, while leadership is more focused on purpose? You should also begin to take more careful note of the leaders around you. Keep noticing; observe them carefully.

John P. Kotter distinguishes leadership and management in a set of short assertions that are worthy of note: "Management is a set of processes that can keep a complicated system of people and technology running smoothly. The most important aspects of management include planning, budgeting, organizing, staffing, controlling, and problem solving. Leadership is a set of processes that creates organizations in the first place or adapts them to significantly changing circumstances. Leadership defines what the future should look like, aligns people with that vision, and inspires them to make it happen despite the obstacles."[6] Note the leadership verbs: *create, adapt, define, align, inspire*—all with respect to a vision. These are not only noticeable, but imitable characteristics.

I've had conversations about the leadership–management distinction with Fred Gluck, retired managing director of McKinsey & Co. He looks to leaders for the "big picture," for change and adaptability, as well as strategy, whereas managers deal with operations, effectiveness, and efficiency. The leader's responsibilities focus on the whole enterprise; managers have their focus on operating units. So, how do they deal with people? Leaders, according to Gluck, inspire, motivate, engender trust, and build confidence; managers attend to hiring and firing, maintenance of quality, deploying the appropriate skills, and measuring performance. The "ultimate responsibility for both leadership and management always remains with the leader of an enterprise or of a specific unit within the enterprise," says Fred Gluck. "Leaders may choose different balances, but delegation cannot be abdication."[7]

Just by keeping your eyes open you will meet leadership models in ordinary life. In your lived experience of school, sports, summer camp, volunteer activity, employment, and military service, you will encounter leaders. Models of leadership are waiting to be found in good literature like Shakespeare's dramatic presentation of King Henry V, as well as in many films and lots of fiction. Most people will meet their model leaders in the pages of history books; that will be our point of departure for this exercise of looking at leaders.

In what follows it would be a mistake to look for an order of preference on my part, or my judgment of superiority in a given leader's effectiveness. There is surely something imitable in the style and achievements of each of the leaders presented here. Readers are encouraged to pick and choose imitable characteristics that appeal to them. You are also encouraged to get deeper into the reading habit and search library and bookstore shelves for attractive biographical, historical, and literary presentations of leadership lives. Recall that one of my students saw admirable qualities in the life of the notorious gangster Lucky Luciano, who, understandably, does not make the lineup I will be presenting here. Readers can add to or subtract from my list as they wish. The point is that I want you to begin noticing leaders in life and literature, and to become accustomed to deciding for yourself what you want to learn from them as you internalize their principles and develop your own leadership style.

## THE KENNEDY BROTHERS

In chapter one, you learned from Ted Sorensen something about the leadership style of President John F. Kennedy. The President's brother Robert was attorney general in the Kennedy administration. Robert Kennedy's legal counsel was Nicholas deB. Katzenbach, whose 2008 memoir[8] provides a window on the attorney general's leadership style:

> Bobby was clearly the leader [in daylong, relatively informal meetings of a small group charged with developing a strategy for this new administration's campaign against organized crime], and not simply because he was attorney general. He impressed the group with his factual knowledge, and he encouraged free-flowing discussion and differing views. He was quick to appreciate suggestions, to praise efforts, to push for more without being critical. You could sense that this varied group was prepared to follow him and wanted desperately to please him, to find the facts that were needed, however difficult the task might

be. I began to realize then, if I had not already seen it, that Bobby
had the capacity to become an exceptional leader.[9]

And Katzenbach added that Robert Kennedy "led in a way that was open
and aboveboard, with shared intelligence, no secrets, no favorites. . . . A
positive spirit—the desire to do a good job—permeated the whole department."[10] There is a causal relationship between what Katzenbach observed
as openness at the top and the positive spirit that permeated the entire Department of Justice.

Those glimpses of the Kennedy brothers—JFK and RFK—given
by men who knew them well and viewed them as model leaders, are useful
for the project this chapter undertakes, namely, looking at leaders with an
eye to imitating their leadership qualities. It is one thing to read about leadership in the abstract; it is quite another to see it in the flesh. So think of
the rest of this chapter as a portrait gallery or theater where you can "see"
some leaders up close and decide for yourself if there is anything there that
you would like to imitate.

## FRANKLIN DELANO ROOSEVELT

In the context of political leadership, Joseph Alsop reminds us that
you have to be elected before you can lead. So he offers what he calls "Rule
One" of Leadership: "You have to be a good politician in order to get the
chance to be a great statesman. And from the standpoint of Rule One, the
[presidential] campaign Roosevelt waged in 1932 deserves to be included
as a model in every primer for aspiring American leaders."[11]

Many books are available to introduce interested readers to the intricacies of political campaigns. This book is not one of them. I recall hearing the late Paul Tully, a professional political campaign manager, reply to
a question about what he wanted to do in the administration of the candidate
he was managing, should that campaign be successful, by saying simply,
"Nothing. I do politics. I don't do government." Those who just "do politics"—and the journalists who observe them—have written scores of books
about the process. The process of campaigning is interesting and necessary,
and it cannot be avoided by those who seek elective office. But there's more
to leadership than the campaign. Elected leaders must first be emergent
leaders; the qualities that help them emerge are those that occupy our interest in this book.

What was it about FDR that enabled him to emerge? Intelligence was not his strongest suit; temperament was. He was an outgoing, genial, engaging, smiling, pleasant person. He was likeable. A combination of good looks, family wealth, a famous family name, a respectable mainline religious affiliation, and education in the "right" schools (despite modest academic achievement there) qualified him for admission to the ranks of the elite without barring his acceptance by the broader population of his day and age. He did not have the "touch" of the common man, but he was able to stay in touch with the nation. His commanding voice did not carry the accents and vocabulary of the less-well-educated majority in America. But he was somehow able to communicate and to gain the trust of ordinary people, a task surely made easier by the existence of widespread fear in people's hearts during the Great Depression and their anxiety in the months leading up to and during World War II. Roosevelt's general acceptance by the people was public acknowledgment of what Joseph Alsop sees as FDR's "central achievement on the home front," namely, the fact that "on a very wide front and in the truest possible sense, Franklin Delano Roosevelt included the excluded."[12]

## WINSTON CHURCHILL

Steven F. Hayward's small book, *Churchill on Leadership: Executive Success in the Face of Adversity*,[13] is a useful guide to the character and qualities of one of the world's great leaders. As the subtitle suggests, Hayward is interested in describing Churchill's executive style, not in providing a comprehensive biography. His purpose and mine coincide, so I will rely on him for identification of the leadership characteristics available for imitation by anyone willing to take a closer look at Churchill.

As we have already seen, character, integrity, honesty, creativity, intelligence, and persistence are among the qualities we look for in our leaders. Steven Hayward identifies four essential aspects of character that explain the effectiveness of Churchill's leadership. What set him apart from other politicians, says Hayward, were "candor and plain speaking, decisiveness, the ability to balance attention to details with a view of the wider scene, and a historical imagination that informed his judgment."[14] It was Churchill's view that typical politicians hemmed themselves in by platitudes because of their reluctance to offend and their readiness to compromise. Churchill favored candor and plain speech. Although he sometimes preferred to delay than to decide (in the hope, perhaps, that the delay would obviate the need for a decision), he was more often than not impressively decisive.

Much has been written in praise of Churchill's historical imagination. He himself made the famous remark that "the longer you look back, the farther you can look forward," a point of view that Hayward quotes and immediately underscores by quoting the British historian Sir John H. Plumb, who wrote: "History, for Churchill, was not a subject like geography or mathematics, it was part of his temperament, as much a part of his being as his social class and indeed, closely allied to it. . . . It permeated everything which he touched, and it was the mainspring of his politics and the secret of his immense mastery."[15] The point is further reinforced by Isaiah Berlin: "Churchill's dominant category, the single, central, organizing principle of his mind and intellectual universe, is a historical imagination so strong, so comprehensive, as to encase the whole of the present and the whole of the future in a framework of a rich and multicolored past."[16]

The importance of looking back (knowing history) in order to be able to see into the future cannot be overemphasized. There is a caution, however, that must be mentioned. Generally speaking, people prefer to live in the immediate past. They can be unduly influenced by past experience. They—that is, all of us—are subject to "anchored thinking." We must beware of the false sense of complacency that can reach out from the past and impede movement (change) to the future.

Like Roosevelt, Churchill was said to be imperturbable. A fiery orator but calm thinker, Churchill became a great leader. Read any good biography of Churchill and you will discover that he was not afraid to take risks, nor was he afraid to take responsibility. He was a master speaker and superb writer. He could see the big picture without losing attention to detail; he was very well organized. Moreover, he was a kind and magnanimous person; he even regarded himself as a "servant."[17]

## ABRAHAM LINCOLN

The 16th president of the United States makes everyone's list of model leaders. Abraham Lincoln's "moral integrity is the strong trunk from which all the branches of his life grew,"[18] writes biographer Ronald C. White Jr. That "strong trunk" makes him a great model and there is much to imitate in "all the branches of his life." Ronald White's recent biography is one of the best of the hundreds of Lincoln books now in print.

During the 2008 presidential campaign in the United States, candidate Barack Obama was asked in a nationally televised interview to identify one book, apart from the Bible, that he would take with him, if elected, into the White House. His reply: Doris Kearns Goodwin's 2005 bestseller *Team of Rivals* (Simon and Schuster). This book carries the subtitle, "The Political Genius of Abraham Lincoln." It is an account of President Lincoln's leadership during the Civil War. Upon election, Lincoln put together a leadership team made up of his strongest rivals in the campaign for the presidency, hence the title of the Goodwin book. Obama did something similar. Senators Joe Biden and Hillary Rodham Clinton, along with New Mexico Governor Bill Richardson, competed against Obama in the long primary season of 2008. Taking a page from the Lincoln playbook, President Obama selected Senator Biden to be his vice president, Hillary Clinton to become his secretary of state, and he nominated Bill Richardson, who later withdrew from consideration, for secretary of commerce.

Early in the Obama administration, the *Harvard Business Review* published a "conversation" with Doris Kearns Goodwin under the title, "Leadership Lessons from Abraham Lincoln."[19] HBR editors thought that with the nation suffering a severe economic downturn in 2009, readers would be interested in learning something from Lincoln on how to lead in turbulent times. There is indeed an application waiting to be made in the world of business of the leadership principles that worked so well for Lincoln in politics.

Noting that Doris Kearns Goodwin had written books not only on Lincoln, but also on Presidents Franklin Roosevelt, John Kennedy, and Lyndon Johnson, HBR asked her: "What, in your opinion, are the essential qualities of a successful leader?" Her response: "I can't emphasize strongly enough the fact that you've got to surround yourself with people who can argue with you and question your assumptions. It particularly helps if you can bring in people whose temperaments differ from your own."[20] And Goodwin went on to say, "You also have to be able to figure out how to share credit for your success with your inner team so that they feel a part of a mission. Basically, you want to create a reservoir of good feeling, and that involves not only acknowledging your errors but even shouldering the blame for the failures of some of your subordinates. Again and again, Lincoln took responsibility for what he did, and he shared responsibility for the mistakes of others, and so people became very loyal to him."[21]

Noting that Lincoln and Roosevelt made no secret of taking breaks from their official responsibilities, Goodwin said, "As a leader you need to know how to relax so that you can replenish your energies for the struggles facing you tomorrow."[22] She observes that Lincoln had "an extraordinary amount of emotional intelligence. He was able to acknowledge his errors and learn from his mistakes to a remarkable degree. He was careful to put past hurts behind him and never allowed wounds to fester."[23]

Lincoln, famous for his self-deprecating humor, was a famous storyteller. One of his most famous quips was directed to a critic who accused him of being "two-faced," prompting Lincoln to reply: "If I were two-faced, do you think I'd be wearing this one?"

"I was once accosted," Lincoln told his portrait painter Francis Carpenter in 1864, "by a stranger who said, 'Excuse me, sir, but I have an article in my possession which belongs to you.' 'How is that?' I asked, considerably astonished. The stranger took a jackknife from his pocket. 'This knife,' he said, 'was placed in my hands some years ago with the injunction that I was to keep it until I found a man uglier than myself. I have carried it from that time to this. Allow me to say, sir, that I think you are fairly entitled to the property.'"[24]

## BARACK H. OBAMA

Barack Obama announced his candidacy for the presidency of the United States in 2007, two days before Lincoln's birthday on February 10th in the Land of Lincoln—the State of Illinois. Indeed he made the announcement in Springfield, the state capital that Abraham Lincoln, as a state legislator, voted to establish. It is no secret that the first African-American president of the United States has a special affection for the Great Emancipator.

Evidence that Obama adopted Lincoln's team-of-rivals viewpoint appeared in an article about Vice President Joseph R. Biden Jr. published in the *New York Times*[25] in the third month of the Obama administration. "Speaking Freely, Sometimes, Biden Finds Influential Role," is the way the front-page headline characterized Mr. Biden's position. The news story reports that Mr. Obama "has come to see Mr. Biden as a useful contrarian in the course of decision-making." "Rahm Emanuel, the White House chief of staff, said that 'when there's group-think going on, the vice president tends to push the envelope in the other direction.'"[26]

According to the news story, Mr. Obama has noticed "an institutional barrier sometimes to truth-telling in front of the president," and the president went on to say to the *Times* reporter: "Joe [Biden] is very good about sometimes articulating what's on other people's minds, or things that they've said in private conversations that people have been less willing to say in public. Joe, in that sense, can help stir the pot."[27] Obama apparently likes that; Lincoln surely did.

Although not a rival, former treasury secretary and Harvard president Lawrence H. Summers was invited into the Obama inner circle to be the president's chief adviser on economic policy. This is a new stand-alone, next-to-the-Oval-Office arrangement. Summers was not asked to chair the President's Council of Economic Advisers, which is housed across the street from the White House in the Old Executive Office Building. Summers is inside and down the hall because he is an expert on the economy and that's where the problems were when Obama took over. "Barack thinks with his mind open and Larry thinks with his mouth open,"[28] remarked Harvard law professor Charles Ogletree, who knows both men well. That apparently is the way the president likes it. Another Harvard law professor, Lawrence Tribe, said a lot about the leadership qualities of both men in a few well-chosen words: "The president's affability and inclusiveness might help nurture those same qualities in Larry, even though those haven't been among Larry's notable strengths."[29]

A turning point in Obama's bid for the presidency came in the winter of 2008, when race became an issue in the campaign. Offensive remarks by Obama's former pastor, the Reverend Jeremiah Wright, were being used, sometimes quite unfairly, against the candidate. So Obama suspended his campaign for a few days to write a speech that was delivered at the Constitution Center in Philadelphia on March 18, 2008 under the title "A More Perfect Union."[30] As you will note a little later in this chapter, former Pennsylvania Governor William W. Scranton called it the greatest speech on the topic of racism since the Emancipation Proclamation.

Candidate Obama said that over 221 years ago, just across the street from where he was speaking, the framers of our Constitution wrote, "We the people, in order to form a more perfect union;" and "with these simple words, launched America's improbable experiment in democracy." The document they produced "was stained by this nation's original sin of slavery." They "embedded" the answer to the slavery question in the Constitution's guarantee of liberty and justice for all, said Obama, but "words on a parchment would not be enough to deliver slaves from bondage, or provide men and women of every color and creed their full rights and obligations as citizens of the United States. What would be needed were Americans in successive generations who were willing to do their part . . .

to narrow that gap between the promise of our ideals and the reality of their time."

Acknowledging that much progress has been made, the candidate said he was running for president to work for unity, "to continue the long march of those who came before us, a march for a more just, more equal, more free, more caring, and more prosperous America." It was about much more than race, but "the fact is that the comments that have been made and the issues that have surfaced over the last few weeks reflect the complexities of race in this country that we've never really worked through—a part of our union that we have yet to perfect."

He talked about the past legacy of segregated schools, legalized discrimination, lack of economic opportunity for black men, the absence of basic services in so many urban black neighborhoods. He cited an array of contemporary social problems and said he was running in order to promote the unity that would enable the whole country, working together, to do something about them.

As president, Mr. Obama has demonstrated many qualities that belong in a leader's toolkit, notably decisiveness, effective oral communication, and a clear passion for the job.

In an interview with Richard Wolffe shortly after he won the presidency, Obama said,

> I think that we learned an awful lot about what it takes to put an effective organization together during the campaign. I mean, running a huge, multibillion-dollar bureaucracy is obviously different than running a political campaign. On the other hand, the campaign itself was big enough that I had a sense of what worked and what didn't in executing, on the one hand, and messaging on the other.
>
> And I think that if you think of the presidency just as a bureaucratic job, then you will not be effective. If you think of it only as a rhetorical, political job, you will not be effective. And I think that our goal has been to say, how do we function as good managers and good stewards of government and reform it and clean it up and make it work and make it tight? But let's not lose sight of the fact that we also have to persuade the American people as to where the country needs to go. And those two things have to work in concert, in tandem, to be effective.[31]

There they are—persuasion (messaging) and organization (executing)—key elements of effective leadership.

## NELSON MANDELA

Anyone who wants to lead should know about the remarkable life of Nelson Mandela. Born the son (some accounts say grandson) of an African chief in 1918, he is now retired after serving as president of the African National Congress and as the first democratically elected president of South Africa. "His achievement has been dependent on mastering politics in its broadest and longest sense, on understanding how to move and persuade people, to change their attitudes. He has always been determined, like Gandhi or Churchill, to lead from the front, through his example and presence, and he learned early how to build up and understand his own image."[32]

A twenty-seven year imprisonment (part of it for passport violation—leaving his apartheid-poisoned country without permission) served as Mandela's prep school for leadership. The South African presidency was, so to speak, his diploma, and the 1993 Nobel Peace Prize was his lifetime-achievement award. But to understand both the model and the man, I recommend a book by John Carlin, *Playing the Enemy: Nelson Mandela and the Game That Made a Nation.*[33] That game was the 1995 World Cup rugby championship match hosted by the Springboks, the South African national team, who had long personified white supremacist rule. Their fight songs were racist and, of course, under apartheid, the team was all-white.

Carlin writes that South Africa had experienced a "peaceful transfer of power from white rule to majority rule, from apartheid to democracy. . . . No country had ever shepherded itself from tyranny to democracy more ably, and humanely."[34] He set out to write a book "about a country whose black majority should have been bellowing for revenge but instead, following Mandela's example, gave the world a lesson in enlightened forgiveness."[35] And the major symbolic event through which the human factor that produced the "South African miracle" emerged was a sporting event, the 1995 Rugby World Cup, similar to the football Super Bowl in the United States, but truly unique in this instance.

The Brazilian soccer star Pelé once said, "Sport has the power to change the world. It has the power to inspire, the power to unite people that little else has. . . . It is more powerful than governments in breaking down racial barriers."[36] This proved to be the case in South Africa where, despite the fact that the black Mandela had been elected president, the racial hatred remained.

Mandela used the World Cup as an occasion to close the racial divide. Edward Griffiths, CEO of the rugby federation cooperated by inventing a slogan for the Springbok campaign: "One Team, One Country." Another influential white, Morné du Plessis, former Springbok captain who now served as manager of the team, persuaded the team to act in such a way as to convince the entire country, especially black South Africa, that the slogan meant what it said. As a rugby hero, he had credibility, especially among white South Africans; he and Mandela had become friends.

> Du Plessis came up with the idea of teaching the Springboks to sing the "black" half of the new national anthem, "Nikosi Sikele." He and Mandela shared the same mission impossible: persuading black South Africans to perform an historical about-face and support the [Spring]Boks. Mandela was doing his best within the ANC, sending word out to his people that now "they" were "us." Du Plessis did his bit by urging the players [one, but only one, black was now on the team] to behave respectfully in public. He knew that things could go terribly wrong if before the start of each World Cup game black people were to see the Springboks singing the Afrikaans and English words of "Die Stem" with gusto but making no effort to sing "Nikosi Sikele."[37]

Nelson Mandela, for his part, wore a green Springbok jersey and cap on the day of the championship game against the favored New Zealand team. Minutes before the kickoff, Mandela, wearing the green cap and jersey, stepped onto the field in front of 62,000 fans. His appearance electrified the crowd whose shouts of "Nelson! Nelson! Nelson!" filled the stadium and, by virtue of television, were heard around the world.

"The symbolism at play was mind-boggling. For decades, Mandela had stood for everything white South Africans most feared; The Springbok jersey had been the symbol, for even longer, of everything Black South Africans most hated. Now suddenly, before the eyes of the whole of South Africa, and much of the world, two negative symbols had merged to create a new one that was positive, constructive, and good. Mandela had wrought the transformation, becoming the embodiment not of hate and fear, but generosity and love."[38]

Before appearing on the field, Mandela visited the Springbok players in their locker room. There was quiet and tension in the room, but when he entered, the tension broke. François Pienaar, the Springbok captain, later recalled the scene. "Suddenly there he was. I didn't know he was coming, and even less did I know that he was going to wear the Springbok jersey. He was saying, 'Good luck,' and he turned around and on his back there was this number 6, and that was me. . . .

"You know, the passionate supporters, they're the ones who wear the jersey of their team. So now here I am seeing him walking into the dressing room, in this moment of all moments, dressed like another passionate fan, but then I see that it is my jersey that he is wearing. There are no words to describe the emotions that ran through my body."[39]

And here are the words Mandela used to encourage the team: "Look here, chaps. You are playing . . . one of the most powerful teams in the rugby world but you are even more powerful. And just remember that this entire crowd, both black and white, are behind you and that I'm behind you."[40] He then went around the room shaking hands and sharing a few words with each player.

It worked; they won the game in overtime. Among other things, it was a great victory for the humanity of Nelson Mandela. His pre-game visit to the locker room provides a nice lead to a literary example of another leader mingling with his men on the evening before battle.

## KING HENRY V

Shakespeare provides you with a good model of leadership in his dramatic portrayal of the person of King Henry V of England. Just before the Battle of Agincourt (1415) during the Hundred Years' War, "King Harry" goes into the field and mixes in person with his men, who are ready but outnumbered, on the night before battle. I always imagine him standing by their campfires as he reminds them that

> This day is called the feast of Crispian:
> He that outlives this day, and comes safe home,
> Will stand a tip-toe when the day is named,
> And rouse him at the name of Crispian.
> He that shall live this day, and see old age,
> Will yearly on the vigil, feast his neighbours,
> And say "To-morrow is Saint Crispian":
> Then will he strip his sleeve and show his scars.
> And say, "These wounds I had on Crispin's day."
> Old men forget: yet all shall be forgot,
> But he'll remember with advantages
> What feats he did that day: then shall our names,
> Familiar in his mouth as household words,
> Harry the king, Bedford and Exeter,

Warwick and Talbot, Salisbury and Gloucester,
Be in their flowing cups freshly remember'd.
This story shall the good man teach his son;
And Crispin Crispian shall ne'er go by,
From this day to the ending of the world,
But we in it shall be remember'd;
We few, we happy few, we band of brothers;
For he to-day that sheds his blood with me
Shall be my brother; be he ne'er so vile,
This day shall gentle his condition:
And gentlemen in England now a-bed
Shall think themselves accursed they were not here,
And hold their manhoods cheap whiles any speaks
That fought with us upon Saint Crispin's day.

These inspiring words draw an immediate response from the Earl
of Salisbury that the French are arrayed for battle "and will with all expe-
dience charge on us." This prompts a famous line from King Henry, "All
things are ready, if our minds be so."

Henry's presence and words prepared their minds; his was prepared well in advance. This, of course, is a task of leadership. What Shakespeare had King Henry do on stage, Nelson Mandela did in a rugby team's
locker room. The venue can be a stadium or a battlefield. The test of leadership is being there and having something to say.

This Saint Crispin's Day speech is said to have been John F.
Kennedy's favorite selection from Shakespeare. His wife invited the British
actor Basil Rathbone to present this passage at a White House dinner on
April 30, 1963.

## MOHANDAS K. GANDHI

Through his commitment to the principle of nonviolence, Mohandas K. Gandhi (known worldwide as "Mahatma" Gandhi, an honorific San-
skrit title meaning "great soul") offered the world, as Margaret Bourke
White once put it, "a way out of its madness." Sadly, that offer remains,
for the most part, untaken and untried. But the idea and the ideal of nonviolence remain. What the world needs now is more people like Gandhi who
are willing to "model the way" of nonviolence.

Eknath Easaran, commenting on how Gandhi "made himself the force of nonviolence," reports that, once, when a reporter asked Gandhi for a message to take back to his people, he replied with "a hurried line scrawled on a scrap of paper: 'My life is my message.'"[41]

For many reasons, the remarkable life of Gandhi is worth knowing about and studying carefully. For purposes of this book, Gandhi presents a compelling model of principled leadership.

As Michael N. Nagler describes him, "Gandhi was an inveterate tinkerer; in a country where the bonds of tradition have always been strong, he was making changes in his way of living, chipping away at imperfections, right up to the day he died. His manual for all this experimentation—his 'spiritual reference book,' as he called it—was the Bhagavad-Gita."[42] This is a classic Hindu scripture.

Gandhi was born in India in 1869. Shy as a child and not a good student, he found his way to London to study law. Three years later he returned to India, credentialed but ill-prepared to practice law there. He relocated to South Africa and took a position in a Muslim law firm. It was in South Africa, a nation where the white minority ruled and the black majority included, in the eyes of the whites, the significant Indian population that had settled there, that Gandhi found purpose in his life. He discovered what he called the "true practice" of law. "I had learnt to find out the better side of human nature and to enter men's hearts. I realized that the true function of a lawyer was to unite parties riven asunder."[43]

He began to see opportunities for service in the practice of law. He had no interest in profit or prestige. He became an advocate for poor Indians in South Africa, especially those who came as laborers and found themselves in what amounted to a system of legalized slavery.

> When the black plague broke out in the squalid Indian ghetto of Johannesburg, the sick and dying were taken to an abandoned quarantined building where a heroic English nurse spent long hours alone caring for them. Many years later she related that in the evening at the height of the epidemic a small figure appeared at the door. She shouted a warning: "Get out! This is plague." But the man quietly replied, "It's alright. I've come to help you."
>
> She recognized him as a leader in the Indian community and let him in. He went straight to the sick. As she saw him bend over a dying man covered with vermin, she said, "Leave him; I'm used to it." But Gandhi attended the man himself and whispered back, "He is my brother." And he stayed throughout the night until relief came.[44]

Gandhi found himself committed to the ideal of selfless service. "The domestic struggles in South Africa were the training ground where Gandhi learned the demanding art of living for others rather than himself. Later he would apply the same lessons on a global scale, so that in the end the whole world became his family."[45]

In his first year in South Africa, Gandhi was treated badly by a railway car conductor who first evicted him from his first-class compartment because of his dark skin, and then, when he protested, had a policeman eject him altogether from the train in the mountain town of Maritzburg. Gandhi spent a cold night there in the unlit railway station without overcoat and luggage, which had been taken by the officials. He made the decision then "never to yield to force and never to use force to win a cause."[46] Notice the two-way street—never to yield to, never to use.

Years later, having returned to India, he led a nonviolent fight against the greatest empire in the world (the British), and won. Details of the great salt march and other leadership achievements in his native India can be learned from the history books. The point to emphasize here is twofold. First, Gandhi's conviction that "there comes a time when an individual becomes irresistible and his action becomes all-pervasive in its effects. This is when he reduces himself to zero."[47] And the other consideration to emphasize is his understanding of the essence of the principle of nonviolence, namely, "that it must have its root in love. Its object should not be to punish the opponent or to inflict injury upon him. Even while non-cooperating with him, we must make him feel that in us he has a friend and we should try to reach his heart by rendering him humanitarian service wherever possible."[48] This is the way Gandhi confronted power; this is the way Gandhi led.

## MARTIN LUTHER KING

An interesting window on Martin Luther King's approach to leadership is provided by a routine budget document distributed to the members of the Dexter Avenue Baptist Church in Montgomery, Alabama for their "prayerful consideration" and subsequent adoption, when he became their pastor in 1954, at age 25. Reverend (not yet Doctor) King prefaced the document with a few paragraphs stating his understanding of leadership. "When a minister is called to the pastorate of a church," he wrote, "the main presupposition is that he is vested with a degree of authority." He then spelled out that presupposition as follows:

> The source of this authority is twofold. First of all, his authority
> originates with God. Inherent in the call itself is the presupposi-
> tion that God directed that such a call be made. . . . Secondly,
> the pastor's authority stems from the people themselves. Implied
> in the call is the unconditional willingness of the people to ac-
> cept the pastor's leadership. This means that the leadership never
> ascends from the pew to the pulpit, but it invariably descends
> from the pulpit to the pew. This does not mean that the pastor is
> one before whom we must blindly and ignorantly genuflect, as
> if he were possessed of some infallible or superhuman attributes.
> Nor does it mean that the pastor should needlessly interfere . . .
> assuming unnecessary dictatorial authority. But it does mean that
> the pastor is to be respected and accepted as the central figure
> around which the policies and programs of the church revolve.
> . . . It is therefore indispensable to the progress of the church
> that the official board and membership cooperate fully with the
> leadership of the pastor.[49]

There's a strong suggestion of the "vertical" approach here (leadership "descends from the pulpit to the pew"), but there is also a hint of
the center-of-the-circle approach in King's reference to himself as the "central figure around which" activities revolve. He softened the authoritarian
tone of that statement by appending 34 specific recommendations for financial management to be discussed and eventually accepted for the good
order of the congregation. He also encouraged widespread participation by
appointing members to newly constituted committees. Taylor Branch notes
that the young pastor developed good rapport with the less sophisticated
members of his congregation by never asking them, "What are you
doing?"—a potentially embarrassing question for those who "were just
farming or doing the white folks' laundry." Instead, the new pastor "always
looked his members squarely in the eye and asked them *how* they were
doing, usually following with a personal question about their health or the
kids."[50]

Taylor Branch offers an interesting comparison of the King and
John F. Kennedy personalities: "What King had envied in President
Kennedy was his self-esteem and his lack of perceptible angst. Although
politically on the defensive nearly every time King communicated with
him, Kennedy always possessed an independent sense of well-being. By
contrast, King was personally self-conscious. He worried about his looks,
his tough skin, about what people thought of him and whether they might
find out that he had ghostwriters for his books."[51]

King was, without doubt, a great leader. His stature as a leader increased as his official authority decreased. He had no formal authority when he led the civil rights movement; he had enormous moral authority, however, and it was on the strength of that moral authority that he rose to greatness. As a young pastor, he probably never even thought of the possibility of a distinction between authority (his office as pastor) and leadership (his pastoral ministry).

Commitment to his core values of justice and nonviolence provided Dr. King with an inner compass. Courage to speak truth to power and to face the ever-present threat of assassination freed him to lead from the front.

These few paragraphs serve only to post the name of Martin Luther King at the top of the list of model leaders; they don't pretend to provide anything more than a simple introduction to his approach to leadership. His writings—including "A Letter from the Birmingham Jail" and his famous "I Have a Dream" speech—and his creative and courageous leadership marches chronicled by Taylor Branch and others should be studied by anyone aspiring to a position of leadership. The importance of courage simply cannot be overemphasized in assembling a list of qualities that belong in the leadership toolkit.

## ANNE MULCAHY

When the *New York Times* interviewed Xerox CEO Anne Mulcahy for the "Corner Office" feature of the Sunday Business Section,[52] the first two words in the opening question put to her were, "You led." She did indeed lead a turnaround at Xerox beginning in 2001, and she restored confidence at the top of a corporate giant that was embarrassed by ethical lapses and stood on the brink of bankruptcy. In the process, she has provided both example and encouragement to female aspirants to positions of leadership in business.

So the *Times* wanted to know, "What lessons did you learn from that experience?" She replied, "When you have that window of opportunity called a crisis, move as quickly as you can, get as much done as you can. There's a momentum for change that's very compelling. I think we took good advantage of it."[53] Notice the leadership qualities hidden in that answer: optimism (seeing crisis as a "window of opportunity"), decisiveness ("move as quickly as you can"), persistence ("get as much done as you can," don't fail to ride that "momentum for change").

The *Times* asked another question: "Looking back over your career, do you recall a certain insight that put your career on a different trajectory?" In replying, she first noted that she came up through sales but reached a point "where I felt like I was just running out of steam." So she chose to go into human resources. "I didn't do it so much because of leadership development or career aspirations. I did it just simply because I thought it was really interesting. I'd always believed that human resources could be a very powerful part of an organization and often wasn't. So I kind of threw my hat in that ring, wound up running human resources for Xerox worldwide. That was a decision that certainly changed my career path and reinforced the power of leadership for me."[54] Tucked away inside that reply is the suggestion that she chose to move closer to Xerox people, the employees instead of the customers, and in the process perhaps gave those leadership qualities of empathy and intuition a chance to grow.

Not surprisingly, the interviewer asked, "As chief executive, how do you stay in touch with people at all levels?" Her reply is instructive for would-be leaders as well as veterans in the leadership ranks:

> I stay in touch by staying in touch. You've got to be out there. You've got to be visiting your operations. You've got to be doing town meetings. You've got to be doing round-tables. There are plenty of avenues for getting feedback, but there's nothing that substitutes for the dialogue that you can have with people on the ground, with your customers in terms of how they view the company. . . .
>
> This is not an arm's length exercise. You've got to get up close and personal. You've got to give people permission to give you tough news, not shoot the messenger, thank people for identifying problems early and giving you the opportunity to solve them. So I think part of it is the way you handle candid feedback, but the other part is being present.
>
> Nothing replaces sitting around a table and really asking people what's working, what's not working, what's getting in their way, how do we help. I do a lot of that and I think it is the most important thing I do.[55]

This is a good description of center-of-the-circle leadership as opposed to being parked on the top of a pyramid.

One additional comment that will be a helpful takeaway, for anyone looking at the leadership qualities of Anne Mulcahy, deals with "the most important list" she keeps. When asked about that she replied, "I'd say my contact list. I'll at times run down my contact list, and it's hundreds of names in my BlackBerry, just to think through who I haven't spoken to, who do I need to touch, what contact do I need to make, is there a customer I need to call. It's a great way of ensuring that you really have a system of making sure not too much time goes by between you reaching out and talking to someone, either on your team or external to the company, who you really need to be close to."

Years ago the nation's major telephone company ran ads in print and on radio and television that urged all of us to "reach out and touch someone." When you do that by telephone, you do not literally touch anyone, but you do indeed stay in touch with others. And that is something leaders have to do. Failure in that regard will be acknowledged by some (I would include myself among them) as a major weakness; not infrequently, it is the explanation for failures in leadership.

Anne Mulcahy turned over the Xerox CEO responsibilities in July 2009 to Ursula Burns, the first African-American female ever to lead a Fortune 500 company.

## BARBARA BOGGS SIGMUND

Service as the elected mayor of Princeton, NJ (1983–90) certainly admits Barbara Boggs Sigmund to the leadership ranks. As the daughter of Hale Boggs, longtime majority leader of the U.S. House of Representatives, and Lindy Boggs, who filled her husband's seat in Congress as a representative from Louisiana after his tragic death in a plane crash in 1972, "Mayor Barbara" was raised on politics. Her mother Lindy, a leader in her own right, served in Congress for twenty years and then became U.S. ambassador to the Vatican. Barbara's sister, Cokie Roberts, is a well-known political analyst on network television and public radio. Her brother Tommy is one of Washington's most effective lobbyists.

Sadly, Barbara, who was a devout Catholic, died of cancer in 1990 at age 51. Before her death, however, she sent a public letter to Pope John Paul II urging him to "bring back Mary." Excerpts from that letter will explain why she belongs in this chapter and why young women, as well as young men, need compelling models of leadership. Here are her words to the pope: "Modern women need Mary to validate female strength-in-gentleness in the world of power. We are entering that world inexorably but uncertainly; jealous of both our femininity and our detachment. We resist taking on the 'pinstripes of the oppressor.' But all of our archetypes of power are male ones: the warrior, the team, the old bulls and the young. We need a model of our own on the grand scale." And she drew this conclusion: "So bring back Mary . . . to celebrate the need for the tough tenderness of femaleness in the life of the world, to acknowledge that charm and kindness can still entice God to dwell among us."

There it is again—the power of persuasion. Women have no corner on that quality, of course, but they come by it naturally and possess a sufficient supply to warrant more space for them today in the corner offices of organizational life.

## JACK WELCH

Writing in the *Wall Street Journal*, January 23, 2004, Jack Welch, the retired chairman and CEO of GE, spoke of the "four essential traits of leadership." He listed them as (1) energy, (2) the ability to energize others, (3) having an edge ("the courage to make tough yes-or-no decisions—no maybes"), and (4) the ability to execute. If a candidate for a leadership role has all four of these, says Welch, "then you look for a final trait—passion. By that I mean a heartfelt, deep and authentic excitement about life and work." But, according to Welch, you cannot even start to think about the Four E's until you get a solid yes on two questions:

FIRST: Does the leadership candidate have integrity? That means, does he or she tell the truth, take responsibility for past actions, admit mistakes and fix them? Does he demonstrate fairness, loyalty, goodness, compassion? Does she listen to others? Does he truly value human dignity and voice? These may seem like fuzzy, subjective questions, but you have to get a strong "AMEN" in your gut to all of them to even consider a person as a leader.

SECOND: Before applying the Four E's, you have to ask, is the candidate intelligent? That doesn't mean a leader must have read Kant and Shakespeare. . . . It does mean the candidate has to have the breadth of knowledge, from history to science, which allows him to lead other smart people in a world that is getting more complex by the minute. Further, a leader's intelligence has to have a strong emotional component. He has to have high levels of self-awareness, maturity and self-control. She must be able to withstand the heat, handle setbacks and, when those lucky moments arise, enjoy success with equal parts of joy and humility.[56]

There's nothing there that we haven't seen earlier in these pages, except perhaps for passion. Welch's list is long, but familiar: integrity, fairness, loyalty, goodness, compassion, ability to listen, respect for human dignity, intelligence, an emotional component (no robots or martinets need apply!), self-awareness, maturity, self-control, toughness, and the ability to put humility in harness with joy when things are going particularly well.

With the assistance of *Business Week* editor John A. Byrne, Jack Welch wrote a best-selling autobiography[57] in which he describes himself as "brutally honest and outspoken . . . impatient and, to many, abrasive."[58] He also acknowledged that he had the "smarts and passion" to run GE, and that, of all the basic ideas that served him well, integrity was at the top of the list.

Echoing Lincoln, Welch cited his mother as "the most influential person in my life." "If I have any leadership style, a way of getting the best out of people, I owe it to her."[59] She helped him overcome a childhood speech impediment, impressed upon him the value of competitiveness, built up his self-esteem, and gave him self-confidence.

Nowhere, to my knowledge, does Welch acknowledge an intellectual or managerial debt to Abraham Lincoln, but he does welcome candor and argument around the table where decisions are made. "I loved the 'constructive conflict' and thought open and honest debates about business issues brought out the best decisions," writes Welsh. "If an idea couldn't survive a no-holds-barred discussion, the market-place would kill it. Larry Bossidy, a good friend and former GE vice-chairman, would later liken our staff meetings to Miller Lite commercials. They were loud, raucous, and animated."[60]

Like President Kennedy, Welch found it difficult to fire people. "It's the toughest and most difficult thing we ever do." But here's how he did it. "If I learned anything about making this easier, it's seeing to it that no one should ever be surprised when they are asked to leave. By the time I met with managers I was about to replace, I would have had at least two or three conversations to express my disappointment and to give them the chance to turn things around. I would follow up every business review with a handwritten note. Some may not have appreciated my candor, but they always knew exactly where they stood."[61]

## KEVIN W. SHARER

In the "Corner Office" feature of the Sunday Business section of the *New York Times* on March 29, 2009, there was an interview with Kevin Sharer, chief executive of Amgen. The interviewer, Adam Bryant, asked, "Do you recall some insight about leadership and management that put your career on a different trajectory?" The Amgen CEO replied that he would point to four things: (1) His father, a Navy aviator in World War II, began speaking to him about leadership when he was a child. (2) Sharer was later chief engineer on the construction of a submarine in the 1970s; he had to train the crew, work with the shipyard, and get things organized "or I just would have been crushed." (3) He was hired by McKinsey while in his early 30s and learned "how to think as a top manager at a young age." And (4) he was hired to do business development strategy for Jack Welch at GE and "to be that close to the center of GE in those exciting times and watch Welch at his peak, close up, was instructional and inspirational."

"I've certainly learned other things in the intervening years, but I think the family background, submarine, McKinsey, GE experience was foundationally important and I draw on it to this day."[62] Asked about the "intangibles in leadership," he replied, "Leadership is not about charisma and it's not about style. It's something about authenticity. It's something about integrity. It's something about willingness to take risks. It's something about the ability to make others feel part of a larger thing. It's part of being able to articulate the social architecture in a way that others can understand, believe in and follow."

After his appointment was announced, but before he became CEO, he talked to the top 150 people in the company one-on-one for an hour. He had asked them beforehand to consider several questions: What three things would you like to see us keep? What three would you like to see changed? What would you like me to do? What is it that you're afraid I'm going to do? And what else, if anything, would you like to talk about?

This tactic enabled him to become better known and it obviously gave him greater knowledge of the company. The responses from the top 150 people in the company became components of a strategic plan for the company he would lead.

Another tactic that worked for Sharer was putting himself on the block for an annual performance review involving the management team and conducted by the company's director of human resources. This, says Sharer, has deepened his "self awareness"; he compares the evaluation process to seeking help to correct his golf swing!

## RICK WAGONER

Leaders sometimes fail. A good example is George Richard (Rick) Wagoner Jr., who was Chairman and CEO of General Motors until March 29, 2009, when he agreed to a White House request to resign the position he had held for nine years. The situation was not unlike the one the former chancellor of Austria described: "Two men sat down together at a table. One had a machine gun and the other held a fountain pen. Both were loaded." In 1938, in that situation, he signed an agreement with Hitler and then resigned as Germany seized Austria.

Wagoner met on March 27 with Steven Rattner, the so-called car czar whose proper title was Auto Industry Adviser to the Secretary of the Treasury. He is an investment banker whom President Obama recruited one month earlier to lead the Treasury Department's auto-industry task force. Through Rattner, the Obama administration used the threat of withholding funds authorized to help the ailing automobile industry to force Wagoner out of office. What led up to this leader's downfall?

Wagoner grew up in Richmond, Virginia. He was recognized as best all-around student in his graduating class from John Randolph Tucker High School. He went on to Duke (where he played basketball) and then to the Harvard Business School for an MBA in 1977. His first job was as an analyst in the treasurer's office at General Motors. He moved up from there to become chief financial officer in 1992, executive vice president for North American Operations in 1994, and president and chief operating officer of GM in 1998. Two years later, he was CEO and was then elected chairman in 2003. His career seemed to contradict the belief that "there is no escalator to the top." A few months before he became chairman, a *Business Week* cover story commented, "CEO Rick Wagoner has fixed many of GM's problems. But he still has to deal with thirty years of management mistakes."[63] That was something of an understatement. *Business Week* cited "weak brands and gargantuan pension payments." And things just got worse.

The cover story portrayed a "self-effacing" Wagoner and admired his "low key style." His "greatest achievement" [up to then, 2003] was that "against all odds, Wagoner is making real progress in energizing GM's torpid culture. He broke with GM tradition by recruiting two respected outsiders for key positions—Robert A. Lutz as head of product development and John Devine as vice chairman and chief financial officer. And he gave them extraordinary leeway to fix the company's problems."[64] (Lutz stayed

on with Wagoner; he retired as vice chairman for global product development in 2009. In December 2005, Devine was replaced as chief financial
officer by Frederic "Fritz" Henderson, who emerged as the immediate successor to Wagoner as chairman. Eight months later, Henderson was ousted
by an impatient board.).

Here's more from *Business Week*: "Wagoner's willingness to let
others shine is a classic trait of leaders who have boosted their companies
to exceptional performance, says Jim Collins, author of *Good to Great*. As
a longtime GM insider, Wagoner has other advantages: He knows what
brutal facts need to be confronted, and he can assess which veterans can
handle key jobs. Says Collins: 'Wagoner has the opportunity to take it back
to great.' But the odds are stiff—only 11 of 1,435 companies Collins studied
made such a lasting transformation. And those that did required an average
of seven years to get breakthrough results."[65] Wagoner, as the whole world
now knows, did not make it. Why?

Those healthcare costs and pension obligations tell part of the story.
President Obama's impatience figures in as well. His March 30, 2009 announcement on the auto industry spoke directly of "a failure of leadership
. . . that led our auto companies to this point. . . . Our auto industry is not
moving in the right direction fast enough to succeed in a very tough environment. . . . I'm absolutely confident that GM can rise again, providing
that it undergoes a fundamental restructuring. As an initial step, GM is an-
nouncing today that Rick Wagoner is stepping aside as Chairman and CEO.
. . . It will take new vision and new direction to create the GM of the future."

Wagoner failed to produce a satisfactory business plan to justify
additional federal support. The president gave GM sixty days to come up
with a better plan. When the CEOs of GM, Ford, and Chrysler first appeared before a Congressional Committee in November 2008 to request
federal loans (popularly referred to as a "bailout"), they drew ridicule from
the national press for using their corporate jets to fly to Washington instead
of taking less expensive modes of transportation. Next time they appeared,
they drove from Detroit. Ford decided to decline federal assistance.
Chrysler was told by Mr. Obama, speaking after consultation with experts,
to find a merger partner. The president then reminded both GM and
Chrysler that bankruptcy was an option that could give them protection
from creditors while not jeopardizing their continued existence.

Had Mr. Wagoner come to Washington hat in hand, with a commercial boarding pass in his pocket and a viable business plan in his brief-
case in late 2008, he might have avoided losing his job in 2009.

## SHEILA C. BAIR

From teller in a small-town bank during her college years to chairman of the Federal Deposit Insurance Corporation (FDIC) is a career path that led Sheila Bair to be named, in 2008, the second most powerful woman in the world by *Forbes* magazine. No disgrace to be ranked second to Germany's chancellor Angela Merkel.

No small achievement either to move from a philosophy major in college to a law degree from the University of Kansas in the 1970s, to a teaching post at the law school of the University of Arkansas, on to the General Counsel's office of the former U.S. Department of Health Education and Welfare, and then to a succession of Washington appointments as research director, deputy counsel, and counsel to Senator Robert Dole; commissioner and acting chairman of the Commodity Futures Trading Commission; vice president for government relations for the New York Stock Exchange; and assistant secretary for financial institutions at the Treasury Department.

Before joining the FDIC in 2006, she was the Dean's Professor of Financial Regulatory Policy at the Isenberg School of Management at the University of Massachusetts Amherst.

As a bank teller in the early'70s, Sheila Bair got to know the "little people" who carried savings passbooks and made monthly mortgage payments (typically 30-year, fixed-rate payments they could afford). She knew how important it was to the little people in small towns to have their savings deposits insured. She also knew how important it was for local bank lenders to be honest and open with their mortgage borrowers. This knowledge was there to guide her judgment decades later when she saw early signs of what became known as the subprime mortgage crisis that triggered the economic meltdown of 2008–9.

In an introduction to its special "Women to Watch" eight-page supplement in the November 10, 2008 edition, the *Wall Street Journal* asked: "Who made our annual list of women who are poised to make an impact on the world of business? For starters, think financial crisis." Number one on the list of fifty "women to watch" in 2008 was Sheila Bair. Here is how the *Journal* introduced her:

> One day this past April, Federal Deposit Insurance Corp. Chairman Sheila Bair saw a stark reminder of the human side of the foreclosure crisis. Attending a foreclosure-prevention workshop

in Los Angeles, she saw hundreds of homeowners of all back-
grounds lined up for hours to be admitted to the event, where
they desperately hoped to receive help or advice that would
allow them to keep their homes.

For Ms. Bair, the outspoken and politically savvy head of
FDIC, the images of so many borrowers trying to salvage their
lives left an impression.

"This myth of all these people making sophisticated calcu-
lations and trying to game the system, that wasn't it. . . . These
were just regular people, working families trying to hold onto
their homes. They were scared and I saw a lot of fear on their
faces, and I think that struck me more than anything."

The event . . . solidified in Ms. Bair's mind that the federal
government needed to take much more aggressive action to stem
the record number of foreclosures at the center of the growing
economic crisis. It also reinforced her belief that compassion
should be a key part of the equation for policymakers.[66]

In June 2009, she received a Profile in Courage Award at the
Kennedy Library in Boston, an award given to public officials who have
exhibited "political bravery." She qualified because of her efforts, even
though unsuccessful, to get the Bush Administration to address the subprime mortgage crisis.

As a member of the Commodity Futures Trading Commission in
1993, she was the lone commissioner to vote against a provision that re-
laxed federal oversight of the high-flying Enron Corporation—essentially
an energy trading company dealing in futures contracts—from anti-fraud
regulation. It was well before the Enron implosion of 2001, but she saw
the potential for fraud in what Enron was doing. She favored tighter regulation to prevent it, but did not prevail. The experience, however, strengthened her resolve more than a decade later to take her pro-consumer and
pro-regulation sympathies public and influence policy in the Obama Administration as she continued to chair the FDIC.

## WILLIAM W. SCRANTON

Less well-known now that he is in his early nineties and out of the
public eye, former Pennsylvania governor William W. Scranton is still a
model leader. He not only served as governor (1963–68, when there was a
one-term limit on that office in Pennsylvania), he was also a U.S. Con-
gressman, this country's ambassador to the United Nations, a bank presi-

dent, and an unsuccessful challenger to Arizona Senator Barry Goldwater for the Republican nomination for President in 1964. He was a World War II Air Transport Command pilot, who finished law school after the war and later served on many corporate boards including IBM, A&P, Pan American Airlines, The New York Times, Scott Paper, and H. J. Heinz Company. His bloodline runs back to the Mayflower.

During my years (1975–82) as president of the University of Scranton in his hometown, I often saw the former governor walking briskly on downtown sidewalks and picking up trash as he went along, then dropping paper cups, wrappers, and soda cans in corner receptacles that invited citizens to "Help Keep Our City Clean." He led by example; I've been picking up trash ever since!

During the Obama campaign, Governor Scranton agreed to a newspaper interview[67] in which he disclosed that he, like Obama, had Abraham Lincoln for a leadership paradigm. "I hate oppression. My whole theory of life is that almost everybody . . . can excel if you give them the chance." He called Mr. Obama's March 2008 speech on racism "the best on the subject since the Emancipation Proclamation," and has kept a copy of the speech on his desk. Noting that change is more than a political slogan and something that seldom comes easily, this elder statesman said, "All politicians talk about changing Washington. Changing the Congress of the United States is not a simple task, no matter who is president. When I was there [in Congress], it was run by seniority, which is wrong, but now it's run by money, which is worse. Government run by money is tyranny. We're supposed to be a free country, and you're not if some lobbyist is running you."[68]

The Public Broadcasting System (PBS) outlet for Northeastern Pennsylvania (WVIA) produced a documentary on the life and achievements of Governor Scranton when it launched its "Great Pennsylvanians" series in 2004. This is worth viewing by anyone who doubts the effectiveness of the low-key, self-effacing, out-of-the-limelight leadership style that characterized Bill Scranton and that is much appreciated and widely admired in his home state.

## NELL MINOW

Nell Minow is former president of Institutional Shareholder Services; former head of Lens Governance Advisors, a shareholder-activist investment firm; and co-founder and now chair of the Corporate Library, which provides research on corporate governance issues. Despite multiple credentials of her own, she is invariably referenced as the daughter of former Federal Communications Commission chairman Newton Minow who, back in the days of the Kennedy Administration, came up with a famous phrase to describe television in America: "vast wasteland."

The "Corner Office" feature in the Sunday Business Section of the New York Times—which I urge my leadership students to read and to which I've referred earlier in this chapter—asked this opening question of Ms. Minow in a recent interview: "What are the most important leadership lessons you've learned through the years?" Here is her answer: "I noticed that there was something very definitional in who was included in somebody's 'we' and 'them.' I found generally that the more expansive the assumptions were within somebody's idea of 'we'—the larger the group that you had included in that 'we'—the better off everybody was. I started to really do my best to make sure that my notion of 'we' was very expansive and to promote that idea among other people." And when asked to expand on that, she added, "I also learned a lot about being a manager from being a mom. When I first became a professional manager, I was pregnant for the first time, and so I grew up with both responsibilities at the same time. You have people saying the same two things to you all day long, which is, 'Look what I did.' And you say: 'It's really good. Do some more.' Or they say, 'He took my stuff.' And you have to say, 'Tell him to give it back.'" She then explained, "You're constantly trying, whether you're raising children or dealing with employees, to get them to take responsibility for their own issues. In both cases, you're trying to make people more independent and bring them along."[69]

Thinking about the "importance of we," as Nell Minow does, is a good way to summarize what you are likely to find when you begin looking, as we've been doing in this chapter, at leaders—major and minor, elected or appointed, widely recognized or relatively unknown. The leadership "we" is always superior to a leadership "I." This is true even in crisis situations that require a strong "I" to be seen and heard throughout the crisis. The would-be leader who overworks the perpendicular pronoun in speech and directives to the followership during tense and tight situations, and, worse, prepares for those public moments by withdrawal and isolated pondering, is certain to fail.

There is little if any room at the very top of the pyramid for a leadership "we," but lots of room on that sawed-off platform a little lower down where the leadership group meets around a table to discuss and debate, analyze and challenge, reexamine and reassure. Some ridicule this as the "bogat" method of management—"bunch of guys around a table"—but none should fail to see the wisdom underlying the leadership "we" approach to running the organization in good times and in bad.

It should be obvious by now that there are many leadership styles, just as there is a wide variety of leaders in organizational life. A useful image as well as a very helpful set of categories for understanding this is provided in a book I recommend to anyone interested in learning about leadership. The book is *Primal Leadership*; the authors are Daniel Goleman, Richard Boyatzis, and Annie McKee.[70] The image they employ to illustrate the fact that there are different leadership styles that can be used at different times by the same leader, is a set of golf clubs. Use the club that best suits your need at a particular time and location on the course.

Under the heading, "The Leadership Styles in a Nutshell,"[71] they are listed as (1) visionary, (2) coaching, (3) affiliative, (4) democratic, (5) pacesetting, and (6) commanding. They are more fully explained, of course, in the book. The last two are to be used with caution, if at all. The first four presuppose competence, experience, a measure of wisdom, and a familiarity with the foibles of human nature. The entire book is must reading for those who want to lead.

John Sosik and Don Jung wrote a book called *Full Range Leadership Development*.[72] They have a lot to say about "transformational leadership" (which, they explain, "inspires followers . . . to perform beyond expectations"[73]) but express their preference for a "full-range model of leadership" as an "important organizing mechanism for pulling together the leadership literature."[74] Their book does indeed serve that purpose and is well worth consulting. It departs from trait-based, "great man," innate-quality explanations of leadership and opens the door to an exploration of the "four I's" of transformational leadership—namely, "idealized influence, "inspirational motivation," "intellectual stimulation," and "individualized consideration."

Inspirational motivation is the quality I want to highlight here. It would have a leader (1) "talk optimistically about the future," (2) "talk enthusiastically about what needs to be accomplished," (3) "articulate a compelling vision of the future," (4) "provide an exciting image of what is essential to consider," and (5) "express confidence that goals will be achieved."[75] The book you now hold in your hand will help you cover those bases. I mention them here only to suggest that exercising full-range leadership is going to give your talents a very full stretch!

This chapter now ends, but the practice of "looking at leaders" should continue for anyone interested in influencing the behavior of other humans. Leaders are everywhere. You can't miss them, but you have to know what you're looking for. The first two chapters of this book will have served their purpose if they provided you with a framework, a range-finder, through which you can observe the service of leadership in the world around you. The shorter chapters that follow will introduce you to the tools you will need to be a responsible and effective leader.

I think it was Yogi Berra who once remarked that "you can see a lot by just observing." Well, any time is a good time to observe, and to be convinced that it is never too late to learn.

## NOTES:

1. (San Francisco: Jossey-Bass, fourth edition, 2007).
2. Ibid., 14, 29.
3. Ibid., 183.
4. Ibid., 23.
5. Adapted from a December 4, 2006 PowerPoint presentation at The Commonwealth Club, London, by Susan Sarfati, president and CEO, the Center for Association Leadership.
6. *Leading Change* (Boston: Harvard Business School Press, 1996), 25.
7. Private conversation in Philadelphia, June 25, 2008.
8. *Some of It Was Fun: Working with RFK and LBJ* (New York: Norton, 2008).
9. Ibid., 26–27.
10. Ibid., 27.
11. *FDR: 1882–1945* (New York: Random House Gramercy, 1982), 108.
12. Ibid., 10–11.
13. (New York: Random House Gramercy, 2004).
14. Ibid., 3.
15. Ibid., 9.
16. Ibid.
17. Ibid., 120.
18. *A. Lincoln: A Biography* (New York: Random House, 2009), 5.
19. (April 2009): 43–47.
20. "Leadership Lessons from Abraham Lincoln: A Conversation with Historian Doris Kearns Goodwin," *Harvard Business Review* (April 2009): 44.
21. Ibid.
22. Ibid., 45.
23. Ibid.

24. Bob Blaisdell, ed., *The Wit and Wisdom of Abraham Lincoln* (Mineola, NY: Dover, 2005), 15.

25. Mark Leibovich, "Speaking Freely, Sometimes, Biden Finds Influential Role," *New York Times* (March 29, 2009): 1, 16.

26. Ibid., 16.

27. Ibid.

28. Jodi Kantor and Javier C. Hernandez, "A Harvard Lightning Rod Finds Path to Renewal," *New York Times* (December 7, 2008).

29. Ibid.

30. For a link to a transcript of this speech, go to httm//www.masnbc.msn.com/id/23690567/-52k-cached.

31. Richard Wolffe, *Renegade: The Making of a President* (New York: Crown, 2009), 304.

32. Anthony Sampson, *Mandela: The Authorized Biography* (New York: Alfred A. Knopf, 1999), xxiv.

33. (New York: Penguin, 2008).

34. Ibid., 3.

35. Ibid.

36. Quoted ibid., 4.

37. Ibid., 173.

38. Ibid., 223.

39. Ibid., 228.

40. Ibid.

41. *Gandhi the Man: The Story of His Transformation* (Tomales, CA: The Blue Mountain Press, 1997), 140.

42. Ibid., 8.

43. Ibid., 22.

44. Ibid., 25.

45. Ibid., 33.

46. Ibid., 42.

47. Ibid., 150.

48. Ibid., 156.

49. Taylor Branch, *Parting the Waters: America in the King Years 1954–63* (New York: Simon and Schuster, 1988), 114–15.

50. Ibid., 118–19.

51. Ibid., 918.

52. "The Keeper of That Tapping Pen," *New York Times* (March 22, 2009), 2.

53. Ibid.

54. Ibid.

55. Ibid.

56. "Four E's (a Jolly Good Fellow): Do the Democratic Presidential Candidates Have What It Takes to Lead?" *Wall Street Journal* (January 23, 2004).

57. *Jack: Straight from the Gut* (New York: Business Plus, 2001).

58. Ibid., xii.

59. Ibid., 4.

60. Ibid., 42–43.

61. Ibid., 44.

62. "Feedback in Heaping Helpings," *New York Times* (March 29, 2009): 2.

63. *Business Week* (February 10, 2003), 52.

64. Ibid., 53.

65. Ibid., 55

66. Michael R. Crittenden, "Sheila Bair, Chairman, Federal Deposit Insurance Corp.," *Wall Street Journal* (November 10, 2008), R3.

67. Chris Kelly, "We Are in This Together," (Scranton) *Sunday Times* (September 28, 2008): D1, D6.

68. Ibid., D1.

69. "Think 'We' for Best Results," an interview with Nell Minor conducted by Adam Bryant in *New York Times*, (April 19, 2009): BU 2.

70. Daniel Goleman, Richard Boyatzis, and Annie McKee, *Primal Leadership: Learning to Lead with Emotional Intelligence* (Boston: Harvard Business School Press, paperback 2004).

71. Ibid., 55.

72. John J. Sisik and Don I. Jung, *Full Range Leadership Development: Pathways for People, Profit and Planet* (New York: Psychology Press, 2010).

73. Ibid., 14.

74. Ibid., xviii.

75. Ibid., 120–31.

# CHAPTER THREE

## A LEADERING ATTITUDE

On February 20, 1962, America's pioneer astronaut John Glenn blasted into orbit as part of the space race between the United States and the Soviet Union. We were behind in that race and John Glenn's success in orbiting the earth three times on that sunny day many years ago did much to restore American prestige and advance our progress in space exploration.

Glenn's Mercury spacecraft was named "Friendship 7." In it, John Glenn risked his life as he traveled at 17,500 miles per hour 160 miles above Earth. His autopilot function failed and he had to pilot the spacecraft manually for reentry. The world watched on television and listened to Mission Control wonder aloud whether the space capsule's heat shield would hold while reentering the earth's atmosphere, because, as the spacecraft began its second orbit, Mission Control received a signal that the heat shield was loose. Its function, we knew, was to prevent the capsule from burning up during reentry.

Normally the retrorocket package would have been jettisoned after the rockets were fired to slow the capsule for reentry. In this case, however, Glenn was ordered to retain it to hold the heat shield in place. As he struggled to maintain control of the spacecraft, John Glenn watched as huge chunks flew past the window and he wondered whether it was the heat shield breaking up. The world held its breath at reentry time. The heat shield held. If it hadn't, John Glenn and his capsule would have been incinerated.

During those tense moments of flight maneuvers and instructions, Mission Control frequently used the word *attitude* referring to the attitude of the space craft. I was intrigued by that vocabulary and soon realized, of course, that they were talking about the tilt, the direction of incline, the bias, the position of the capsule. It had to be tilted so that the heat shield would be there, if indeed it was still attached to the spacecraft, to make first contact with the earth's atmosphere. It was there. It held. John Glenn lived to tell the story of the flight. History was made. The mission was a success.

"Have in you the same attitude that is also in Christ Jesus," wrote St. Paul in his Letter to the Philippians (2:5), thus inviting them to have a tilt, a bias, a direction, an attitude of humble service. Their tilt could not be simply a nod or salute to Christ Jesus. More is required of the Christian than a membership card. There has to be commitment to the values of Jesus, a fidelity in following his way, a willingness to imitate him, to internalize his world view, to adopt his convictions, to make them one's own, to internalize them. In other words, if you are a Christian with the controls of your own life in your own hands (manual control, no autopilot), you have, Paul urges, to tilt your life as Jesus tilted his. And what was his tilt, his bias, his attitude? Paul outlines it for you: "Though he was in the form of God, [Jesus] did not regard equality with God something to be grasped. Rather, he *emptied* himself, taking the form of a slave coming in human likeness; and found human in appearance, he *humbled* himself, becoming obedient to the point of death, even death on a cross."

A NASA news release on June 4, 2002, forty years after the famous Glenn flight, announced that something called the Global Positioning System is now "determining the attitude, position, and speed of the International Space Station. This is the first successful use of GPS data in attitude control of a spacecraft, NASA officials and scientists believe. It is working well, feeding information on the station's attitude to systems that control its orientation in space. GPS also is providing more precise speed and position data than had been available. 'As far as I know, no one else is using GPS operationally for attitude determination,' said the Johnson Space Center's Susan Gomez, chief engineer of the Space Integrated Global Position System/Inertial Navigation System."

Here on earth, as our feet of clay try to find their way on the journey of faith, the word of God, preserved for us in the books of the Bible, can function as a "positioning system," an attitude setter. With or without religious faith, you can cultivate biases (or permit a secular culture to cultivate them for you) that run counter to the biases that were part of the attitude that Jesus cultivated for himself and those who would follow him.

The verse from Philippians is just one of many readings that can be factored into a personal (as distinct from global) "positioning system." There is one I like from a non-Christian source that echoes Philippians and can function within anyone's personal positioning system. It is from Mahatma Gandhi, who said, "There comes a time when an individual becomes irresistible and his action becomes all pervasive in its effect. This comes when he reduces himself to zero."[1] This, as I suggested back in chapter two, and as Gandhi demonstrated in his remarkable life, is an attitude that is indispensable for effective leadership.

This describes the poured-out life, the emptying out of self in service for others. Don't mistake this for doormat spirituality. The upside for you, as it was for Jesus, is also articulated by Paul in the Philippians text: "Because of this, God greatly exalted him and bestowed on him the name which is above every name, that at the name of Jesus every knee should bend, of those in heaven and on earth and under the earth, and every tongue confess that Jesus Christ is Lord, to the glory of God the Father" (2:10–11).

If you are a Christian, all this can make sense to you even though you can't expect to find any bended knees before you. You can and do, however, bet your life on the glory that awaits you in Christ Jesus your Lord, if you make his attitude your own. Even for the unbeliever, there is the upside of knowing that those whom you have led will achieve free and fuller lives because of you.

The range of possible attitudes that leaders can adopt is wide and varied. Not all are good, and no one attitude is the best for all occasions. An attitude of optimism is needed in times of crisis. When things look bad, the leader must be looking up. There is a time for "grim determination," but that time is also a time for resolute hope that is visible in the person of the leader. Consider Joseph Alsop's observations on the imperturbability of Franklin Delano Roosevelt: "Roosevelt could never have been a great war president, as I think he was, without his total imperturbability and firm belief that any disaster could only be temporary, which quite largely derived from his Christian faith. In bad times, as his wife later wrote, he literally and humbly believed God was with him and would never desert him. And why not, for his chief adversary [Hitler], as he saw it, was one of the truly wicked men of the 20th century, and who can say Roosevelt was not fighting for good against evil?"[2]

Imperturbability is a reflection of attitude. In time of war, both soldiers and civilians look for calm self-assuredness in their leaders. Roosevelt had exactly the right temperament to deal with crises in war or peace. He demonstrated that well before the outbreak of war when he led the nation during the Great Depression.

The expression I've used for the title of this chapter, "a leadering attitude," has a nice ring to it. It usually finds its way into conversations about leadership when the names Winston Churchill and Franklin Delano Roosevelt come up. And it is remarkable how often emotional attitude comes to the fore in discussions of the leadership style of Barack Obama. Commentators admired, and the voters seemed to approve, his even-tempered "cool" during the televised debates in the 2008 campaign that led up to his election. Early in his presidency, Mr. Obama appeared on the Sunday evening CBS Television progam"60 Minutes" with Steve Kroft. That interview, along with an appearance on the "Tonight Show" with Jay Leno, a "Face the Nation" interview with Bob Shieffer, and a one-on-one with Charles Gibson on ABC television's "World News Tonight" prompted some to say that this new president had fashioned for himself a network-hopping version of Roosevelt's famous "fireside chats."

Throughout the campaign, Obama projected a calm and disciplined image. On a campaign visit to Philadelphia, the candidate sat down with the editorial board of the *Philadelphia Inquirer* for a wide-ranging conversation in which he said, "I've got a temperament that would serve me well as president. I don't get too high when things are high. I'm not too low when things are low. I've gotten my share of knocks and made some mistakes during the campaign, and I think I have held pretty steady throughout. That actually can serve you well as president."[3]

After persuading over 65 million people to vote for him, he carried his steady, calm, cool image (and style) with him into the White House.

Martin Luther King was another great leader who knew how to keeps his cool. His commitment to nonviolence undoubtedly helped shape his temperament. He was imperturbable but not fatalistic. And, of course, he was a powerful speaker.

President Harry S. Truman's biographer, David McCullough, says that that president's "subordinates found him invariably cheerful and positive. He was never known to make a rude or inconsiderate remark or to berate anyone, or to appear the least out of sorts, no matter how much stress he was under."[4] McCullough says this despite his subsequent account of the outburst of presidential fury in a "scathing" letter Truman wrote to David Hume, music critic of the *Washington Post*, who published a negative review of the presidential daughter Margaret Truman's singing performance in a public concert at Constitution Hall in December 1950.[5] Presumably, this demonstration of fury was the exception to the rule.

The steady, cool, even-tempered, imperturbable personality is desirable in a leader, but it should be open to adaptation. The good leader must be properly assertive, even effusive on occasion. He or she has to be a lively speaker. The passion and emotion must be there even though the underlying personality is calm and under control.

## Leadership Competencies, Leadership Styles

This is perhaps as good a place as any to make the point that there are leadership competencies and leadership styles, and that the sensitive leader will have first mastered the competencies and then will alternate the styles (by putting his or her leadership on manual, not autopilot) to match the shifting winds and changing challenges that constitute the leadership context. No leader is going to exhibit the same style all the time, nor will the same set of skills or competencies be employed in equal proportions all the time. Like John Glenn in the space capsule, the leader has to manage the "tilt," the "attitude." So it's important to note that attention to the "leadering attitude" is going to involve the management of a medley of leadership competencies and styles.

Underlying any executive's style is an attitude and, as the 2008 economic meltdown in the United States demonstrated, an arrogant attitude on the part of some CEOs, coupled with their questionable competence as to what was happening or was about to happen in their companies and in the economy, brought them down. Some pleaded the "perfect storm" defense, but that didn't wash with the *Washington Post* business writer Stephen Pearlstein, whose harshly critical essay appeared under the title, "A Perfect Storm? No, a Failure of Leadership": "The reason the perfect storm is such an appealing metaphor for these shipwrecked captains of industry is that it appears to let them off the hook. After all, who can blame you if the ship goes down in one of those freak once-in-a-century storms that result when three weather systems collide?"[6]

Sebastian Junger's account of the shipwreck that popularized the notion of the perfect storm makes it clear that the skipper of the Andrea Gail ignored warnings that the ship was headed for disaster.[7] Sam Zell, the Chicago real estate tycoon who made the smart move of selling out at the top of the commercial real estate cycle only to make the bad move of buying the Tribune Company's newspaper and broadcast properties just as circulation and advertising revenues were about to plummet, was no victim of a perfect storm, wrote Pearlstein. "The only perfect storm to hit the Tribune was the one that resulted from the collision of Zell's ego, his arrogance, and his utter ineptitude in running a media empire, along with a total disregard for the financial well-being of thousands of employees, whose retirement assets he commandeered for a financing scheme that gave him control of the company while putting in very little of his own money."[8]

Pearlstein concludes his reflections on the problems of the media companies, automobile manufacturers, and banks by saying, "What capsized the economy was not a perfect storm but a widespread failure of business leadership—a failure that is only compounded when executives refuse to take responsibility for their misjudgments and apologize." It should come as news to no one that "pride goeth before a fall."

Daniel Goleman (who introduced the idea of emotional intelligence into the leadership literature) co-authored a book with Richard Boyatzis and Annie McKee: *Primal Leadership: Learning to Lead with Emotional Intelligence*.[9] Primal leadership simply means being intelligent about your emotions. *Primal,* as these authors employ the term, means being first in two senses—original and most important. Emotional intelligence, which is at the origin of any instance of genuine leadership, and which these authors also rate as most important, is there at the controls in any leader's "space capsule." Reflect on the leadership styles and competencies that these authors identify.

The leadership styles[10] are (1) visionary, (2) coaching, (3) affiliative, (4) democratic, (5) pacesetting, and (6) commanding. The last two can be counterproductive. The pace set by the leader can be too swift and thus unsustainable by others; the commands (except in genuine crisis situations) can generate a negative resistant reaction. So the amalgam of these competencies you select for your particular style of leadership has to be carefully fashioned.

The leadership competencies[11] are (1) self-awareness, which presupposes an accurate self assessment and sufficient self confidence; (2) self-management, which implies self-control; (3) social awareness, which requires empathy, political sensitivity, and a commitment to service; and (4) relationship management, which assumes that the leader can inspire others and then foster teamwork and collaboration. This fourth competency includes what the authors identify as being a change catalyst, which they describe this way: "Leaders who can catalyze change are able to recognize the need for the change, challenge the status quo, and champion the new order. They can be strong advocates for the change even in the face of opposition, making the argument for it compellingly. They also find practical ways to overcome barriers to change."[12]

Surely, there is an emotional side of all good leadership. If you are unemotional, it is unlikely that you will succeed in inducing others to follow. Chapter 5 of this book will focus on the leadership tool of oral communication—public speaking as well as effective speech in smaller groups. An emotionless, monotonic voice induces sleep, not action. A listless body behind that voice speaks louder than the words; the message it conveys is that the speaker is unconvinced of the truth of what he or she is saying, indeed that the speaker suffers from a deficit of self-confidence. The unemotional speaker—hiding behind a podium or slumped in a chair—is an embodiment of neutrality, an emotional Switzerland incapable of persuading, unable to convince.

A strong leadering attitude will have come to terms with emotions in a very positive and quite productive way. Intellect alone will not move others to action.

After their discussion of strategy and leadership development exercises at the Unilever Corporation, Goleman, Boyatzis, and McKee had this to say:

> For most leaders, and even most managers, it is not more clarity about the strategy that will make the difference. It is not yet another five-year plan, and it is not another mundane leadership program. What makes the difference is finding passion for the work, for the strategy, and for the vision—and engaging hearts and minds in the search for a meaningful future. One more intellectual planning exercise is not going to get people engaged, and it certainly won't change a culture. Even the best leadership development programs, if conducted in a vacuum, do little to foster the kind of change that organizations need today.[13]

The trick is to find the person with a leadering attitude that is conditioned to making this happen.

It is instructive to note that another good book on leadership is titled simply, *The Catalyst*.[14] The subtitle promises that reading the book can help you become "an extraordinary growth leader." Without endorsing that promise, let me help readers who, at the moment, may be trying to recall explanations of the role of a catalyst from their high school chemistry classes, by letting the authors of this book on leadership explain why they chose *The Catalyst* for their title.

> We chose the word *catalyst* carefully in looking for a good way to describe our leaders. Catalysts drive action. But there's more.

In science, the term *catalyst* refers specifically to an agent that
is *required* to activate a particular chemical reaction. In other
words, chemical catalysts don't just make things happen; they
make things happen that wouldn't happen at all without them.
They accomplish this by reducing the barriers that would, under
normal circumstances, prevent a reaction. That is exactly how
the growth leaders—our corporate Catalysts—overcame growth
gridlock and the terror of the plug [a reference to the number
that's been pulled out of thin air and "plugged" into a company's
budget or strategic plan to make it work] in their organizations.[15]

To meet those corporate catalysts, you'll have to read the book.

I once knew a business executive who jokingly referred to his cus-
tomary cocktail hour before dinner as a period of "attitudinal adjustment."
Relax, lighten up, leave your business worries at the office. A good leadering attitude is something you will carry with you wherever you go—in the
office and out, at the conference table, in the board room, in your walk-
around contacts in the workplace, and in conversations with suppliers, customers, and competitors. Your leading attitude is you. Behind the flexible
repertoire of competencies and styles is the leader you have grown to be.

## THE ADAPTIVE LEADER

Ronald Heifetz, Alexander Grashow, and Marty Linsky have writ-
ten a book that incorporates into its title the notion of an adaptive leader.[16]
The ability to adapt—essential for good leadership—is not unrelated to the
possession of the right leadering attitude; that's why I want to discuss adaptive leadership here. Heifetz, a psychiatrist, is the author of *Leadership
Without Easy Answers*,[17] and, with Marty Linsky, he wrote *Leadership on
the Line: Staying Alive through the Dangers of Leading*.[18] Many years of
teaching about leadership in the Kennedy School of Government at Harvard, together with his consulting work on leadership around the world,
have gained for Heifetz a well-deserved reputation as a leading theorist on
leadership. He is best known, perhaps, for employing the metaphors of the
"dance floor" and the "balcony above" to gain an understanding of the practice of leadership (on the floor). And from an observation post above (the
balcony), it is possible to figure out what is or is not happening below so
that one can come up with the right "diagnosis" in order to lead effectively.

Remember, Heifetz is a physician; he knows well that if you are wrong on your diagnosis, you will surely be wrong on your prescription.

Anyone who has been there knows that pressures to adapt are part of the very environment of leadership. Rigidity simply will not work, which is not to say that principled decision-making and strong convictions are of no consequence. They are. Unlike laws, principles have no loopholes. They cannot be broken; they can only be applied. How to apply them, how to time their application, and how to bring others into the application flow are all questions of adaptability on the part of the leader. Heifetz and his colleagues write, "The single most important skill and most undervalued capacity for exercising adaptive leadership is diagnosis."[19] Their research and teaching interest focuses on "leading adaptive change, with all the dangers, ambiguity, setbacks, and improvisations that leadership journeys involve."[20] Hence the importance of diagnosis—getting up on the balcony—to size up the situation carefully and correctly before taking action. For Heifetz, "adaptive leadership is an iterative activity, an ongoing engagement between you and groups of people."[21]

I recall that, many years ago, a business consultant remarked to me, "Iterative—that's just an elegant word for messy." He was speaking in the context of strategic planning and the point he was making was clear. Situations change. So do assumptions. Plans change accordingly. Planning is therefore iterative. The planning process can easily appear messy, even sloppy, but that just serves to remind that it is unavoidably human. So the leader has to be human too—reading the human landscape accurately, being sensitive to human emotions, hopes, and fears, and relating in a human way to other humans who are looking for leadership. All of these considerations factor into the proper attitude—the "tilt"—the good leader has toward those he or she is privileged to serve.

## OPTIMISM

"The fundamental task of leaders is to develop confidence in advance of victory, in order to attract the investments that make victory possible—money, talent, support, loyalty, attention, effort, or people's best thinking."[22] That is Rosabeth Moss Kanter speaking. She is a professor at the Harvard Business School and former editor of *Harvard Business Review*. Con-fidence (with faith) means what it says. You have faith in yourself, in your product or service, in your associates, and in all the surrounding, interacting forces that create the market within which your organization operates. Even if yours is not a commercial operation, you are still in a market of sorts and there are people there who need to share your faith and catch your optimism. So a faith-based optimism might be viewed as a component of a good leading attitude. Not religious faith necessarily, although there is no reason to exclude religion from life in the secular realm of leadership—but faith nonetheless. A good leader must have confidence; a charismatic leader exudes confidence. As far back as biblical times, the warning was posted that no one is going to follow an "uncertain trumpet" into battle (1 Corinthians 14:8). Without a blast of the bugle, there will be no charge, and without the charge, there will be no victory. "Onward, with confidence," is the message an effective leader must project by word and example.

The effective leader will invariably be a hopeful person, a person capable of communicating and inspiring hope in others. I'm puzzled at the way the word "hopefully" worked its misapplied way some years ago into our American vernacular. That adverb means "in a happily expectant way." Like "cheerfully," it conveys a mood. Hope is substance; hopefulness is style. "Hopefully" suggests a bounce in your walk, some lilt in your voice.

Are you really full of hope and happily expectant when you say, "hopefully"? Or are you struggling with doubt and trying to sound brave? Instead of saying, "hopefully," you should probably be saying, "(from the depths of my doubt and uncertainty) it is to be hoped" that this or that outcome will emerge.

Hope is an engine to drive your dreams into the unknown future. That's what leaders have to do, and it takes the right leading attitude to do it.

Just as sorrow can make you sorrowful, hope can make you hopeful. From the inside, the hopeful mood feels good. From the outside, it is typically seen as something light, bright, and cheery, although it can work just as well under cover of seriousness. For the religious person, hope is an anchor that connects one securely to God.

There is a wonderful book, *Images of Hope*, written back in 1965 by a Jesuit priest by the name of William Lynch. He was a genuine Christian humanist. He points, in the best humanistic tradition, to "imagination as healer of the hopeless." Lynch saw hope as "the very heart and center of a human being." And he says that hope must be tied to the life of the imagination. I'll let Fr. Lynch speak for himself:

> I define hope. . . as the fundamental knowledge and feeling that there is a way out of difficulty, that things can work out, that we

as human persons can somehow handle and manage internal and external reality, that there are "solutions" in the most ordinary biological and physiological sense of that word, that, above all, there are ways out of illness.

What [I'm] saying is that hope is, in its most general terms, a sense of the possible, that what we really need is possible, though difficult, while hopelessness means to be ruled by the sense of the impossible. Hope therefore involves three basic ideas that could not be simpler: what I hope for I do not yet have or see; it may be difficult; but I can have it—it is possible.

Hope looks to the next step, whatever it is, whatever form the step may take. If there is hope, I take [the step]. We are too much inclined to think of hope as an emergency virtue that saves itself for a crisis (one that is really meant for use in moments when there is not much or any hope at all!). The truth is that [hope] is present in each moment as it looks to the next. [Hope] is present everywhere, in the flowing of the bloodstream and in every small action. I would not breathe if I did not hope that the air around me would respond to my call.[23]

A good leader is a waiting, wishing, hopeful person, who, precisely because he or she lives by hope, steps out to meet the demands of the present day en route to an unknown future.

For his "Corner Office" feature in the *New York Times*, Adam Bryant asked Robert A. Iger, CEO of the Walt Disney Company, to identify the "most important leadership lesson you have learned." Iger replied,[24] "What I've really learned over time is that optimism is a very, very important part of leadership. However, you need a dose of realism with it. People don't like to follow pessimists." And then he added, "I've also learned to listen better and manage reaction time better."

When asked about how he goes about hiring, Iger replied, "Carefully." He elaborated on that by quoting Warren Buffett: "When you hire someone, you look for brains, energy and integrity, and if they don't have the third, integrity, you better watch out, because the first two will kill you."[25] As important as optimism is to a good leading attitude, it has to be tempered by realism; and it never hurts to have a good sense of humor.

I don't think I'd use the expression "nasty optimism" to describe the leading attitude of folk singer Pete Seeger who has been the Pied Piper of the social protest movement in America for more than a half century. But that's what Bruce Springsteen sees behind Pete's "somewhat benign, grandfatherly façade," and so described him in the presence of thousands at a ninetieth birthday party for Seeger in Madison Square Garden on May 3, 2009. Mr. Seeger is "a stealth dagger through the heart of our country's illusions about itself," said Springsteen, and the *New York Times* agreed editorially, saying that Springsteen got it "exactly right."[26]

Pete Seeger is an American leader as well as an American icon. He has absolutely no authority of position (and never has had any) but he's a genuine leader who has had an impact in the pursuit of peace and protection of the environment. His attitude is upbeat, hopeful in the future, considerate of and committed to future generations. So, he's an optimist, a serious one, but never nasty. And he's a great leader.

Larry Bossidy, longtime right-hand man to Jack Welch at GE and later an outstanding CEO both at Allied Signal and Honeywell, reflected on five decades of personal experience in business and listed what he sees as prerequisites for effective leadership: (1) know enough about the business to participate in decisions at all levels of the business; (2) embrace realism in everything you do; (3) set clear goals and be careful not to set too many; (4) reward good people in your organization; (5) coach your people; and (6) know yourself.[27] This, in my view, is a nice way to package the practical with the theoretical in articulating the right attitude you might expect to find in an effective business leader.

Your leading attitude will be shaped by your deeply held personal values. Some of those values will never change in terms of your belief in and commitment to them. There can be, however, a rearrangement of the ranking of your priorities, from time to time, as circumstances change and the need to adapt arises. This rearrangement comes into play in the strategic planning that leaders engage in. Noel Tichy and Warren Bennis touch on this in their comparison of the values that guided Jack Welch during his years as CEO of GE and those that influenced his successor in that post, Jeff Immelt.

> The values that Welch emphasized included speed, simplicity, self-confidence, boundary-lessness, and the four E's, which in Welch's words are: "Energy to cope with the frenetic pace of change. Energize, the ability to excite, to galvanize the organization and to inspire it to action. Edge, the self-confidence to make tough calls with yesses and noes and very few maybes, and Execute, the ancient GE tradition of always delivering, never disappointing."
>
> Immelt has changed the values to be: imagine, solve, build, and lead. These four values are the ones that he feels will support

the right behaviors throughout GE to execute on his growth strategic judgment. It means that all of the hiring and promotions screens at GE ask how well people have done and can be expected to do with regard to these values. Do they have imagination? Can they innovate, and have they done so in the past? Can they solve problems? Have they taken innovative ideas and turned them into solutions for customers? Can they take innovation that solves a customer need and build it into a viable business? And, finally, can they develop and lead others to grow through innovation?[28]

The Tichy-Bennis book is all about judgment, and the subtitle promises to explain "how winning leaders make great calls." Throughout their book, they demonstrate that effective leaders have a winning attitude and that their attitudes are shaped by intelligence, information, and by values that are internalized and clearly communicated. In this chapter, I've referred to attitude as a tilt or bias. Subsequent chapters, notably chapter twelve, "The Ethical Leader," will discuss higher values that a leader might want to internalize and how an understanding of those values might be communicated to those the leader wants to lead.

Back in chapter one, I mentioned that I'm grateful to William Taylor and Polly Labarre for introducing me to the notion of "humbition," which is operative in the leadership style of those who run SEI Investments in Oaks, Pennsylvania. Tichy and Bennis spotted the same characteristic in some of the executives with whom they have consulted. They describe it in the less colorful and more academically flat expression, "the paradoxical combination of self-confidence and humility to learn."[29] Whatever label you give it, it describes a great leading attitude. Tichy and Bennis see it in Jeff Immelt, "a leader with an insatiable thirst for being better, who invested himself in self-knowledge creation."[30] And they make their case by offering this excerpt from a talk that Immelt gave to an incoming class of MBAs at the University of Michigan:

> The first part of leadership is an intense journey into yourself. It's a commitment and an intense journey into your soul. How fast can you change? How willing are you to take feedback? Do you believe in self-renewal? Do you believe in self-reflection? Are you willing to take those journeys to explore how you can become better and do it every day? How much can you learn? Can you look in the mirror every day and say, gee, I wish I had done that differently, boy I think I've got to do better here. . . .

> You've got to be willing to do an intense journey into yourself.
> . . . I've been lucky, you know, because I've got to do things that
> I love with people that I love. But more than anything else, the
> burning desire inside me was to get the best out of what I could
> be and go on that journey.[31]

That is advice well worth heeding. But as you do, wrap it in these words of wisdom from an unknown source: "Humility is not thinking less of yourself; it is thinking less about yourself." The "intense journey into yourself" is an important one to take, just don't become overly enamored of the destination!

I want to close this chapter with a thought that is in the spirit of what you've come across earlier in this book from the mind of Mahatma Gandhi. It relates to the importance of taking that journey into yourself. It relates to having the right leading attitude. I recall once being of some assistance to a young woman who found herself at a career crossroads, an important decision point in her life. I encouraged her to focus on her feelings and deepest desires. I gave her an idea from an ancient Hindu text. She carries it now, years later, tucked neatly in her address book: "You are what your deep driving desire is/ As your desire is, so is your will/ As your will is, so is your deed/ As your deed is, so is your destiny."[32] Your deeply felt desires are the place to begin looking for the direction in which you might be called to do great deeds.

## NOTES:

1. Eknath Easwarab, *Gandhi the Man* (Tomales, CA: Nilgiri Press, 1997), 150.
2. Joseph Alsop, *FDR: 1882–1945* (New York: Random House Gramercy, 1982), 241.
3. Larry Eichel, "Next Up: Test of Obama as Leader," *Philadelphia Inquirer* (November 9, 2008).
4. David McCullough, *Truman* (New York: Simon & Schuster, 1992), 434.
5. Ibid., 829.
6. "Perfect Storm Warning: Don't Take It as an Excuse," *Washington Post* (December 10, 2008): D1 and D4. The quoted lines are from page D1.
7. Sebastian Junger, *The Perfect Storm: A True Story of Men against the Sea* (New York: Harper, 1997).
8. "Perfect Storm Warning: Don't Take It as an Excuse," D4.
9. (Boston: Harvard Business School Press, 2002).
10. Ibid., chapter four, 53–69.

11. Ibid., summarized in appendix B, 252–56.

12. Ibid., 256.

13. Ibid., 239.

14. Jeanne Liedtka, Robert Rosen, and Robert Wiltbank, *The Catalyst: How You Can Become an Extraordinary Growth Leader* (New York: Crown Business, 2009).

15. Ibid., 7.

16. *The Practice of Adaptive Leadership: Tools and Tactics for Changing Your Organization and the World* (Boston: Harvard Business School Press, 2009).

17. (Cambridge, MA: The Belknap Press of Harvard University Press, 1994).

18. (Boston: Harvard Business School Press, 2002).

19. *The Practice of Adaptive Leadership*, 7; see note 16 above.

20. Ibid., xii.

21. Ibid., 8.

22. Rosabeth Moss Kanter, *Confidence: How Winning Streaks and Losing Streaks Begin and End* (New York: Three Rivers Press, 2004), 19.

23. William F. Lynch, S.J., *Images of Hope: Imagination as Healer of the Hopeless* (New York: Mentor–Omega, 1966), 24–25.

24. "He Was Promotable, After All," *New York Times*, Sunday (May 3, 2009): DU 2.

25. Ibid.

26. Lawrence E. Downes, "Still Singing," *New York Times* (May 5, 2009): A26.

27. Presentation to the National Catholic Roundtable on Church Management, Wharton School, University of Pennsylvania, Philadelphia, June 27, 2008.

28. Noel M. Tichy and Warren G. Bennis, *Judgment: How Winning Leaders Make Great Calls* (New York: Portfolio, 2007), 166.

29. Ibid., 238.

30. Ibid., 241.

31. Ibid.

32. These words are from one of the Upanishads, ancient Indian philosophical treatises; this saying appeared on a bookmark and no precise reference was given.

# CHAPTER FOUR

## LEADERS LISTEN

"In his case, the ears are merely ornamental." I'll always remember an unhappy faculty member making that comment about a pompous college president. And I have to admit that he was right.

Ears—listening, hearing ears—are, like perceptive eyes, essential to good leadership. (I'm not unmindful of the fact that visually impaired or hearing-disabled persons can lead effectively. My point is simply that awareness of what others are saying or have said, together with a grasp of the interconnected dimensions associated with any reality that can be seen, belong in the leadership toolkit.)

We've discussed leadership styles and "leadering attitudes" in earlier parts of this book. To put the emphasis in this chapter on listening is to underscore the importance of many things, not the least of which is the willingness to consult. Ask for advice. Seek help. To consult is not a sign of weakness. You don't have to take all the advice you receive, but you should not insulate yourself against advice, particularly advice that could prove helpful to you. In some cases, you will not get it unless you ask—hence, the importance of asking. Of course, you don't have to follow the advice you receive, but that should be your choice based on consideration of an array of options before you. To enlarge your array of options by simply asking for advice is an indication of wisdom, not weakness.

Don't think that you have to have an immediate comment on everything you hear. But you should be aware that your immediate response, especially if it is a rejection of the suggestion offered, is likely to discourage subsequent suggestions, some of which might have been helpful. For instance, a college president, who was worried about retaining enrolled students when the 2009 recession hit so many families, rejected out of hand a suggestion that he might offer from unrestricted reserve funds "lines of credit" to enable students—financially strapped, but already enrolled—to stay in school. "We're not a bank," he said by way of dismissing the suggestion. The one who made the suggestion thought to himself (but did not say aloud), "But you might consider acting like a foundation; you can offer 'life-lines' to students in need. These would be grants, not loans, and the recipients would be asked to sign a nonbinding pledge to participate, as best they could in future years, in alumni annual giving." Not a bad idea. It was, however, never heard because the leader showed no interest in listening.

## I'M ALL EARS

For many years, the gossip circuit at all levels of society and in most corners of the world has been informally wired by the widespread admission that, "I'm all ears."

Now, in the cell phone era, we are always and everywhere "all ears" all the time. Cell phones have to be banned from classrooms and put on vibrate in exclusive clubs and restaurants, but, across all divisions of age, class, and sex, cell phones have given the human ear a degree of anatomical prominence it has never known before. Nonetheless, just because it is there is no reason to conclude that the ear will always be used. "Those who have ears to hear, let them hear" is a biblical prompting that bears repeating in our day. And in heeding that advice, be sure to note that there is a huge difference between careful listening and all the tweeting, texting, and e-mail volleyball that can clutter up our avenues of communication every day.

James J. Schiro, CEO of Zurich Financial Services, was asked by the *New York Times*, "What is the most important leadership lesson you've learned?" He replied, "It's the ability to listen, and to make people understand that you are listening to them. Make them feel that they are making a contribution, and then you make a decision. You've got to have a sense of inclusiveness."[1] Note that listening is, in his view, the most important leadership lesson he learned along the way to the top. That's a remarkable statement.

If you open yourself to listening, you will, on occasion, "get an earful." But you can always filter out the vengeful and unfair portions of what unfriendly critics might pour into your auditory canal; to shut yourself off, however, from hearing the rest of what they might have to say is not wise.

On another occasion, that same "Corner Office" interviewer asked Eduardo Castro-Wright, vice chairman of Wal-Mart Stores the same question. His immediate response repeated much of what you have already seen in this book, namely, "Walking the talk is the most important lesson. There's nothing that destroys credibility more than not being able to look someone in the eye and have them know that they can trust you. Leadership is about trust. It's about being able to get people to go to places they never thought they could go. They can't do that if they don't trust you." And he continued with some thoughts on the importance of listening: "I think the best source of strategy is your customer and the people who work for you. I'm not saying there's no room for a vision statement or anything like that. I'm just saying that we tend to spend too much time on that and not enough on the more practical, down-to-earth requirements that drive business. . . . I walk around the store and approach customers and ask them if they have any recommendations for us. And I typically also will go to the back of the store and talk to associates and ask them questions about their jobs. I always tease them that they can tell me whether their store manager's good or bad. Almost always you get enormous insight from those who spend their days taking care of customers."[2]

In another "Corner Office" interview that appeared under the headline, "Knock-Knock: It's the C.E.O.," Terry J. Lundgren, the chief executive of Macy's was asked, "How do you stay in touch with people throughout the company?" His reply: "I just go and pop into a store. I have the cell phone number of every store manager, and I call them, and 95 percent of the time they're there. . . . I literally do it every week somewhere. And so we walk through the floor, and they have had no time to prepare for my questions, they've had no time to prepare the store. I always make it a good experience. I learn as much by going through a store as anything I do, because I'm learning and seeing exactly what our customer is seeing."[3]

Lundgren also stays in touch with employees by a monthly webcast for 55,000 people and he regards this as "a great communications vehicle. People feel like they know me in this gigantic company of 170,000 people."[4]

### HOW TO RUN A MEETING

Strong leadership presence (not overbearing or dominant, just consciously being present to others), a good leadership voice (pleasant, appropriate volume, clearly audible), and leadership listening (being acoustically attuned) are all prerequisites for the conduct of a good meeting. Just as it is a truism that if you refuse to listen, you will never lead, it is also true that the listening leader is the one, when in the chair, who is most likely to succeed in making a meeting productive. Without saying so aloud, think to yourself, when you call the meeting to order, "I'm all ears."

Any regular participant in organizational life will enjoy reading *Death by Meeting: A Leadership Fable* by Patrick Lencioni.[5] The extended subtitle to this book informs the reader that it is "about solving the most painful problem in business." The most painful problem? Yes, for many who have been in the world of work at the management level beyond those exciting, early, getting-to-know-you days, meetings are a form of slow death. "When is this going to end?" they ask themselves, when they should be thinking about creative forms of pain relief—making meetings interesting.

So let's talk about meetings, staff meetings, in particular—how to run them, keep them moving, and how to prevent them from running on forever. The ability to listen is the skill you need in order to run a meeting well.

A staff meeting in business or anywhere else should always be a pause in the flow of mainline organizational activity—a pause with a productive purpose, of course, but a pause nonetheless. It should never be a substitute for mainline productive activity. Nor should it ever be permitted to become what an unbiased observer might judge to be a waste of time. Meetings, whether you like them or not, are necessary on a regular basis for the smooth operation of any organization, but they can, if not well planned and managed, become a waste of time.

The typical meeting should really be a non-event, just a pause on the way to a definite, measurable outcome. If no expected outcome is anticipated, the meeting becomes an outcome in itself. It becomes, in fact, a meaningless event of absolutely no consequence.

So, what needs to happen for meetings to be productive? First, there should be an agenda—a list of what is to be decided and what needs to be discussed so that a good decision can be made. Facts inform discussion. Discussion paves the way for decisions. Someone, therefore, has to assemble and distribute the factual information needed for informed decision making. Uninformed discussion (no facts) is nothing more than pooled ignorance, which has zero potential for making any contribution to real progress.

Assuming that the meeting starts on time and all participants know why they're there, the chairperson (the one functioning as a convener, facilitator, and enabler) should provide early proof that his or her ears are not merely ornamental. Those around the table should be invited to comment upon and approve the agenda. They might also be given an indication of the expected time of adjournment.

It helps if agenda items that are not merely informational—items, in other words, that call for action—can be phrased, if possible, in question form so that there can be an up-or-down, yes-or-no resolution. Opinions pro and con should be heard (notice again the importance of listening) before votes are taken. Not everything has to be voted on, of course. The sensitive and skillful chairperson will be able to read a consensus and let a proposition be adopted "without objection."

It also helps if the person in the chair politely inquires, "Does everyone else agree with that, or see it that way?" when an opinionated, dominant participant—who may often be in error, but is never in doubt—attempts to derail discussion or makes a questionable assertion. With no reinforcement from the group, the off-the-wall point can simply be dropped and not permitted to impede progress.

It is particularly helpful if the chair invites an occasional expression of opinion from silent, sphinx-like members of the group. The listening leader will be aware of those who have not spoken. Some of them may be angry. Some simply refuse to acknowledge that there is "an elephant in the room" that they prefer not to talk about. Nonparticipatory meetings create a vacuum waiting to be filled by the voice, opinions, and pre-packaged decisions of an insensitive executive accustomed to a command-and-control management style. Attendees at nonparticipatory meetings tend to see early adjournment as the "solution."

The importance of "naming the elephant" is stressed by Heifetz, Grashow, and Linsky in their book *The Practice of Adaptive Leadership*. Their point is that all of us, beginning in childhood, take our cues from persons in authority. "Therefore, when you are the authority, you have to model the simple act of naming the sensitive issues simmering under the surface, because if you do not, the odds are high that no one else will."[6] Not to name the elephant is to fail to lead an effective meeting.

Every staff meeting (as well as other roundtable-type discussions) can benefit from the inclusion of a routine "go-round," an expected opportunity for each participant to mention anything of importance that has happened since the group last met, or soon will occur, in his or her area of responsibility. This exchange of information is always appreciated and adds to the efficiency and smooth functioning of the organization.

Detailed minutes need not always be taken, but meeting highlights and a list of decisions made should be recorded and distributed in advance of the next meeting. As a nation, Americans tend to neglect to read the minutes of the last meeting. Any organization will do better in the future if it is aware of what it has discussed and decided in the past.

Regular, relatively brief, always open and honest meetings will strengthen the fabric of organizational life.

Not all experts will agree with everything I've said so far about the conduct of meetings, and the author I mentioned earlier, Patrick Lencioni, would be one of them. If you read his *Death by Meeting*, and I strongly recommend that you do, you will notice that he uses the strategy-tactic distinction, with their respective long-run and short-run frameworks, as a classification device in naming and planning meetings. As we shall see, he discusses daily, weekly, monthly, and quarterly meetings that should be a routine part of organizational life but will differ in purpose and duration—the daily "check-in" meeting of top managers lasts five minutes; the weekly tactical meeting runs for one hour; the monthly strategic meeting runs abut the length of a movie; and the quarterly off-site session goes for six hours or more.

Lencioni thinks, for example, that staff meetings should be held weekly and they should focus on tactics. "Weekly tactical meetings will start with everyone giving a sixty-second report about what they're working on that week," he says, and they involve "going around the table and asking every person at the meeting to report on the three primary activities that are on their plate for the week. And everyone gets only one minute."[7]

## ALTERNATE APPROACHES

What about the agenda? There is none, at least not at the beginning of the meeting. Lencioni recommends that the quick around-the-table reporting session be followed by a "progress review," a routine reporting of critical information. This is in the form of "metrics" relating to items like revenue, expenses, customer satisfaction, inventory and other pre-selected measurables that are important to a given industry or organization. Just four or five of these at any given go-round; this should take no more than five minutes for each participant. No lengthy discussion should be permitted during this "progress review" of any of the underlying problems. You are now, perhaps, fifteen or twenty minutes into the weekly tactical meeting and only then, according to Lencioni, do you start to talk about agenda for that meeting.

> This makes sense because the agenda should be based on what everyone is actually working on and how the company is performing against its goals, not based on the leader's best guess forty-eight hours prior to the meeting. Trying to predict the right priorities before these critical pieces of information are reviewed is unwise.
>
> Leaders of meetings must therefore have something I call *disciplined spontaneity*, which means they must avoid the temptation to prepare an agenda ahead of time, and instead allow it to take shape during the meeting itself. While this might mean sacrificing some control, it ensures that the meeting will be relevant and effective.[8]

I made a case earlier on to have an agenda in place before meetings begin. I appreciate Lencioni's point and I don't want to say "pay your money and take your choice." I recognize the risk of not having an agenda going in and would simply suggest that you give Lencioni's way a try and stick with it if it works; otherwise take the pre-fixed but flexible, adjustable agenda approach.

The weekly tactical meeting should focus on the resolution of issues and the clarification of what the organization wants to achieve.

The monthly strategic meeting should be just that—strategic. It respects the distinction between strategy and tactics and the corresponding distinction between long- and short-run considerations. Weekly meetings should not get bogged down in discussions of long-run issues; if they arise, just park them for later consideration at the monthly strategic meetings, which, it goes without saying, should not get engaged with tactics. Regular strategic meetings are essential to the health of an organization. They should run for at least two hours, follow a leisurely pace, and not attempt to cover too much. Strategic meetings require preparation. They presuppose research and depend on good data.

A fourth type of regular meeting that every organization should have is what Lencioni calls the "quarterly off-site review." This is not a mini-vacation for the leadership team; it is rather a day or two spent apart from the rush of routine activity in order to reflect together on how the strategy is holding up, how the team is doing, what personnel issues are going unattended, and what's happening with the competition and in the wider world within which the organization operates. It sometimes helps to bring in experts from the outside to inform the conversation as well as facilitators who can keep the conversation on track.

Good meetings—all four types—will not be a waste of time; they will instead save the precious time of key individuals while moving the whole organization forward. Their success will, in no small measure, depend on the leader's ability to listen.

Meetings should also begin on time. The Macy's CEO, Terry Lundgren, asked how he ran meetings, replied, "First of all, and people know this about me, the meeting's at 8:00. You're not there at 8:01. You're here at 8:00, because the meeting's going to start at 8:00. And I've had to tell a couple of people that now and then: 'You have a tendency to be an 8:02 person or an 8:03 person, and it's not good by me. So from now on, I would like you to be here at 7:55. Everybody else will be here at 8:00, but you need to be sitting in your chair five minutes before that just because you haven't demonstrated to me that you can do that.' I will tell you this—every time that I have told a person this, it's solved."[9]

Meetings between and among key players of an organization that is geographically dispersed are taking place on the Web with greater frequency now that airfares and the price of gasoline are putting pressure on travel budgets. Similarly, meetings with customers, suppliers, and others with whom an organization wants to be in touch, are taking place more often now by means of interactive audio and video technology. Someone with good ears still has to convene, facilitate, and run the meeting; all participants have to listen carefully. If it is audio-only (a telephone conference call), the convener has to "call the roll" and ask participants to be sure to identify themselves whenever they speak. If it is videoconferencing, participants have to stay awake and resist the temptation to multitask in full view of all.

Any meeting will be a better meeting to the extent that attention is paid to the placement of chairs, the size of the room (relative to the size of the assembled group), and the possibility of eye contact between and among all gathered at or around the table. If at all possible, avoid a theater-like setting for a meeting that you expect to be participatory. A theater is designed to focus the attention of the viewer. If the attention of all is focused on one forward point (podium, chart, or screen), those who are seated in rows and can see only backs of their colleagues' heads are not likely to feel encouraged to contribute to the discussion. Circular seating, whenever possible, is preferable. Similarly, breakout groups are welcome relief in large assemblies; they also increase the probability that all will have an opportunity to be heard.

## LISTENING RECEPTIVELY

I was present at the creation of Bread for the World (BFW), a Christian citizens' lobby founded by Lutheran pastor Arthur Simon is 1974. Art recruited me first to participate in a small advisory group that helped him shape the idea, and then as a member of the board of directors of the resulting organization that now has a membership of over 60,000 and has, over the years, made a major impact—on behalf of the hungry poor—on U.S. policies aimed at alleviating hunger at home and abroad.

Art is a good listener. You have to be if you are responsible for organizing people around an issue. Hunger is the policy canopy under which BFW thinks and acts. But under the broad heading of world hunger, there are multiple possibilities when it comes to focusing the effort around a single issue, as BFW does each year. In his memoir, Art Simon addresses that question:

> To members and staff alike, the choosing of policy targets is crucial. Not long after Bread for the World was up and running, we began developing criteria to guide us in the selection of issues and give us a consistent frame of reference against which to test possibilities. These criteria compel us to ask, among other things: Is a proposed target clearly a hunger issue? If it becomes U.S. policy, what difference might it be expected to make for hungry people? Is it an issue that the membership has been prepared to act on? Is it one that can be explained clearly? Would Bread's role be apt to make a significant difference in the outcome? Questions such as these guide us. The selection of issues evokes intense and sometimes heated discussion, because much is at stake and staff members feel deeply involved. The process is always informed by Bread members and activists whom we poll, as well as church leaders, coalition partners, and congressional offices. Recommendations ultimately come from the staff, and decisions are made by our board of directors. The process is not simple, but each year it helps us determine targets of opportunity on which Bread seems to have the best chance of helping hungry people. Focus is essential.[10]

Focus is indeed essential and, over the years, Art Simon proved himself to be a focused listener. He heard all suggestions and concerns, evaluated them with care, and then presented a focused policy proposal for approval by the board. I chaired that board for many years and watched the process align itself with the purpose of the organization—to help the hungry poor.

Art Simon would be a good example of a servant-leader. That style of leadership will be discussed more fully in chapter thirteen. The category takes its name from the title of a famous book by Robert Greenleaf.[11] A prominent keeper of the flame and proponent of the servant-leadership idea is Larry Spears, who identifies listening as an essential characteristic of the servant-leader:

> Traditionally, leaders have been valued for their communication and decision-making skills. Servant-leaders must reinforce these important skills by making a deep commitment to listening intently to others. Servant-leaders seek to identify and clarify the will of the group. They seek to listen receptively to what is being said (and not being said!). Listening also encompasses getting in touch with one's own inner voice, and seeking to understand what one's body, spirit, and mind are communicating. Listening, coupled with regular periods of reflection, are essential to the growth of the servant-leader.[12]

"Listen receptively"—what a great phrase! I find myself using it from time to time as a window through which I can look back into countless board rooms and committee meetings and see persons in positions of authority who failed as leaders because they failed to listen. If only they had "listened receptively" and acted upon what they heard! Not only would the result have been good for them; it would have been immeasurably better for their organizations.

Of capital importance for anyone who would lead is acceptance of the fact that you have to quiet yourself enough in order to listen. This means time out for reflection—by yourself, apart from the crowd, away from the noise. You have to choose solitude from time to time in order not simply to think, but to listen to what your gut might be trying to tell you, indeed to what your God might be calling you to do.

Peter Senge recalls that, for Robert Greenleaf, the first impulse of the servant-leader was always to listen and not to talk. And Senge quotes with approval the retired chairman of Motorola who once said, "My job is to listen to what the organization is trying to say, and then make sure that it gets forcefully articulated."[13]

John Sperling is a former history professor who became a pioneer in the for-profit educational business as founder of the University of Phoenix, a $10-billion company. He is a complicated person and controversial educator whose profile in *The Chronicle of Higher Education*[14] makes interesting reading. For the information of would-be leaders, *The Chronicle* reports: "Despite his fondness for conflict, [Sperling] doesn't demand the floor in meetings. 'I speak as little as possible because when I talk I don't learn,' he explains. He tends to sit back quietly, waiting for the right moment to interject. When he has a point to make, he will spring to life, leaning over the table, raising his voice, wagging his finger. It's as if he has been waiting for the action to begin."[15]

Reducing what you hear to writing will be discussed in a subsequent chapter. Hearing what you hear—"getting it," as we often say—is a function of listening. It is not wide of the mark to say that only those who listen are qualified to lead. Testing their ability to listen receptively and retain what they receive, is a trial-and-error challenge for those who appoint, vote, or otherwise select persons for leadership positions.

The bankruptcy of General Motors in the summer of 2009 is a watershed event in the history of American business. Not surprisingly, all eyes focused on Fritz Henderson, 50, the new CEO whose boss and mentor was Rick Wagoner, whom you met in chapter two. Wagoner was ousted; Henderson was chosen by the board to take over. Shortly after GM went into chapter 11, the *New York Times* ran an article, "G.M. Insider Wants to Show He's Tough Enough."[16] Henderson, according to the *Times*, had to prove that his 25 years with the company (his entire career) was an asset, not a liability, as he faced up to the turnaround challenge at the giant company. The newspaper wanted to know what he would do first. "I have to listen," he told the *Times*; "Listening to others is a key skill." The company, as he knew it, "has always been very open and collaborative and I don't want to change that."[17] Sadly for him, and not all that long into his chairmanship, Fritz Henderson was ousted by his board; they faulted him for not listening.

Both empathy and intuition, if they are to have a place in the leadership toolkit, can grow with age and experience. A reliable detection device for the presence of empathy is the willingness to listen. "Empathy—which includes listening and taking other people's perspectives—allows leaders to tune into the emotional channels between people.

. . . And staying attuned lets them fine-tune their message to keep it in synch."[18] This observation comes from business consultants who work with executives in many parts of the world. They're interested in the "primal" aspects of both intelligence and leadership; they have great respect for the emotions in the process of decision making. They also appreciate the importance of listening. "The best [business] communicators are superb listeners—and listening is the key strength of the democratic leader. Such leaders create the sense that they truly want to hear employees' thoughts and concerns and that they're available to listen. They're also true collaborators, working as team members rather than top-down leaders. And they know how to quell conflict and create a sense of harmony—for instance, repairing rifts within the group."[19]

## TWO EARS, ONE MOUTH

Each of us carries an anatomical reminder that listening is twice as important as speaking. You have two ears and one mouth. So utilize your ears to full capacity, not simply for your personal growth in learning but for the good of the organization you might be called upon to lead. "Where has all the innovation gone?" the business commentators ask, particularly in times of great need for new ideas to spur economic recovery and growth.

The listening leader will also be an asking leader—asking on a regular basis for innovative ideas, new ways of doing things. This is particularly important in business but applicable as well in every other form of organizational life. Asking will not violate the two-to-one ratio of ears to mouth, so long as the question is short and the answer is encouraged to be sufficiently detailed to convey the possibility of a new or improved product or service that will enhance the enterprise.

At least once a month, there should be provision made in a regular staff meeting for an innovation roundtable: Any new ideas? Any ways we can improve? Any needs we're not attending to? The listening leader will want to know.

## SUMMING UP

By way of summary in this important consideration of listening— the incorporation of listening into the leadership toolkit—listen to Isabel Lopez, whose essay on "the personal development path" to becoming a leader appears in Larry Spears's book of essays cited earlier:[20]

We must learn to empathize. This entails learning to walk in someone else's shoes. Being able to empathize is a sign of our maturity. Sympathy, on the other hand, only allows us to feel sorry for someone else. The outcome of acceptance and empathy is that we will not reject the other and will therefore be practicing "unlimited liability."

To develop this characteristic, try the following exercises. When someone brings you a problem, an issue, or an idea, listen first. Don't assume you know what they want. Just listen. Listening is an intense activity. You may want to ask someone to talk to you for five minutes while you listen. After they have finished, repeat what you heard. Did you hear what they were saying? The more emotional the conversation, the more intense is the listening required. Ask yourself the following questions:

- Was I able to concentrate?
- Did I have other thoughts running through my head while the other person was talking?
- How often was I framing solutions to what I perceived was the "problem" rather than listening?

Although the practice of listening is intense, the opportunities to practice present themselves all the time.

## NOTES:

1. "The C.E.O., Now Playing on YouTube," *New York Times* (May 10, 2009): BU2.

2. "In a Word, He Wants Simplicity," *New York Times* (May 24, 2009): BU2.

3. *New York Times* (April 12, 2009): BU2.

4. Ibid.

5. Peter Lencioni, *Death by Meeting: A Leadership Fable* (San Francisco: Jossey-Bass, 2004).

6. Ronald Heifetz, Alexander Grashow, and Marty Linsky, *The Practice of Adaptive Leadership: Tools and Tactics for Changing Your Organization and the World* (Boston: Harvard Business Press, 2009), 167.

7. Peter Lencioni, *Death by Meeting: A Leadership Fable*, 146, 238

8. Ibid., 239.

9. "Knock-Knock: It's the C.E.O.," *New York Times* (April 12, 2009): BU2.

10. Arthur Simon, *The Rising of Bread for the World: An Outcry of Citizens against Hunger* (Mahwah, NJ: Paulist Press, 2009), 109–10.

11. *Servant Leadership: A Journey into the Nature of Legitimate Power and Greatness* (Mahwah, NJ: Paulist Press, 25th anniversary edition, 2002).

12. Larry C. Spears, ed., *Reflections on Leadership: How Robert K. Greenleaf's Theory of Servant Leadership Influenced Today's Top Management Thinkers* (New York: John Wiley& Sons, 1995), 4–5.

13. Peter M. Senge, "Robert Greenleaf's Legacy: A New Foundation for Twenty-First Century Institutions," in Larry C. Spears, ed., *Reflections on Leadership*, 229.

14. Thomas Bartlett, "Phoenix Risen: How a History Professor Became the Pioneer of the For-Profit Revolution," *The Chronicle of Higher Education* (July 10, 2009): 1, A10–A13.

15. Ibid., A11.

16. Bill Vlasic, "G.M. Insider Wants to Show He's Tough Enough," *New York Times* (June 16, 2009): B1.

17. Ibid., B4.

18. Daniel Goleman, Richard Boyzatis, and Annie McKee, *Primal Leadership: Learning to Lead with Emotional Intelligence* (Boston: Harvard Business School Press, paperback 2004), 49.

19. Ibid., 69.

20. Isabel O. Lopez, "Becoming a Servant-Leader: The Personal Development Path," in Larry C. Spears, ed., *Reflections on Leadership*, 153.

# CHAPTER FIVE

# LEADERS SPEAK

Speaking is one of the most important things a leader does. Not just public speaking, which is, of course, an indispensable instrument in the leadership toolkit, but also clear, persuasive oral communication in a one-on-one setting or in small groups. Recall that you were told, while still in school, that rhetoric is the art of persuasive communication. The leader communicates in written and spoken words and, as Howard Gardner has noted, "How to understand the world and its complexity and subtlety, and yet communicate directly to dispersed individuals with limited expertise, is perhaps the fundamental issue facing leaders today."[1] It is the issue before you in this chapter and the next.

In a lengthy feature, "So, You Want to Be an Entrepreneur," the *Wall Street Journal*[2] raised ten questions to help you "see if you have what it takes." Here is number 7: "How persuasive and well-spoken are you?" And the importance of this question is stated plainly: "Nearly every step of the way, entrepreneurship relies on selling. You'll have to sell your idea to lenders or investors. You must sell your mission and vision to your employees. And you'll ultimately have to sell your product or service to your customers. You'll need strong communication and interpersonal skills so you can get people to believe in your vision as much as you do. If you don't think you're very convincing or have difficulty communicating your ideas, you might want to reconsider starting your own company—or think about getting some help." This applies to being in business for yourself or working for someone else; in either case, you have to be able to communicate effectively.

James J. Schiro, CEO of Zurich Financial Services, recalls asking Colin Powell what he viewed as the most important thing associated with leadership. The former Chairman of the Joint Chiefs of Staff and U.S. Secretary of State said, "The most important thing is the troops have to understand where they are going."[3] Again, note the need for clear communication. Asked about any rule of thumb he might have with regard to keeping the message simple, Schiro replied, "I say, 'Three slides, three points.' You really can't manage more than three or four things at most, but I like to see it in three slides."[4]

Countless people confess to fear—in some cases, immobilizing fear—when it comes to speaking in front of a group. This is a fear that can and must be overcome. The sooner this fear is confronted head-on, at any age, the higher the probability that a potential leader will become a genuine leader. So, regardless of your age, if you want to lead, be on your feet and speak up whenever an appropriate opportunity presents itself. This doesn't mean sounding off to fill any gap of silence in a meeting, or waving your hand to answer every question that is addressed to the entire class, but it does mean having something to say and saying it clearly, concisely, and in a pleasant voice that others can hear, whenever the circumstances are right.

If you are in school, consider participation in dramatics and debating. If you are out of school, look around for an onstage opportunity in community theater. Let me mention a book here that I will be drawing from in chapter nine, where I'll discuss "remembering as presence" and point out that an actor's training can be quite useful in the practice of leadership. The book is *Leadership Presence: Dramatic Techniques to Reach Out, Motivate, and Inspire.*[5] More on that later; for the moment just note that some experience on the stage in your developmental years can be enormously helpful later on in organizational life.

The classroom is often where it all begins. Whenever I have a chance to facilitate the process, either in the classroom or in sessions with out-of-school adults, I say to the speaker, "Let your voice bounce off the back wall of this room." Whether it is a classroom, auditorium, meeting hall, or conference room of any size or shape (both size and shape of the gathering space have important acoustical implications), I encourage the speaker to imagine his or her voice as a ball to be thrown against the back wall.

With or without a microphone, the spoken word must be audible throughout the area where listeners are assembled. This is so obvious that it puzzles me that so many would-be speakers don't get it. The best way to assure that an acoustical connection will happen is to imagine your voice as a ball thrown out and bouncing back. "Can you hear me in the rear?" is a useful question to ask at the outset. An added invitation to "raise your hand and let me know if you are having any difficulty hearing me," is never going to draw a complaint from the audience.

Few things frustrate an audience more than the inability to hear what a speaker is saying. When such frustration emerges, the self-activated time-to-take-a-nap mechanism —standard equipment between every pair of ears—comes into play. People empower speakers to speak, not by giving them a podium, but by lending them their ears, as the saying goes. Speakers have to be aware that this is a loan that can readily be foreclosed. If I can't hear you, I just tune out.

## THE MICROPHONE

For many young people, the earliest observation of a microphone in use is associated with pop singers or standup comedians. Notice how the typical handheld mike is right there in front of the mouth; think of it as if it were an ice-cream cone. If the handheld microphone is within "licking distance," you are going to be heard. But you are also at risk for the annoying "pop" that Peter Piper's peck of pickled peppers has been warning against for years. Once you hear a "pop" (if you don't hear it, you should know that you're the only one in the auditorium who doesn't!), lower the microphone an inch or two and speak "over the mike" so that the next punchy "p" or bomb-like "b" will not annoy your hearers.

Similarly, keep your mouth in proper alignment with a stationary floor-stand microphone, particularly as you look to left or right. Imagine the mike as a fixed point around which you turn when you look left or right (as you should, by the way, in order to maintain eye contact with your audience). This means that your head will turn a bit to the right when you want to look left, and to the left when you want to look right, but the distance between your lips and the mike will not change. The proper distance is usually just an inch or two, this measure should be determined by a "mike check" before you begin.

Far too many speakers make the mistake of thinking that a microphone is like a telephone and they use their telephone tone, volume, and phrasing when they speak into a microphone. Often the result is that the volume is too low, the pace and phrasing too fast, and the tone too conversational to make a good public speaking impression. Note that I said "too conversational," because I wouldn't want you to avoid a lively conversational style altogether. Just be aware that the normal conversational pace is a bit fast and that phrases all too easily run on to one another. The spoken sentence needs the elocution equivalent of a space bar.

Critically important is the use of "sense phrases" when you speak in public. A sentence of normal length can be broken into several sense phrases that enhance the interpretation provided by the speaker while conveying the meaning the sentence contains. If those sense phrases are not spaced properly and presented distinctly (not with long pauses, just punctuated by brief intervals), the syllables tend to collide in mid-sentence. They create an echo chamber that is not present in ordinary conversation. In an auditorium or large room, syllables can bounce into one another. The echo makes it difficult to hear some words that are part of the sentence and could be essential to the meaning.

Another important consideration is maintaining your volume all the way to the end of the spoken sentence. Too often, speakers drop their voices, reduce the volume, and soften the tone, so that the sentence glides inaudibly to its unheard end. What is not heard will, of course, neither instruct, persuade, nor impress.

Before moving on from the microphone, I'd like to warn against what I call the "interrogative declarative." This began spreading like a virus among America's youth in the 1990s when up-tics found their way into declarative sentences so that a straightforward self-identification, for example, instead of falling directly on the ear of the hearer, sounded something like this: "Hi, I'm Becky? And I'm from Syracuse?"

I'll leave it to the linguists and psychologists to suggest what might be going on here. I tell myself that it has something to do with generational tentativeness. I don't really know. But I've been hearing it for a long time now wherever young people gather. Ask them what their major happens to be in college, and you learn that they may have started in biology but "Now I'm in political science?" as if to say, "I hope that's alright with you." I won't overwork the point here. Let me simply suggest that the reader listen attentively and notice whether or not the interrogative declarative is still making the rounds. It surely does not strengthen any oral presentation.

## THE VOICE

I recommend to my students a small book by Morton Cooper, *Change Your Voice, Change Your Life.*[6] It helps them locate their true natural voice, recognize that it is a tool, and become convinced that it can be improved upon and strengthened. It also makes them aware, probably for the first time, that each person has a distinctive "voice image."

I point out the importance of considering the thoracic quality of a speaker's voice. This simply means paying attention to the chest and abdomen and noticing how so few people use that anatomical region while speaking, and how many prefer to speak completely from the neck up—not to mention the legions whose vocal production is localized in the nasal area. Get your voice out of your sinuses, I often think to myself as I listen to the young; get that voice out of your head! And while you're at it, give belly breathing a try! (I'll explain what I mean by that in just a moment.) Imagine, as you listen to a friend, that if you could unscrew her head and hold it a yard or two off to the side, the quality of the sound of the speaking voice would not change. That's because the thorax is not at all engaged in the process of producing the sound. Your voice is more than your vocal chords. Notice how often the sound of a pleasant voice seems to be coming from the waist up. That's the way it should be.

Tell a person to take a deep breath and, chances are, his or her upper chest will rise along with a corresponding constriction of the vocal cords. Everything tightens up, including what might best be described as the resulting "pinched" voice.

Proper breathing for effective speech means that a deep breath should be felt as putting pressure on the wall of the lower abdomen. Let the deep breath push out a bit against your belt; then you'll know that you are preparing the way for better sound. You will be demonstrating your understanding that the body can function much like a cello in providing a chamber for fuller, richer, mellower sounds. The analogy is not perfect, but the vocal cords can be thought of as the strings on a violin or cello, and the chest and abdomen likened to the chamber fashioned by high quality wood that creates the acoustical environment from which the rich sound emanates. Take a few "belly breaths" to get a feel for how this works.

With proper breathing and a simple set of voice mechanics almost anyone can produce a pleasant, even commanding, speech sound, and thus claim a distinctive voice image. Vocal strain is so common because the mechanics of proper speech are so largely ignored. Damage can be done to vocal cords and medical help will sometimes be necessary. But just about anyone who wants to can improve his or her speaking voice and, in the process, enhance the confidence and influence essential for effective leadership.

Those who want to polish up their speaking skills would be well advised to try the buddy system—select a friendly partner with whom the skills can be practiced and the desired improvement achieved. A voice-projection volley—back and forth—will be helpful; a friendly critique of tone and pace will be welcome.

"A Voice Can Speak Volumes" is the title of a commentary page article in the *Philadelphia Inquirer* that urged readers to "be certain that you sound like someone an employer would want to hire."[7] This was valuable advice as the unemployment numbers soared in early 2009. "During that job interview," writes Orlando Barone, "in response to questions, you want to convey authority, assurance, and confidence. You want to show that you know what you're talking about and that what you have to say is important. You want to eliminate false starts, long pauses, and the use of 'ums.' You should avoid shifty, 'nervous' eyes, and a voice that shakes or cracks." Notice that he said "long" pauses. A short pause to think before you speak is fine; it helps you avoid giving the impression that you are a know-it-all. Just don't pause too often or too long. The writer of the *Inquirer* article is co-author of a 2009 book, *Your Voice is Your Business*. Indeed it is and you should be paying attention to it!

## THE HANDS

Many speakers have no idea what to do with their hands. Males try to bury them in their pockets; females often fold them in front or pick up something to hold onto. There is nothing wrong with resting your hands on the podium and lifting them now and then to reinforce (that is, visually underline) a point. Sports fans who watch retired coaches and veterans of the game provide half-time television commentary during major college or professional contests, might, if they stop to think about it, conclude that these "experts" would be speechless if they were unable to project both hands in front of them and shift them to the right and left as the analysis proceeds. Excessive hand motion can distract from the speech. But awkward immobility of the hands can generate discomfort in the audience, too.

No doubt about it, your hands can become dead weights at your side when you stand to address a group. The trick is to employ the natural elbow bend or break, and thus keep your hands above your waist, allowing for an appropriate palm up or palm down gesture, or a broader sweep to make your point. Use your hand to "count off" those three or four major points in your speech. Use your finger to point, when the context permits it, to persons or objects that relate to the message you are delivering. But always let your hand movement be graceful and natural. Your hands can serve as light-touch punctuation marks, or they can be, quite literally, heavy-handed distractions.

Some speakers retreat to a quiet room on occasion, play appropriate music and observe their hand motion in a mirror as they "conduct" the orchestra as an exercise in graceful hand movement. This can carry over easily and naturally to the podium for use in front of an audience.

An itchy nose will sometimes require attention; any audience will understand that. But excessive scratching of the forehead, frequent flicking hair away from the eyes (a special problem for females), buttoning or un-buttoning your suit jacket (which, by the way, should be buttoned while facing an audience)—all these will dilute the strength of your presentation and possibly annoy your listeners. So will swigs of bottled water or sips from a glass, unless irrigation of the throat is absolutely necessary.

Just as your two feet should be planted firmly on the floor (no rocking back and forth, up and down, one side to the other; no shifting weight as if to signal your desire to hightail it out of there!), so your hands should be strong, firm, and measured in their movement in service of your words. Your hands should be seen and not heard, obviously, but, if seen, they will make whatever it is you have to say more likely to be received and understood according to your intent. The point of it all is communication; the hands can help, as can your entire body. Be present to your audience. The way you stand in front of others is itself a statement.

## THE PAUSE

A pause is the white space on your vocal page. Your listeners need it in order to follow and digest your presentation. An opening pause is often recommended, just to establish your presence and connect with your audience. This should take only a moment and be accompanied by the movement of your eyes across the room—left to right, front to back. Too long an opening pause will generate discomfort in your audience; just the right amount sets the stage for your remarks.

Punctuate your speech with timely pauses. If you have the audience in the palm of your hand, as the saying goes, you can sense their presence to you and yours to them in the language of silence. Silence can be eloquent. Don't be afraid to introduce it periodically, but not too frequently, at the end of a sentence or paragraph. And you should know that high praise can come your way at the end of your presentation in the form of a moment of audience silence before a burst of audience applause.

I mentioned above, in my comments about proper use of a microphone, that it is important to deliver your message in "sense phrases." That means an awareness on your part that, if you are not careful, you can permit your syllables quite literally (and audibly) to bump into each other causing a collision of sounds that smothers meaning. What an audience cannot hear, it will not understand.

## NON WORDS

*Um, you know, like, okay, I mean, sort of, ahhh, uhhh*—these are all non-words. Not only are they shuffled in and out of ordinary conversational exchanges, they all too often find their way into formal presentations. The *ahhh*s usually win the day if you happen to be counting. And that's exactly what some irritated listeners do—count the number of *ahhh*s and *uhhh*s and *um*s that come from the mouth of a public speaker.

Void of any meaning at all, these utterances are a form of punctuation for some speakers, ponderous pauses for others. The *ahhh* is the first sound out of the mouth for some highly intelligent, well-educated, executive-level pubic speakers. Many are totally unaware that they are producing these distracting sounds. "I don't do that," said a participant in an executive speech development workshop when the facilitator first raised the subject. "Right," said the professional instructor, "I lie; the tape tells the truth. Let's listen to the tape." That's usually all it takes to get the attention of the one in need of help, but the habit is not easily broken. Yet it must be broken for anyone who has it and wants to become an effective public speaker.

Some criticized the press early in 2009 for being unkind to Caroline Kennedy when she expressed to the Governor of New York her interest in the U.S. Senate seat vacated by President Barack Obama's choice for Secretary of State, Hillary Rodham Clinton. "We weren't unfair to her; we just quoted her," reporters said in their own defense. The *New Yorker* reported in a short article, "Eliza Doolittle Dept. Correcting Caroline,"[8] that the daughter of the former president "met with a couple of [New York] *Times* reporters recently and said 'you know' a hundred and thirty-eight times. Speaking to the *News* and on NY1 she broke two hundred."

All of us do it, just not that frequently. And all of us should get rid of the *you know*s even though linguistic experts give non-words the elegant labels of "discourse markers" or "pragmatic particles." Just get rid of them!

## A KEEPER'S FILE

It is already late, but not too late to begin developing your keeper's file. I got that term from Gerry Roche, senior chairman of Heidrick and Struggles, the executive search firm. He files away anecdotes, stories, jokes, and a wide range of wise sayings that can be employed from time to time in the many speeches he gives each year. You can organize yours around the seasons of the year, the stages of life, sports, business, religion, family, or file folders in alphabetical order—whatever set of bins or categories that you find congenial. Fill up the notebooks or file drawers; you'll be dipping in regularly to find material that will enliven your presentations and reinforce your central points.

A storyteller friend of mine, Frank Moynihan, produces family-focused, values-oriented films in clay animation. He likes to quote what he identifies as an old Indian proverb: "Tell me a fact and I'll learn. Tell me a truth and I'll believe. But tell me a story and it will live in my heart forever."

Here's a story a former student of mine sent to me recently. Naturally, it is now housed in my keeper's file.

> Parents of a young girl diagnosed with a potentially fatal blood disease were unsuccessful in locating a donor with a compatible blood type for a needed transfusion. They discovered that the girl's six-year-old brother had the right blood type, so the youngster's mother, together with the physician attending to her daughter, sat down to explain the problem and ask if the boy would donate blood to save his sister's life. He did not answer right away and said he would need some time to think about it. A couple of days later he told his mother okay, he would do it. So the physician brought brother and sister to the clinic and stretched them out on tables side by side. He drew a half pint of blood from the boy and transfused it immediately into the arm of the girl in the sight of her brother. The boy could see the effect. In several minutes, color began to return to his sister's cheeks. Then the boy motioned to the doctor to bend over to hear a question he wanted to ask quietly. "Will I start to die right away?" he asked.

The child had thought, when he was asked to donate blood to save his sister's life, that he was being asked to trade his life for hers. No wonder he needed a few days to think it over!

Stories, sayings, proverbs, one-liners—all are useful at one time or another. Personal reflections—narratives of events in which you took part—always make your speech more interesting. Abraham Lincoln, often referred to as America's greatest leader, was also widely regarded as one of this country's greatest storytellers. Use your Internet search engine, or go to any library or bookstore, and search for books on the "wit and wisdom" or the "leadership principles" of Abraham Lincoln. You will be impressed with the power of storytelling as a tool of leadership.

Similarly, look for books of Winston Churchill's famous sayings—serious and humorous. One of the qualities that made him such an effective leader was his mastery of the spoken word. In his book *Churchill on Leadership*, Steven Hayward devotes a chapter to Churchill the communicator.[9] In it, he quotes from a short reflection on "The Scaffolding of Rhetoric," written by Churchill when he was a 24-year-old army officer in India. In it, the young Churchill lays out "four constructive principles of effective communication" that served him well throughout his lifetime: (1) correctness of diction, (2) rhythm, (3) accumulation of argument, and (4) analogy.

As you build your personal reference library of useful stories, quotations, and anecdotes, set some time aside for occasional "presentations" of those snippets by you before your bedroom or bathroom mirror. Be mindful of the sense phrases; be attentive to the pace. The practice will polish your delivery and deepen your memory; it will also serve to remind that your search for quotable material never ends.

## HOW ABOUT HUMOR?

Should you tell jokes to warm up your audience, to render them benevolent? Only if the jokes are really good, and only if they fit. "Before we begin, I want to tell you a joke." Never do this. "I heard a funny story the other day and I want to share it with you." Forget it. "You'll really laugh at this." Don't count on it. "Did you ever hear the one about . . . ?" They probably did and, even if they didn't, they don't want to hear it now.

Humor is a welcome ingredient in almost any speech. Better to work it in as you go along; the unexpected arrival will heighten the humor. Your keeper's file should include a collection of one-liners and good jokes. Funny stories can always enliven a presentation, but first ask a friend—not only whether the story is funny, but if your telling of the story does it justice. Some very good speakers cannot handle humor. They know it, don't use it, and thus retain their reputations as being "good speakers."

## EYE CONTACT

When Communispond was launched in 1969 as a subsidiary of J. Walter Thompson, the advertising agency, it had this self-defining slogan: "To Speak as Well as You Think." Now, some 600,000 clients later, Communispond employs another: "Inspiring Passionate Performance." The objective, however, is still the same—providing executive speech development for men and women in managerial positions in every corner of corporate America.

One of the exercises these men and women experienced when I observed the operation in the 1970s, involved sitting in a semicircle (there were usually about a dozen executives participating in a given workshop) and one group-member would stand as the designated speaker in front of the others. The speaker would be instructed to establish eye contact with someone in the semicircle who raised his or her hand, and maintain that contact until that hand was lowered and another was raised. The speaker then had to lock-in eye contact with the person whose hand was aloft and hold the contact until that hand came down and another went up. And so it went around the semicircle.

The point, of course, was to get some practice in maintaining eye contact, an absolute requirement for effective speaking. Participants were typically surprised at how difficult it was, at first, to hold the contact. They were also encouraged by the facilitator to note how "shifty" various speakers appeared to be when their eyes kept moving to the right and left instead of remaining fixed on the eyes of one listener for a short interval and then consciously moving to establish eye contact with another.

Body language is spoken everywhere. The message of shiftiness and mistrust is communicated, unwittingly but most convincingly, through the eyes. Shifty eyes; shifty character. That is not a message most speakers want to deliver.

Tim Malloy, a partner in an executive speech development practice located in Cyberspace at www.PublicSpeakingSkills.com, advises clients to "lock, talk, pause." He means lock-in on eye contact with someone in your audience, speak for a moment or two, and then with a punctuating pause, make eye contact with another member of the audience as your narrative continues. As an alternate way of making the same point, Tim says, "Never think you are speaking to a group of individuals; speak to individuals in a group." This is another way of helping speakers not to forget that communication is, in fact, comm-YOU-nication.

The eyes are useful means of communication. Raised eyebrows say something. Intense eye contact (not too intense, just the right degree) commands attention. And what Tim Malloy calls the "aerosol" spray of measured, deliberate eye contact with your audience is going to hold the attention of your hearers and convince them that you are speaking just to them.

Here again, it is advisable to pair off with a partner for some practice. If you are shifting your glance, you need someone you trust to tell you that you are coming across in a "shifty" manner.

Eye contact is important for any subject of a television interview. If the questioner is in another studio or city and you are full-face on camera, be sure to fix your eyes directly on the camera that is on you. Look it "in the eye," and hold that look as long as the red light above the camera lens is on. If you are in the studio sitting across from the interviewer, look at the interviewer, not at the camera, and just be comfortably aware that your conversation is being telecast to others who are listening in. It is not at all necessary for you to be looking at the audience. It is useful to maintain eye contact with the interviewer and, from time to time in order to avoid an uncomfortable "locking in," simply shift your glance not to the camera but over the interviewer's shoulder and then back again to his or her eyes as you would in a normal, off-camera conversation.

A useful tip for speakers in what might become a hostile question-and-answer session (such as a CEO meeting with shareholders, an executive holding a press conference, an NFL coach in a post-game interview with reporters, a college president meeting with angry students) relates to eye contact. While responding to a hostile question, the speaker should hold eye contact with the questioner until the midpoint of his or her very last sentence. Then, while still speaking, the speaker's eyes should shift away to connect with the next questioner. Otherwise, the speaker is open to an immediate follow-up from the hostile questioner and will find him- or herself "pinned," instead of free to move on to the next question from a perhaps less hostile questioner.

## OUTLINE OR WRITTEN TEXT?

No one will recommend that you memorize your speech and then stand in front of an audience to deliver it. Chances are, you will appear wooden and unnatural. There is an even better chance that you will forget what you wanted to say, lose your train of thought, and fall into the open pit of an embarrassing pause. So write it out. Before you speak, reduce your thoughts to paper.

This does not mean that every word must be written down beforehand. Some speakers write their opening and closing paragraphs, and lay out in between a list of the points they want to cover. Typically, they practice beforehand how any or all of those points might be developed.

Some speakers prefer to have a complete text before them—every sentence written out—some words or phrases underlined for special emphasis. This requires that the speaker be a good interpretive reader. It also requires attention to the maintenance of eye contact with the audience as the speech is read. I learned long ago that it is helpful to select a 16-point typeface for ease of reading a full-text speech. (I also convert the print to bold face in order to make the reading even easier.) Of itself, this does not solve the problem of eye contact, so I keep one hand, alternating left and right, on the page and run my finger down the text as I read, thus holding my place during those intervals when, knowing what the next line or two says, I lift my eyes from the text to meet the eyes of my hearers. Some reader-speakers are afraid to lift their eyes for long because they are afraid of losing their place. The finger-on-the-page is an insurance policy against losing your place. And that amounts to one less worry that a nervous presenter might otherwise communicate to his or her audience.

It is not a sign of weakness to have your speech completely written out. It can indeed be a sign of respect for your audience that you take the time to think about what you want to say and put your thoughts on paper. Writing it all out beforehand gives you an opportunity to polish your phrases, introduce compelling imagery, fashion some attractive alliteration, and pay attention to style. Any audience will appreciate that.

## STRUCTURE OF THE SPEECH

One veteran speech-maker shared with me, many years ago, his rendition of some well-known advice. He said to do *this* when you get up before a group: "Tell them what you are going to tell them. Then tell them what you told them you were going to tell them. And finally, tell them that you told them what you told them you were going to tell them." He was referring to the introduction, the body of the speech, and the conclusion. He believed in order and clarity. (This approach goes all the way back to Aristotle.)

Some speakers work around a set number of points and make this clear at the outset by saying something like, "There are three major points I want to cover in my time with you this evening; I'll talk about life, liberty, and the pursuit of happiness." You may have four or five points to cover, or only two. In any case, let your audience know what's coming. This way, you can assemble your speech block by block.

Every good speech will have a beginning, a middle, and an end. As obvious as that sounds, reflect for a moment and you will probably recall a speech that simply stopped, with no clear ending. Moreover, think of sermons or speeches that made no demands on you, asked you to do nothing when the session concluded. Just as every good salesman will always "ask for the order," every good speaker will leave you with an agenda for future action. That agenda can be a useful summary and fitting conclusion to your speech.

If your speech has no imagery, your speech is in need of improvement.

If your speech is replete with the perpendicular pronoun—"I" . . . "I" . . . "I"—look for an opportunity to substitute *we* or *you* for the frequent references to self. And notice how the mention by name of others who deserve a word of credit or vote of thanks can give the welcome impression that you are not a self-centered, solipsistic, attention-grabbing, praise-collecting bore.

Forgetting for a moment about the mechanics of effective speech, listen to Howard Gardner's comments about the importance of public speaking as he found it in the lives of the major twentieth-century political leaders he studied for his book *Leading Minds*:

> While the majority of the leaders were creditable writers, by and large they were distinguished by their skill at spoken language. They bring to mind President Woodrow Wilson's testimony: "I have a strong instinct of leadership, an unmistakably oratorical temperament. . . . My feeling has been that such literary talents as I have are secondary to my equipment for other things, that my power to write was meant to be a handmaiden to my power to speak and to organize actions." Indeed, if there is a single domain that each [of the leaders discussed] can be said to have mastered, it is the domain of public speaking—speaking directly and convincingly to their various audiences. Roosevelt, Churchill, and de Gaulle were all masters of their nations' respective tongues, and all remain much quoted even decades after

their death. Mussolini was a dramatic speaker graced by a beautiful voice and impressive theatrical gestures. Mao could electrify a crowd with his vivid images, while Lenin's fiery speeches played a notable role in the launching of the Russian Revolution. Indeed, of the various leaders surveyed here, only Stalin seems not to have been an outstanding speaker on the whole, although his speech to the Soviet people after the surprise Nazi invasion is credited with mobilizing patriotism and helping to ensure Germany's ultimate defeat.

Hitler was the most amazing orator of the era. He had discovered both his ability to argue demagogically in small groups in the years before the First World War and his capacities to arouse a mass audience early in the 1920s. From then on, he worked tirelessly to prove his edict that "to be a leader means to be able to move masses."[10]

I doubt that you need any additional persuasion about the importance of oral communication in the leadership toolkit. But let me simply note that after many years of observing business executives in working groups around the world, consultants Daniel Goleman, Richard Boyatzis, and Annie McKee state: "Leaders typically talked more than anyone else, and what they said was listened to more carefully. Leaders were also usually the first to speak out on a subject, and when others made comments, their remarks most often referred to what the leader had said than to anyone else's comments. Because the leader's way of seeing things has special weight, leaders 'manage meaning' for a group, offering a way to interpret, and so react emotionally to, a given situation."[11]

Everything we've covered in this chapter can be wrapped up under the label "Coming Across: Putting Words to Work for You," or "Putting Your Ideas to Work in Words." Words, of course, come alive in both spoken and written form. To make them come alive when you speak, get some emotion into your voice. But enough for now about speaking, let's move on to chapter six, "Leaders Write."

## NOTES:

1. Howard Gardner, *Leading Minds: An Anatomy of Leadership* (New York: Basic Books, 1995), 108.
2. (February 23, 2009): R1, R4.

3. "The C.E.O., Now Playing on YouTube," *New York Times* (May 10, 2009): BU2.

4. Ibid.

5. Belle Linda Halpern and Kathy Lubar, *Leadership Presence: Dramatic Techniques to Reach Out, Motivate, and Inspire* (New York: Gotham Books, 2004).

6. Morton Cooper, *Change Your Voice, Change Your Life: A Quick, Simple Plan for Finding and Using Your Natural, Dynamic Voice* (Los Angeles: Voice and Speech Company of America, 17th printing, 1999).

7. Orlando R. Barone, "A Voice Can Speak Volumes," *Philadelphia Inquirer* (March 1, 2009): D5.

8. "Eliza Doolittle Dept. Correcting Caroline," *New Yorker* (January 12, 2009): 18–19.

9. Steven F. Hayward, *Churchill on Leadership: Executive Success in the Face of Adversity* (New York: Gramercy, 2004), 98–111.

10. Howard Gardner, *Leading Minds*, 260.

11. Daniel Goleman, Richard Boyatzis, and Annie McKee, *Primal Leadership: Learning to Lead with Emotional Intelligence* (Boston: Harvard Business School Press, paperback, 2004), 8.

# CHAPTER SIX

# LEADERS WRITE

In the opening chapter of this book, I quoted Nicholas deB. Katzenbach's description of some of the leadership qualities he observed from working closely with Robert F. Kennedy. Katzenbach later succeeded Kennedy as attorney general and, in that capacity, found that writing well in order to speak effectively was an important part of the job. Just as RFK had a skilled newsman, Edwin Guthman, to assist him in this regard, Katzenbach had former *New York Times* reporter Jack Rosenthal at his side.

> One of the things Jack impressed upon me from the outset was that he had to know what was going on in the department and in my own thinking. If he did not, he would inadvertently say the wrong thing and make us look deceptive. I told him that he was welcome at all staff meetings and that the door to my office was always open to him. When he told me about a speaking invitation I should accept and why, he would suggest a few topics as possibilities, and I would select one. Then we would discuss in general terms what I wanted to say on the subject. Jack would get some young lawyer in the appropriate division to write a first draft incorporating and elaborating on my ideas, which he [Rosenthal] would then edit and rework himself before giving it to me for my comments. I would make changes or suggest some additions and give it back for a final editing. If the lawyer writing the draft disagreed with my thoughts, he was welcome to come to my office and discuss them with me. I learned a lot by preparing speeches. It was typical of Jack's good judgment that the cadre of speechwriters were young but extraordinarily able. They included Adam Walinsky, who later worked on Bobby's [presidential] campaign and ran for attorney general of New York; Peter Edelman, who also worked for Bobby and was

nominated by President Carter for the court of appeals; and Stephen Breyer, who is now an associate justice on the Supreme Court.[1]

Most, not all, but most busy leaders rely on assistance from speechwriters. That's just the way it is. But the point to note here is the importance of interaction with the writers on the part of the one who will literally stand behind the text; that person must be involved in the writing of the speech. This is even more important when others help draft material that will appear in print—memoranda, articles, or books.

There's a joke that makes the rounds where an observer comments on a speech he had just heard. "There were only three things wrong with it: (1) he read it; (2) he didn't read it well; and (3) it wasn't worth reading!" If you didn't write it, there's a good chance that you will not read it well. Moreover, if the humorous comment was aimed at you and if you, in fact, did not read it well, you had better spend some time reviewing the material in chapter five. But if the speech was really not worth reading, attention should be paid to mastering the tools of writing.

## A ONE-SENTENCE SUMMARY

Don't just start to write. First decide what you are going to write about. Choose an idea. Extend that idea into a single sentence. Let that single sentence serve as your thesis, your statement of intent, your proposition to be proved. Don't attempt to move forward unless you have that single sentence nailed down.

Then lay out your thoughts in definable blocks. Build your speech (or your article) block by block. You might think of the blocks (and number them accordingly) as points—your major headings. Don't attempt too many. Three is normally a good workable number. Five is manageable. More than five is too much for a speech, although not excessive for a memorandum or article. The objective is to get to the point and let your hearer or reader know what to expect.

An overconfident young preacher once stepped into a pulpit and gave what he thought was a spellbinding sermon. It was not received well because it had not been easy to follow; it had no "handles," no points, no clearly marked beginning, middle, and end. In fact, it did not end; it simply stopped.

He would have benefited from the advice offered in the last chapter concerning the structure of a speech, namely, "First, tell them what you are going to tell them. Then tell them what you told them you were going to tell them. And finally, tell them that you told them what you told them you were going to tell them."

Bear that in mind as you set out to put words on paper. And when you begin to put words on paper, let them fall like pebbles to the page, that is, directly—the way a pebble falls to the ground. Involuted, drawn-out, "loop-the-loop" sentences serve only to confuse, not to inform. And your objective, of course, in both oral and written communication is precisely that—to inform.

Elementary school used to be universally known as grammar school, and for good reason. Grammar was drilled into children day in and day out, grade by grade, up to a level of competence where they knew the parts of speech and how to assemble those parts into meaningful sentences and paragraphs. Kids could diagram sentences; some found it to be fun. In doing so, all youngsters gained a familiarity with sentence structure. Well-constructed sentences conveyed clear meaning.

The construction project was not always painless, but practice eased the pain and paved the way for style. Call it facility, if you will; some will want to call it a flair for writing. By any name, good style with the written word is a skill that can be acquired with practice. It is a skill without which few will lead effectively, if at all. And, if the truth be told, it is a skill that law firms, corporations, government agencies, and practically all other organizations that are hiring these days will tell you is in pitifully short supply in the ranks of recent arrivals from the halls of academe into the paycheck world of work.

Grammar schools taught the difference between active and passive voice. Voice? What's that got to do with writing? The answer relates back to the pebble-to-the-page imagery. Leaders work in the active voice. They are direct. They have goals. They hit targets. They get things done. The shortest distance between the good idea and the desired outcome is a straight sentence. The essentials of any sentence are a subject, object, and verb. The subject acts, and the verb both conveys and describes the action. If the subject is acted upon, the voice (a property of verbs that indicates the relationship between a subject and the action expressed by the verb) is not active but passive; the subject in this case is the patient, not the agent.

So why be passive? Why say, "We will be met at the airport by Charlie," when you could say, "Charlie will meet us"? There are almost always "bumps" in sentences that employ the passive voice. So avoid it. Be direct.

## VERB POWER

On Saturday afternoons in the autumn, as the football scores are announced over the air, I'm intrigued by what I call the "varsity verb," an action word that has a way of getting the reader into the game. One team does not simply defeat another. Sportscasters use verbs like *trounce, thump, crush, upend,* and *flatten* in tracing the path to victory. The varsity verb has only one target: victory.

In sports, politics, and war—in any contest at all—the object, presumably, is victory. Former Minnesota Senator Eugene McCarthy's sardonic humor is still quoted in Washington gatherings: "Being a successful politician is like being a successful football coach," he once said. "You have to be smart enough to understand the game and dumb enough to think it's important." Not all would agree with that, of course, nor should they. Nor do most of us believe the sideline wisdom sometimes spoken that, "Winning isn't the most important thing; it's the only thing!" The "only thing" that matters in sports, politics, or warfare, our better judgment tells us, *is* "how we play the game." The only thing on my mind at this stage (literally on this page) of this book is good writing. Verbs have a lot to contribute to the quality of your writing. Notice them in the writing of others. Deposit them in your writing bank and spend them out to good effect whenever you write.

I've taught in the business schools at Georgetown, Loyola in Maryland, and St. Joseph's University in Philadelphia. My students—usually senior undergraduates or MBA students—had to write something for me every week. I had a two-tier grading system that I adopted years ago after watching the Winter Olympic figure skating competition on television. Skaters would receive a first bank of marks for "required elements," and moments later, a second bank would appear on the screen for "presentation" or artistic impression. In order to encourage students to pay attention to the quality of their writing, I used an Arabic numeral at the upper right hand corner of the first page of their submission to grade the work for "required elements," and that number went directly to the bottom line, to the grade point average. Then, at the lower left corner of the page, I put a letter grade to evaluate the impression their written work had made—the quality of the visual presentation. This was a message from me to the student—often a

C, D, or F—that did not affect the course grade but did communicate how they came across in writing. I usually told them at the beginning of the course that, as a generation (this has been true for several decades), they had the communications equivalent of bad breath and someone had to let them know. That task was mine. Their task was to work during the semester to raise those F's and D's to higher-altitude B's and A's. Invariably, there would be requests from eager students at the beginning of the course to teach them how to write. My response? Imitate.

I had a paperback edition of a collection of columns written by the late Red Smith of the *New York Times*. I would give it to any interested student with the simple suggestion: "Just read what you like and imitate what you read." David Halberstam, another fine writer, once remarked, "Red Smith's work was not merely unrivaled on the sports page, it tended to be the best writing in any given newspaper on any given day." The sports page was a relatively painless path to imitable prose; that's why I liked to introduce students to Red Smith. But I had a list of other good writers whose work was within reach, whose topics were interesting, and whose style was worthy of imitation. Many on that list were op-ed writers with whom students were free to agree or disagree on the substance of their ideas, while learning to appreciate readability and grace in print—another word for style.

## THE OP-ED PAGE

While we were at it, I offered advice in class that I will repeat here, namely, how to go about writing an op-ed (opposite the editorial page) piece for a newspaper. The students were on their respective ways to leadership positions. It was a safe bet then, and still is, that the op-ed page will be around for quite awhile to influence minds and hearts (that's what leaders do, isn't it?) wherever decisions are made.

First, choose your topic and make sure that it is current. Give a lot of thought to what you want to say and say it concisely in about 500 words; some editors will give you a range of about 700 words, but if you are brief, you have a better chance of finding your way into print. State your thesis, at least to yourself, in a single sentence that can be "built out," paragraph by paragraph, into a compelling essay. Keep your essay jargon-free and steer clear of ideology. Editors are looking for original ideas that have a direct bearing on real-life issues. Controversy is okay; just don't try to substitute authority for thought or emotion for reason. Anecdotes can be helpful; human interest angles enhance the story. Avoid ridicule. Positive over negative is always the preferred route.

To get a sense of what a newspaper likes (not that you cannot choose to disagree with them), read what is on a given op-ed page before you submit an essay for consideration. Get the guidelines for submission and work within them. At the end of your article, be sure to put your name, title, telephone number, e-mail address and, since in some instances you will be paid for your work, your Social Security number. Editors presume that yours is a sole-source submission—that is, that you are not spraying your essay around by means of the simultaneous and multiple submissions route. They may or may not acknowledge your submission. If you hear nothing within two weeks, feel free to send it somewhere else.

Another practical point to be made in connection with op-ed essays is their usefulness in enhancing your resumé when you circulate it to prospective employers. Attach the op-ed to your resumé. This will demonstrate that you are an original thinker capable of stating your ideas concisely and persuasively in print. It sets your resumé apart from hundreds of others that may flow in when an opening is advertised. It also brings to life, in an attractive way, the degrees, dates, awards, and achievements that are listed in cold print on your resumé.

A letter to the editor is another way to exercise influence. Letters are always signed, typically about 250 words in length, targeted on an event or story (cited by date and title) that appeared previously in the paper, and, if your letter has any chance at all of appearing in print, it must be clear and to the point.

To be very practical for a moment, let me provide you with a format for a letter to the editor of any newspaper or magazine. First, create your personal letterhead:

> Your Name
> Street Address
> City, State, Zip Code

Date

Letters Editor
Name of newspaper or magazine
Street Address
City, State, Zip Code

To the Editor:

[Refer in your first paragraph (by title, date, and author) to the article or news story that prompts you to write.]
[Mention the point in the article that prompts your comment.]

[State your agreement or disagreement, or mention a point that the article missed and should, in your view, have covered.]

Sincerely,


Your Name
Your Telephone Number

In order to be able to do this, you will have to read the article carefully, underline the points that you want to comment on, and clarify your main point by reducing it to a single sentence. You should also understand that a "Letter to the Editor" is not a personal letter from you to the author of the article you are commenting on. That's why you begin with the simple salutation: To the Editor.

## IF YOU WANT TO LEAD, LEARN TO WRITE

Once you are in a leadership position, there will be constant demands on your ability to write. So let it be said once again, if you want to lead, learn to write. And here is a tip that will save you a lot of grief when you find yourself in a position where you are responsible for the outcome of a series of negotiating sessions, meetings that could string out over weeks or months.

You certainly won't be in a leadership role for long before you gain an appreciation for the knack of "reducing it to writing" or "getting what we've agreed to down on paper," before moving on. By that I mean it is foolish to walk away from a negotiating session or planning meeting without having consensus on what was discussed and agreed to—not only a verbal understanding, but an understanding that what was said at the point of agreement will be written down, circulated to all participants for their information and reflection, and used as a starting point for the next round of conversation, discussion, and debate about the issues that are on their way to final resolution. The one responsible for getting it down on paper is the leader. He or she does the actual writing or, at the very least, signs off on a draft prepared by someone who was present and was given the assignment to "get it down" on paper. Notice, I did not say "write the minutes." I'm not talking about minutes when I refer to the summary of points agreed to.

What finds its way onto paper will serve as the baseline for the beginning of the next session. Progress is impossible without successive starting lines that are clear and undisputed. Peace will not prevail unless the written summaries are there to shore it up. Clarity, reduced to written form, is the friend of organizational peace and progress.

Let me say so gently, but if you ignore this advice, you do so at the risk of losing your leadership effectiveness. Writing is a tool you will be using all the time.

While conducting research for a book based on interviews with 150 men and women, ages 40 to 55, who had one thing in common—involuntary separation from high-level management positions as a result of corporate downsizing—I had the opportunity to interview more than a few employers in addition to talking to those who had lost their jobs. I learned from one employer a lesson I never fail to pass along to students. He told me that when the list was down to three for a key job in his organization, say, chief financial officer, he interviewed each finalist and, at the end of what was typically a half-hour conversation, he would thank the candidates for their interest and then request each to take a few moments in the reception area to write a short summary of the conversation—major points covered, negotiable points agreed upon, mutual understanding achieved. His secretary would provide typewriter, computer, word-processor, yellow pad, pen or pencil—whatever was needed.

When the summary was written, the candidate (who, by the way, had to work right there without benefit of dictionary, spouse or friend as editor, or any other assistance) left the essay behind and departed. The secretary was instructed to bring the written product in to the CEO, who read it on the spot and, if it was not well written, tossed it into the wastebasket. That candidacy came to an abrupt end simply because the applicant was unable to write well.

When interviewed abut her leadership and management style, Nell Minow, co-founder and chair of the Corporate Library, was asked by the *New York Times* how she went about the task of hiring. After indicating that, in addition to competence, she looked for "passionate curiosity" and a sense of humor, she said, "ultimately, I won't hire anybody who can't write."[2] The interview appeared in the Sunday Business Section of the *Times* in a weekly feature called "Openers" and subtitled "Corner Office." Interviewer Adam Bryant asks prominent CEOs about the influences that shaped them as leaders and, not infrequently, about the qualities they look for in hiring others for top management positions.

One week after the Minow interview, the question-and-answer exchange focused on Richard Anderson, CEO of Delta Airlines. "He Wants Subjects, Verbs and Objects" warned the headline. Predictably, the following question came early in the interview: "Let's talk about hiring. What are you looking for in job candidates?" Here is the Delta CEO's reply: "Typically, when you're hiring a vice president of a company, they already have the résumé and they already have the experience base. And so what you're trying to find out about are the intangibles of leadership, communication style, and the ability to, today, really adapt to change. And there are a lot of ways to go at that. I like to ask people what they've read, what are the last three or four books they've read, and what did they enjoy about those."

Two further questions elicited comments about the importance of writing well:

Q. What are you listening for as somebody describes their family, where they're from, etc.?

A. You're looking for a really strong set of values. You're looking for a really good work ethic. Really good communication skills. More and more the ability to speak well and write is important. You know, writing is not something that is taught as strongly as it should be in the educational curriculum. So you're looking for communication skills.
You're looking for adaptability to change. Do you get along well with people? And are you the sort of person that can be a part of a team and motivate people? Do you have the emotional I.Q.?

Q. And is there any change in the kind of qualities you're looking for compared with five, ten years ago?

A. I think this communication point is getting more and more important. People really have to be able to handle the written and spoken word. And when I say written word, I don't mean PowerPoints. I don't think PowerPoints help people think as clearly as they should because you don't have to put a complete thought in place. You can just put a phrase with a bullet in front of it. And it doesn't have a subject, a verb, and an object, so you aren't expressing complete thoughts.

These are practical points, evidence from the real world of employment that I share with my students by way of motivating them to pay attention to the quality of their writing.

## WORDS IN TIMES OF CRISIS

Back in 2008, US Airways, faced with rising costs, decided to impose new fees on its customers—notably, charges for bags checked and for previously complimentary sodas and soft drinks in economy class. To make that decision in the executive suite is one thing, to impose the fees in flight is another story altogether. So, to explain the change and reduce the risk of having beverages tossed back in the faces of flight attendants requesting payment, the chairman and CEO of the airline wrote a letter under the title of "Changing the Way We Do Business" that appeared in the August 2008 issue of the company's in-flight magazine. Here it is:

> As you've probably read in the news over the past several months, sustained record-high oil prices have created a financial crisis for the airline industry. As a result, US Airways is rewriting its playbook for the way we do business in these challenging times.
>
> In just the last year, the average fuel cost to carry one passenger on a round-trip flight has doubled; since 2000, that cost has more than quadrupled. The numbers are staggering, especially when you consider that consumers are paying roughly the same for domestic airfares as they were in 2000.
>
> To help offset the business-threatening cost of fuel and to continue to provide affordable, reliable transportation for our customers, we simply must change the way we do business. Part of this transformation includes moving to a "pay for what you choose to use" model. In this new model, our intent is to offer services to those customers who want to pay for them, including things like in-flight beverages and meals, checked baggage service, and premium seat assignments. While new and different, this model will help us remain competitive and keep affordable travel throughout the US Airways network.

For our most frequent flyers, our Dividend Miles Preferred members, we'll continue to deliver on items you value most, including exemptions from certain fees, complimentary First Class upgrades, and the best upgrade window in the industry.

So, while change is never easy, and certainly some changes are harder than others, we're working hard to keep building a network that you want to fly at prices you can afford. We're also working hard to keep up our on-time arrival winning streak; at press time, for the past six consecutive months, our airline has finished in the top three among the ten major domestic airlines for on-time arrivals as reported by the U.S. Department of Transportation.

And we're doing this amid what history will likely recall as one of the most dire energy crises of our times.

On behalf of our 35,000 employees, we appreciate that you're flying with us today and we look forward to serving you in the future.

Doug Parker, Chairman and CEO

The letter is well written. Many hands and several drafts probably produced the final product, but ownership of the message belongs to the leader. Notice the frequency of use of the words *change* and *crisis*. Notice the reminder about on-time arrivals. The troubling statistic of fuel cost per flight per customer makes the central point effectively. Few (if any) questions remain unanswered. Plain prose did the job. This is a good example of the written word functioning as a tool of leadership.

Another good example is the letter that appeared as a full-page ad in major newspapers across the country over the signature of the chairman of General Motors two days after GM filed for bankruptcy on June 1, 2009. That day will be long remembered in American business history. The GM leader had to make a statement. Here is the text of his letter, which appeared in many major newspapers, as it appeared in the *New York Times*:[3]

To Our Customers,

While a lot is changing at our company today, one thing is not: our commitment to you, our customers.

We want to assure you that your GM warranty will continue, whether you already own a GM car or intend to buy a new one. Genuine GM parts will be supplied. GM-trained Goodwrench technicians will perform service. Simply bring your vehicle to your GM dealer and you will receive service.

If the dealership you usually visit will be closing, we sincerely apologize and regret that it has affected you. We stand ready to serve with one of the largest dealer networks in America. Please visit GM.com/vehicles/dealer for information on dealers in your area. We pledge to make your next GM experience a remarkable one.

At this critical point in our history, we cannot afford to lose your business. Or your trust. You have our word.

If you are in the market for a new car, I urge you to shop GM. We are open for business, with some of the best vehicles, values and financing rates available. When you come in, I encourage you to be a critical judge of everything—from your experience in our dealership, to the quality of our cars. We owe you nothing but the best. And we will deliver.

General Motors may look different down the road, but we are here to stay. By accelerating work that is already underway and making fundamental changes from top to bottom, GM will be leaner, greener, faster and stronger. We're not just rebuilding our company. We're reinventing it.

Over the coming days, months and years, we will prove ourselves by being more transparent, more accountable and, above all, more focused on you, our customer.

I invite you to track our progress at GMreinvention.com. And on behalf of all the men and women doing the hard work of changing our company for the better, we look forward to showing you the New GM.

Sincerely,

Frederick A. Henderson
President & Chief Executive Officer, General Motors

That's an excellent letter. Now you might say, yes, but Fritz Henderson didn't write it; some spin doctor in his public relations office put it together. Maybe. But he surely had a hand in it, perhaps the defining hand. He would certainly have consulted others as that message moved through various drafts that resulted in this fine outcome. The style is just right. The sentences are short and very much to the point. It is customer-focused. The corporate name is prominent throughout and the salesman-in-chief does not pass up the opportunity to ask for the order. Regrettably, the salesman-in-chief failed to sell himself to his own board of directors and lasted in the job only eight months. Things weren't happening fast enough at GM, so the board fired Fritz Henderson.

Earlier in this chapter I pointed out that sportswriters employ what I like to call the "varsity verb." In the business world, you will notice what might be called the "bottom-line verb." In an opinion piece in *Business Week*, "Words That Pack Power," Frank Luntz claims to have discovered "five words that really resonate in the world of business right now" and suggests that "they should become part of every executive's vocabulary."[4] His five are *consequences, impact, reliability, mission,* and *commitment.* The only one of these that found its way into the US Airways CEO Doug Parker's letter is *reliability,* although synonyms or substitutes for all five are there. Similarly, Fritz Henderson used only one, *commitment,* but echoes of all the others were included. "What these words have in common," says Luntz, "is a desire on the part of those who use them to sound authentic."[5] That's a good word to use as a measure of yourself and your writing—*authentic.* Your aim should be to get authenticity into your writing. Recall that no one follows an uncertain trumpet. In the same way, when the written appeal is bland and inauthentic, the response will be vapid at best.

Luntz's five words "that pack power" and more like them should find their way into the business leader's vocabulary and onto the pages of reports, memoranda, speeches, letters, and advertising copy that business leaders produce.

A good book for any would-be leader to read is *On Writing Well* by longtime professor of writing William Zinsser.[6] This is not a how-to-do-it book with diagrams and drills; it is just a commonsense ("writing is learned by imitation"), down-to-earth ("separate usage from jargon") compendium of principles, methods, forms, and attitudes that will help release the potential you now have to become a better writer.

Not to be overlooked by any would-be leader is the fact that the opportunity to write speeches for a senior executive is a splendid career opportunity for a younger person. Never let that opportunity pass. Notice, in this as in so many other moments in the early stages of your career, fortune favors the well-prepared. Make sure those writing skills are already in your toolkit.

## THE STORYTELLING LEADER

Stories can enhance your message exponentially. You will notice in the "toolkit" you now hold in your hands that, in addition to chapters on speaking and writing, there are chapters that focus on listening and reading. That's where you pick up your stories. Don't rely on memory. How many times have you heard someone say, "I can never remember a joke"? Don't try to remember good stories, write them down and put them in your "keeper's file." That file can be a pack of index cards, a designated computer file, a desk drawer, a cardboard box. You can browse in that box, shuffle the deck, so to speak, when you are looking for new ideas or a good way to illustrate an abstract point. Lincoln did it; so can you.

Here are a couple of examples from my keeper's file. Add them to you own if you wish, or let them nudge you in the direction of searching out your own as you listen and read. (You *are* going to read more, aren't you? Promise me!)

STORY ONE: "Giving an Old Friend New Life," from the world of sports.

> A few years ago, in connection with research for a book I was writing on business ethics, I ran across this interesting definition of character in an account of how the National Football League runs a training camp for rookies in an effort to protect them from various forms of self-destruction. The players are told that "character is what you do when you are angry, afraid, or bored . . . and no one is watching."
>
> That prompted me to wonder how many NFL rookies and veterans alike had noticed that Dick Cass, president of the Baltimore Ravens, while no one was watching, donated a kidney to a longtime friend and law school classmate. He did so quietly, but reporters got wind of it, and, shortly afterward, a headline on the sports page of the *Baltimore Sun* read, "Donation from Ravens' Cass Gives an Old Friend Gift of Life."
>
> A transplant surgeon remarked that donors like Cass "are the closest things to heroes on this earth that you are going to meet." Mr. Cass, whose name at the time was in the early mix of potential candidates to succeed Paul Tagliabue as NFL commissioner, modestly said, "I did some reading and found it wasn't that big a deal. The surgery isn't fun, but other than that, you don't need two kidneys."

Dick Cass has given a compelling example of selfless-
ness in a professional sports culture too often characterized
by arrogance, power, and me-first greed.

STORY TWO: "The Window and the Looking Glass," from nineteenth-cen-
tury Hassidic rabbinical literature.

> A man whose heart was hardened by wealth and who was
> discontent and unhappy, went to consult Rabbi Eisig. The
> rabbi took him across the room and said to the man, "Look
> out the window, and tell me what you see." "I see people
> walking up and down. Then the rabbi held up a looking glass
> in front of him. "Look here now and tell me what you see."
> "I see myself." "So you don't see the others anymore? Con-
> sider that the window and the mirror are both made of glass;
> but, since the mirror has a coating of silver, you see only
> yourself in it, while you can see others through the transpar-
> ent glass of the window. When you were poor, you saw others
> and had compassion on them; but, being covered with wealth,
> you see only yourself. It would be much the best thing for
> you to scrape off the silver-coating so that you can once again
> see other people."

STORY THREE: "Where Does God Live?"

> I remember years ago hearing a story about a father, half
> asleep, shaving one morning at the sink in front of the bath-
> room mirror, with his five-year year-old son standing by and
> observing intently. Apropos of nothing at all that was hap-
> pening there in front of him, the boy asked, "Where does God
> live?" "In a well," answered the dad.
> The boy went downstairs and when the father turned up
> at the breakfast table, his wife, more than a little puzzled,
> asked, "What have you been telling him? He asked you
> where God lives and you said, 'in a well.'" Now, fully awake,
> the father realized what had happened.
> The question took him back to a day in his own young
> childhood in Croatia when he was sitting on the front
> doorstep of his farm house, just off the road, when a band of
> gypsies came along in boots, bandanas, and beards, and one
> of them—a giant of a man—walked up to the well and took
> a drink. Seeing the boy, he walked over, picked him up, and

while holding him aloft asked, "Where does God live?" The frightened child had no reply, so the gypsy carried him over to the well, flipped him around and held him face down looking into the well. "Look down there and tell me what you see." Catching his reflection on the surface of the well water, the boy said, "I see myself." "And now you know," said the gypsy, as he flipped him over once more and placed him on the ground, "where God lives."

You can never have too many stories; that's another way of saying you should never have an inactive keepers file. In the preface to the paperback edition of his book *Leading Minds*, Howard Gardner writes this: "Leaders fashion stories—principally stories of identity. It is important that a leader be a good storyteller, but equally crucial that the leader embody that story in his or her life. When a leader tells stories to experts, the stories can be quite sophisticated; but when the leader is dealing with a diverse, heterogeneous group, the story must be sufficiently elemental to be understood by the untutored or 'unschooled' mind."[7]

So gather them up. Write them down. Use your stories to illustrate your points—in both your written and oral communication. If there is no communication, there will be no leadership. If there are no stories, then the point you wanted to make is that much less likely to be remembered.

And finally, let me give a nod to the new technology. What is new as I write may yield to something a whole lot newer by the time you read this. Next-generation leadership will require familiarity with next-generation communications technology. It's up to you.

## NOTES:

1. Nicholas deB. Katzenbach, *Some of It Was Fun: Working with RFK and LBJ* (New York: W.W. Norton, 2008), 195–96.
2. Interview with Adam Bryant, *New York Times*, (April 19, 2009): BU2.
3. (June 3, 2009): A5.
4. Frank Luntz, "Words That Pack Power," *Business Week* (November 3, 2008): 106.
5. Ibid.
6. William Zinsser, *On Writing Well* (New York: Harper Collins, 30th anniversary edition, 2006).
7. Howard Gardner, *Leading Minds: Anatomy of Leadership* (New York: Basic Books, 1995), ix.

# CHAPTER SEVEN

## LEADERS READ

Reading habits begin in strange ways. My brother always had a flashlight under the covers when we were supposed to be down for the night and sound asleep. My Jesuit friend, the late C. J. McNaspy, a true genius, received a complete set of a popular encyclopedia when he was just six years old. It came from his parents by way of compensation for uprooting and relocating him from New Orleans to Lafayette, Louisiana, where his father took a new job. Over the course of the next year, the six-year-old McNaspy read the entire set, volume by volume, from beginning to end. In the move, he lost some friends but gained a love of learning.

According to the *Wall Street Journal*, Bill Gates became a "diligent learner" at an early age.[1] As a youngster, he read the entire *World Book Encyclopedia* from start to finish and his parents encouraged his reading habit by paying for any book he wanted.

Jack Welch, whom you met back in chapter two, reports that "from the age of six, I got my daily dose of current events and sports, thanks to the leftover *Boston Globe*s, *Herald*s, and *Record*s"—picked up by his father, a railroad conductor on the Boston & Maine commuter line between Boston and Newburyport, MA, when passengers left them behind. "Reading the papers every night became a lifelong addiction. I'm a news junkie to this day," says Welch.[2]

Everyone knows that, as a boy, Abraham Lincoln liked to read. One biographer refers to the "small but steady diet of books he mastered" and writes that in the process, "he learned to rely on his books and his imagination to satisfy his curiosity and intellect."[3] These books, according to his cousin Dennis Hanks, included *Aesop's Fables*, *Robinson Crusoe*, *The Arabian Nights*, along with William Scott's *Lessons in Elocution* and Noah

121

Webster's *American Spelling Book.* And Hanks remarked, "He was a constant and I may say stubborn reader."[4]

## READING EXTENDS YOUR REACH

Many successful leaders will tell you that they enjoy reading history. It might be the history of their country or the world; it might be the history of the organization they lead or the industry or profession within which they lead. Some read military history in order to gain an appreciation of tactics and strategy. Some read biography in search of clues to the development of character. Others like to read speeches not just to get ideas for their own public remarks, but to stay current with what is running through the minds of others. (The journal *Vital Speeches of the Day* immodestly claims to be offering "the best thoughts of the best minds on current national issues" and has been doing so since 1934.)

Some read just for the love of reading and this is always a hopeful sign that they are likely to be well informed and intellectually alive.

Dennis Recio, a Jesuit who teaches English literature at the University of San Francisco, explains what he does by saying, "I teach students to see beyond their own experience." That's what those who are wise enough to read widely—just for the love of reading—are doing; they are seeing beyond their own experience and, in the process, becoming more fully human.

Have you ever taken a long airplane ride seated next to a person who does not read, view, or listen to anything at all? Perhaps that person is thinking. But you have to wonder whether any genuine reasoning—real thinking—is going on, or if it is just idle mental meandering over unimaginative, uncreative brain terrain. The elapsed time in flight, say, from one coast to the other, may represent time well spent in transportation terms, but in terms of the life of the mind, the idle hours aloft are hours of lost opportunity for intellectual growth.

I encourage young potential leaders who are still in school, or in the lower ranks of paid employment in the world of work, to ask senior executives what book may have had an impact on them in earlier years. What book might the elders recommend to them for motivation and instruction?

If they asked, as I did, a high school classmate of mine who is now the retired general counsel of a major oil company, they would get this reply: "Every young person in business *must* read *Silent Alarm* by John G. Blumberg. All of us need the advice in this marvelous small book. It is fiction, but each one of us needs the message. I'm a little too old to change, but I make sure I pass this book on to younger people." I agree; I've read the book and endorse the recommendation.

The same kind of inquiry—what book would you recommend?—can be made at any time with the assistance of a search engine on the Internet. For instance, if you simply type "most influential book" in a search engine slot, you'll be able to examine lists of what computer programmers, entrepreneurs, journalists, and various other surveyed groups recommend. In one instance, the Library of Congress offered a baker's dozen of titles mentioned by respondents who are "out there" and willing to identify books that have had a major impact on their lives. Consider: The Bible; *Atlas Shrugged*, by Ayn Rand; *The Road Less Traveled*, by M. Scott Peck; *To Kill a Mockingbird*, by Harper Lee; *The Lord of the Rings*, by J. R. R. Tolkien; *Gone With the Wind*, by Margaret Mitchell; *How to Win Friends and Influence People*, by Dale Carnegie; *The Book of Mormon*, by Joseph Smith; *The Feminine Mystique*, by Betty Friedan; *Gift from the Sea*, by Anne Morrow Lindbergh; *Man's Search for Meaning* by Viktor Frankl; *Passages*, by Gail Sheehy; and Harold Kushner's *When Bad Things Happen to Good People*. If you haven't read any of these, choose one or two and get busy. But better still, ask those whom you admire and might perhaps want to emulate to tell you about books that may have had a special impact on their lives.

There is no doubt that the writings of Mohandas K. Gandhi had great influence on Martin Luther King, as did the work of Dietrich Bonhoeffer, especially his book *The Cost of Discipleship*. King as well as Franklin Delano Roosevelt and John F. Kennedy acknowledge an intellectual debt to Henry David Thoreau (1817–62), whose book, *Walden*, and essay, "Civil Disobedience," continue to shape the thinking of decision makers.

Both *Walden* (1854) and Rachael Carson's *Silent Spring* (1962) influenced the contemporary environmental movement. To find out why, potential leaders will have to pick up those books and start reading. That, by the way, is the point of this chapter—to encourage movement toward the printed page where ideas that have already influenced others are waiting to influence you.

An easy read is Ralph Waldo Emerson's "Self-Reliance." That essay, read when he was in high school, had a lasting influence on Matt Gillin, co-founder in 1997 of a company called Ecount, which was sold ten years later to Citibank and is now known as Citi Prepaid Services, a leading provider of electronic paperless payment programs. What was it that caught

the young Matt Gillin's eye when he read "Self-Reliance"? Take a look to
see if there's something there that might catch yours. (It is only 58 pages
long.) Here are a few examples:

> There is a time in every man's education when he arrives at the
> conviction that envy is ignorance; . . . that though the wide uni-
> verse is full of good, no kernel of nourishing corn can come to
> him but through his toil bestowed on that plot of ground which
> is given to him to till. The power which resides in him is new in
> nature, and none but he knows what that is which he can do, nor
> does he know until he has tried.[5]

> Whoso would be a man, must be a nonconformist.[6]

> Insist on yourself; never imitate. Your own gift you can present
> every moment with the cumulative force of a whole life's culti-
> vation; but of the adopted talent of another you have only an ex-
> temporaneous half possession. That which each can do best,
> none but his Maker can teach him.[7]

It is interesting to note that in his classic book *On Becoming a
Leader*, Warren Bennis mentions that Norman Lear, a leading writer and
producer in television's so-called golden age, told him that, as a high school
boy, he was profoundly influenced by Emerson's "Self Reliance." Bennis
quotes Lear:

> Emerson talks about listening to that inner voice and going with
> it, against all voices to the contrary. I don't know when I started
> to understand that there was something divine about that inner
> voice. . . . To go with that—which I confess I don't do all the
> time—is the purest, truest thing we have. And when we forgo
> our own thoughts and opinions, they end up coming back to us
> from the mouths of others. They come back with an alien
> majesty. . . . So the lesson is, you believe it. *When I've been most
> effective, I've listened to that inner voice.*[8]

## MOST INFLUENTIAL BOOKS

In May 2009, a small newspaper in the suburbs of Houston asked
school board candidates, "What are the five most influential books you've

ever read?" The editorial rationale for this line of inquiry: "Reading choices can be a rough indicator of a person's personality. Preferences may speak to the reader's intellect, morals, education and interests." All but one of the candidates for school board mentioned the Bible. Other responses gave signals as to where the candidate perched on the ideological spectrum: *The Fountainhead* by Ayn Rand; *The First Billion is the Hardest: Reflections on a Life of Comebacks and America's Energy Future* by T. Boone Pickens; and *The World is Flat* by Thomas Friedman. The fact that the responses will appear in print reduces their reliability as accurate indicators of a person's morals and could point more to aspirations than achievements in the intellectual arena. But I post the question here simply to suggest that you might consider facing up to it yourself right now.

Can you list five truly influential books that have touched your life up to this point? If so, jot the titles down. If not, you had better start reading. Are you curious about books that might have influenced the lives of others who are now established leaders? I'm presuming that you are and would simply encourage you to be resourceful in discovering what those titles are and then reading the ones that appeal to you.

I was surprised when a general sales manager told me that a book that influenced him and which he would recommend to younger colleagues is *Leadership and the New Science: Discovering Order in a Chaotic World* by Margaret Wheatley, who also wrote *Finding Our Way: Leadership for an Uncertain Time*.[9] "The science is not so new anymore," the sales executive told me, "but today's economic changes should be viewed against the scientific theory of quantum mechanics, chaos theory, and self-organizing systems. If business models are going to transform, then this is the direction they will go." He recommends that younger colleagues become better informed on "key concepts like holistic systems, increased self-awareness, relationship-building, and information sharing." You're not going to know this unless you ask. The response you receive may open up some common ground between two generations in the same organization; it can also enhance the quality of colleagueship.

Another executive, in this case the CEO of a venture capital firm, told me that a book on Chinese military strategy that dates back to the sixth century BC is available in English translation and influenced him in understanding business strategy. *The Art of War*, by Sun Tzu, "requires a certain amount of discernment on the part of the contemporary reader," he says, "but I would recommend it as helpful in understanding the importance of setting and fighting for well-defined goals."

*Philadelphia Business Journal*, a tabloid bi-weekly newspaper, runs the "CEO File" as a regular feature. "Stay true to your ethical compass," was the response of J. B. Hillman CEO of IT Evolution, Inc., when asked to mention the most important lesson he had learned. This head of a small IT technical services company identified the most influential book he had read as, *The Art of Happiness at Work* by the Dalai Lama.[10] Another local executive who made the "CEO File" is Widener University President James T. Harris III, whose most influential book is *The Inward Journey*, by Howard Thurman.[11] If your curiosity gets the better of you, you might want to look that one up.

There may be an opportunity in a hiring interview or, later, after you are hired and participating in the annual performance assessment conversation, to ask a more senior person for suggestions about reading. You have to be careful, of course, not to set up an unsuspecting and nonreading elder for embarrassment. So instead of asking what he or she has read and would recommend, take a more indirect approach and indicate you are open to any advice about books or journals that might be interesting and useful as you move along in the organization.

Jonathan J. Hirtle is CEO of Hirtle Callaghan & Co., an investment management firm near Philadelphia. His goal, as reported in *Philadelphia Business Journal*, is to "permanently change the investment industry."[12] The most influential book he has encountered to date is *Built to Last: Successful Habits of Visionary Companies* by Jim Collins and Jerry Porras. Many other business leaders would say the same thing (in fact many did in conversations with me). A good summary of what these authors have to say appears toward the end of the book, where they write, "It would be a mistake to conclude that you could implement any single chapter of this book in isolation and have a visionary company. Core ideology alone cannot do it. The drive for progress alone cannot do it. A BHAG (Big Hairy Audacious Goal) alone will not do it. Evolution through autonomy and entrepreneurship by itself will not do it. Home-grown management alone does not make a visionary company, nor a cult-like culture, nor even living the concept that good enough never is." Why? Because "a visionary company is like a great work of art."[13] Greatness is in the whole composition, not in any of the parts. "[T]he only sacred cow in a visionary company is its core ideology. Anything else can be changed or eliminated."[14]

Recall the suggestion back in chapter one that a leader is an artist. Why then should not the organization he or she leads be considered a work of art? The leader, as artist, will "sculpt," "paint," or "compose" the organization not for the admiration and delight of others, but for the provision of services and production of goods that will meet human needs and serve the common good. Collins and Porras mention the importance of a core ideology in shaping a visionary company; look for a discussion of core values when chapter eight of this book reminds you that "Leaders Think."

I have to confess to a certain degree of skepticism when *The Wall Street Journal* gave us "a glimpse of what the president has been reading" in an article by Karl Rove under the title, "Bush is a Book Lover."[15] The reference, of course, is to the 43rd president, not his father, and the article appeared after the election of Barack Obama but before George W. Bush moved back to Texas.

Rove, the former senior adviser and deputy chief of staff to President Bush, reports that he and the president entered into a book-reading competition that began on New Year's Eve in 2005 and continued at a brisk pace for three years. Their goal was to read a book a week. "At year's end," says Rove, "I defeated the president 110 books to 95," acknowledging that the president lost "because he's been busy as Leader of the Free World." Their 2007 rematch had Rove winning again 76 books to 51, and as they were coming to the end of 2008, Rove was again ahead 64 to 40.

My skepticism was grounded in my own experience of finding time to read amidst mounting demands of administrative responsibility. A book a week is a lot for a busy executive. In any case, an impressive number of books were skimmed or read by President Bush when he occupied the Oval Office. Here, for the record, is Mr. Rove's account of what the President read in 2006:

> Mr. Bush's 2006 reading list shows his literary tastes. The nonfiction ran from biographies of Abraham Lincoln, Andrew Carnegie, Mark Twain, Babe Ruth, King Leopold, William Jennings Bryan, Huey Long, LBJ and Genghis Kahn to Andrew Roberts's *A History of the English-Speaking Peoples Since 1900*, James L. Swanson's *Manhunt*, and Nathaniel Philbrick's *Mayflower*. Besides eight Travis McGee novels by John D. MacDonald, Mr. Bush tackled Michael Crichton's *Next*, Vince Flynn's *Executive Power*, Stephen Hunter's *Point of Impact*, and Albert Camus's *The Stranger*, among others.
>
> Fifty-eight of the books he read that year were nonfiction. Nearly half of his 2006 reading was history and biography, with another eight volumes on current events (mostly the Mideast) and six on sports.

Whew! Think of all the briefings, memoranda, newspapers, and magazines that required the President's attention, not to mention the fact, attested to by Rove and others, that Mr. Bush read the Bible cover to cover each year and incorporated some daily "devotional time" into his schedule. He reportedly watched little television and spent most evenings at home.

## THE REFLECTIVE EXECUTIVE

Bob Holliday, a retired and, by his own admission, now more reflective business executive, told me that he would, at the end of a fifty-year career with a major U.S. corporation, recommend that younger persons in business become acquainted with *The Dignity of Work: John Paul II Speaks to Managers and Workers*, edited by Robert G. Kennedy, Gary Atkinson, and Michael Naughton.[16] This volume presents addresses made over the span of his pontificate by Pope John Paul II to managers, workers, and general audiences that stress not only the dignity of work but the unique dignity of every human person in or out of work. This is a compendium of the Christian vision of management and employment. The recommender says, "This is a book that touched my soul deeply; it has everything to do with leadership and management. I've read it and reread it countless times; it remains undiscovered, sadly, or, even more regrettably, rejected in the business culture because it is so far from the dominant values and cultural norms of our day."

Another book this retired executive recommends is by the late Protestant social ethicist John G. Bennett, *Making a Soul: Human Destiny and the Debt of Our Existence*.[17] "This book caused me to think deeply about how we become spiritual leaders versus material followers. It made me think about how much of my life is spent contributing to the advancement of material things over against the development of the spiritual nature of myself and others. It made me think about the spiritual dimensions of daily work."

And finally he recommends *Hope Is Not a Method: What Business Leaders Can Learn from America's Army*, a book written by former Army chief of Staff General Gordon R. Sullivan with his strategic planner, retired Colonel Michael V. Harper.[18] This book, says Bob Holliday, "contains powerful lessons employed in the transformation of one of the world's largest organizations. It is based on lived reality, not theory."

The Villanova University School of Business introduced a "Read to Lead" feature to its curriculum not long ago. (That's a great slogan!) The idea is to put the same book into the hands of all freshmen in order to—as the school's promotional literature puts it—"connect and inspire all VSB freshmen class members around a common, highly relevant business theme through the collective reading of one book." The reading will not stop there, of course, but the reading habit, accompanied by reflection and discussion, belongs in the business leader's toolkit. For the 2008–9 academic year, the Villanova book was *Pour Your Heart into It: How Starbucks Built a Company One Cup at a Time* by Starbucks Chairman and CEO Howard Shultz and Dori Jones Yang.[19]

The earlier you start reading, the better. And the longer you continue to read, the wider will be your exposure to the human experience. You can learn about distant lands and foreign cultures best by travel. Next best is reading, which, of course, is a lot less expensive. Good literature invites you inside the minds of interesting people—foolish and wise, heroes and cowards, the virtuous and the villainous. The reading experience contributes to your growth as a human being; it also helps develop your leadership potential.

## A FATHER PRESCRIBES

He calls himself "Dr. Bill Quain," not Dr. William J. Quain Jr. He has nothing against his dad; it is just that he prefers informality. And when in print, if he happens to drop the "Dr.," he always adds "Ph.D." after his name lest readers fail to notice that he has academic credentials to back up his popular books on sales, achieving success, and bringing about change. He is a motivational speaker and, until his recent early retirement from the classroom, was a popular college professor. To the surprise of no one who knows him, Bill Quain instructed his daughter Amanda, when she matriculated to his alma mater Cornell, that she had to take the following seven courses—"had to" because he was paying, although he would urge every college student to take them because of their utility later in life. They are Accounting, Personal Finance, Oral Communications, Written Communications, Creative Problem Solving/Adapting to Change, Teamwork, and Sales. (She might have to search around for the one on change and problem solving, but she'll find it.)

In addition, Bill Quain prescribes "The Ten Books Your Child (and you) MUST Read for a Successful Life."[20] Here they are in no particular order of preference:

- *How to Win Friends and Influence People* by Dale Carnegie
- *Who Moved My Cheese?* by Spencer Johnson
- *101 Creative Problem Solving Techniques* by James Higgins
- *Overcoming Time Poverty: How to Achieve More by Working Less* by Bill Quain
- *No Money Down Real Estate* by Carlton Sheets
- *Personality Plus* by Florence Littauer
- *Rich Dad, Poor Dad* by Robert Kiyosaki
- *Chicken Soup for the Soul* by Jack Camfield
- *Click: The Ultimate* Guide *to Electronic Marketing for Speakers* by Tom Antion
- *The Automatic Millionaire* by David Bach

Bill expects his daughter to read all ten early in her college career. He is not one for putting things off until tomorrow.

If you think he overemphasizes the quest for success and money, he would say, fine, make a list of your own that corresponds to what you think is important and let the reading begin. In his view, "If you read one book per month, you are in the top one percent of Americans. Most people stop reading after their formal education stops. You should read something positive every day of your life. Take the time to put some positive into your life. Read good books." This advice is all the more interesting in light of the fact that it comes from a man who, at the age of 14, began losing his vision due to macular degeneration of the retina and is now legally blind.

"Get Lost in Books" is the headline advice to college students accompanying a brief back-to-school op-ed essay in *The New York Times* by Yale English professor Harold Bloom.[21] He suggests that "entering upon an undergraduate education should be a voyage away from visual overstimulation into deep, sustained reading of what is most worth absorbing and understanding: the books that survive all ideological fashions." And the "indispensable canon" he offers is: Homer, Plato, the Bible, Virgil, Dante, Chaucer, Cervantes, Shakespeare, Montaigne, and Milton, acknowledging that "a slightly more arbitrary selection might include Blake, Wordsworth, Austen, Dickens, George Eliot, Hardy, Yeats, and Joyce in England and Ireland," while an American lineup would surely include "Emerson, Thoreau, Melville, Walt Whitman, Emily Dickinson, Hawthorne; and in the twentieth century, Faulkner and the major poets: Robert Frost, Wallace Stevens, T. S. Eliot, Hart Crane." Their difficulty "doubles their value," says Bloom, who adds, "Whatever our current travails, we now have a literate president [Barack Obama] capable of coherent discourse, but too many other politicians are devoid of syntax and appear to have read nothing. Aggressive ignorance in aspirants to high office is another dismal consequence of the waning of authentic education." That's an observation worth pondering for more than a moment or two.

Professor Bloom's article prompted Allison Corbett, a graduate student in English at the University of Colorado at Boulder, to send a letter to the editor of the *Times* expressing disappointment "at how few female authors he had included in his indispensable canon." She went on to suggest that "Virginia Woolf, Daphne du Maurier, Edna St. Vincent Millay, Iris Murdoch, Harper Lee, Toni Morrison, the great biographer Nancy Milford, and Marie Atwood, among others, have more than earned places on a twenty-first-century reading list.[22]

*The Times Literary Supplement* (London) invites Internet surfers to visit www.timesonline.co,uk/definitivelist to discover "the 100 most influential books since World War II." To prime the pump, they list some titles from the 1930s and then direct your attention to later decades where, among other suggestions from the 1940s you will find *The Second Sex* by Simone de Beauvoir, *The Managerial Revolution* by James Buchanan, *The Fear of Freedom* by Erich Fromm, *Darkness at Noon* by Arthur Koestler, *The Great Transformation* by Karl Polanyi, and Joseph Schumpeter's *Capitalism, Socialism, and Democracy*.

Some of the recommended titles from the decade of the 1950s are these: *The Origins of Totalitarianism* by Hannah Arendt, *The Second World War* by Winston Churchill, *A Study of History* by Arnold Toynbee, John Kenneth Galbraith's *The Affluent Society*, David Riesman's *The Lonely Crowd*, and *The Two Cultures and the Scientific Revolution* by C. P. Snow.

Among the most influential books that appeared in the 1960s are these: *The End of Ideology* by Daniel Bell, *Capitalism and Freedom* by Milton Friedman, *The Life and Death of American Cities* by Jane Jacobs, Thomas Kuhn's *The Structure of Scientific Revolutions*, and Thomas Schelling's *The Strategy of Conflict*.

Moving through the 1970s, here are some of the recommended titles: *The Interpretation of Cultures* by Clifford Geertz, *Exit, Voice, and Loyalty* by Albert Hirschman, *A Theory of Justice* by John Rawls, *The Joyless Economy* by Tibor Scitovsky, and Alexander Solzhenitsyn's *The Gulag Archipelago*.

For the 1980s and beyond, here is a representative sampling of the recommendations: *The Capitalist Revolution: Fifty Propositions about*

*Prosperity, Equality, and Liberty* by Peter Berger, *Living in Truth* by Vaclav Havel, *The Rise and Fall of the Great Powers* by Paul Kennedy, *Resources, Values, and Development* by Amartyn Sen, and Michael Walzer's *Spheres of Justice*.

There are no whodunits, westerns, or romantic novels there. No science fiction. Sports is absent from the list. If you have read some of these influential books, great; if not, get busy. If none of these authors or titles is familiar to you, you are way behind—not hopelessly behind, just far behind—on the road to effective leadership.

In an essay titled "Liberal Arts for Leadership,"[23] John Churchill, secretary of the Phi Beta Kappa Society, describes his experience as moderator of a series of week-long discussions, during which college and university presidents shared their reflections on pre-assigned readings from classic texts in the humanities and social sciences. The point of it all was to get a better understanding of the nature of leadership. They discussed Lao-tzu's *Tao Te Ching*, selections from Niccolò Machiavelli's *The Prince*, Martin Luther King's "Letter from a Birmingham Jail," Sophocles' *Antigone*, and Martha Nussbaum's chapter on "Narrative Imagination" from her book, *Cultivating Humanity*. They also discussed Agamemnon and Ulysses S. Grant. They examined the friendship of David and Jonathan in the first book of Samuel.

"It was amazing to me," remarked Churchill, "how quickly the commonalities of responsibility among this group—each one perceiving the kinship of the others in understanding their jobs and their trials—created a rapport. . . . And it was heartening to me to see how readily they bought into the premise," namely, that this kind of discussion could improve their effectiveness as leaders.

Leadership is, you will recall, about influence. It would follow, then, that influential books have a contribution to make to the development of leaders. The books won't be able to influence you if you choose not to read them. And notice that if you happen to be the author of an influential book, you are thereby a leader. You are exercising indirect leadership, of course, but you are a leader nonetheless; and you will never know how many followers you have!

NOTES:

1. (April 2–26, 2009): A8.

2. *Jack: Straight from the Gut* (New York: Business Plus), 8.

3. Ronald C. White Jr., *A. Lincoln: A Biography* (New York: Random House, 2009), 23.

4. Ibid., 31–32.

5. Ralph Waldo Emerson, "Self-Reliance" (Mount Vernon, NY: The Peter Pauper Press, 1949), 9.

6. Ibid., 13,

7. Ibid., 50.

8. Warren Bennis, *On Becoming a Leader* (New York: Basic Books, revised edition, 2003), 28.

9. *Leadership and the New Science* (San Francisco: Berrett-Koehler, 1999); *Finding Our Way* (San Francisco: Berrett-Koehler, 2005).

10. (May 15–21, 2009), 15.

11. (January 9–15, 2009), 13.

12. (November 14–20, 2009), 17.

13. James C. Collins and Jerry I. Porras, *Built to Last: Successful Habits of Visionary Companies* (New York: HarperCollins, 1994), 213.

14. Ibid., 218.

15. (December 26, 2008).

16. (Lanham, MD: University Press of America, 1994).

17. (New York: J. G. Bennett, second printing, 1997).

18. (New York: Random House, 1996).

19. (New York: Hyperion, 1997).

20. That is the title of Chapter 17 in his slim book *College Success for Less: Pay Less and Get More—The Insiders' Guide for Parents*, co-authored with Joseph J. Corabdi and Jack Krutsick (Ocean City, NJ: Wales, 2008), 55–56.

21. (September 6, 2009): 10 wk (News of the Week in Review).

22. (September 13, 2009): 15 wk (Sunday Opinion).

23. John Churchill, "Liberal Arts for Leadership," *The Key Reporter* 74, no. 3 (Fall 2009): 2.

# CHAPTER EIGHT

# LEADERS THINK

The term *critical thinking* is often used to describe a very important instrument in the leadership toolkit. It says something more than intelligence, which, of course is an essential quality of good leadership. Thinking relates to the uses of intelligence, and critical thinking focuses on decision points at the end of a long or short analytical path.

Notice that I referred to critical thinking as an instrument, another word for tool. Dentists have instruments; so do surgeons. Musical instruments are not ordinarily thought of as tools, but to suggest that the thinking tool in a leadership toolkit is also an instrument opens the door of the imagination to consider that this instrument—thinking—can be played like a musical instrument. The result can be part of a symphonic response (the work of many) or a solo performance (the product of one creative mind). Alone, or in the company of others, thought produces ideas, which, in turn, can produce progress.

The expression *thought leaders* is sometimes used to describe major thinkers who influence the direction of thinking in their fields. They are the "academic scribblers" who come up with the theories and new ideas that shape events, even though they themselves remain above the fray. I do not have these theoreticians in mind as I add thinking to the leadership toolkit, although I recognize that they are leaders in their own right. What is up for consideration in this chapter is thought power—the application of intellect to practice for the sake of progress.

## THINKING THINGS THROUGH

I recall many years ago walking past a first-floor dormitory window at St. Louis University where the dorm-room occupant had pasted on his window, for passersby to see, the then popular IBM slogan "Think." The Jesuit who was walking along with me remarked, "It might not be a bad idea for that guy to turn his sign the other way around." That was back when "Teahouse of the August Moon" found its way from Broadway onto film and thus gained a wider audience for a sage remark from an Oriental character who says, "Pain make man think, thought make man wise, and wisdom make life endurable." With or without pain, the path to leadership presupposes facility in thinking things through.

As important as thinking is to leadership—that's why we're devoting this separate chapter to it in this book—it must be said that leaders don't lead by thought alone. Reasoned argument is important, but when all attempts to reason with potential followers fail, the leader has to make an appeal to the heart. Effective leadership won't even consider resorting to force, bribes, or threats; the only alternative is a persuasive appeal, by word or example, to the heart. Why to the heart? Because it is the heart that decides when commitments must be made. But for the moment, at least, let's pay attention to the head.

If what follows in this chapter appears to be excessively cerebral—too reason-ready and stuck between the ears—be assured that other parts of this book attend to the emotional side of leadership, to the need to have stories in the leadership toolkit, to be empathetic and compassionate, to exercise intuition.

Phil Kent succeeded Ted Turner as CEO of Atlanta-based Turner Broadcasting in 2003. Unlike his predecessor (sometimes called "the Mouth of the South"), Kent is a quiet, reflective executive. His three-point "CEO Manual" is worth remembering: (1) carve out time to think, not just react; (2) sabbaticals give you useful perspective; and (3) don't over-schedule; leave time for colleagues.[1] Make room for these three points in your leadership toolkit and never fail to "carve out time to think."

Many years ago, a college friend called my attention to the book *Ideas Have Consequences*.[2] He, though just a youth, was on his way to becoming a genuine intellectual who wrote a few books of his own before meeting death at an early age. Ideas fascinated him. The implications of the book title that he recommended fascinated me. Ideas do indeed have consequences. I've often remarked that the world moves on words and numbers, but both words and numbers are the carriers of ideas. Think, think, and think some more, and then put your thoughts into words. That's what leaders do.

Leaders are constantly being challenged to think of solutions. This is the work of intelligence and imagination. Problems can originate just about anywhere—sometimes in the mistakes of leaders. But solutions come only from leaders. Indeed, the production of a solution may mark the debut of an emerging leader. Those already in the leadership ranks will not remain there long if they fail first to see the problems. (Better perhaps to say this: see the problems first, and then offer workable solutions.) Once the solution is seen, the leader's work of mobilizing the organization's human and moving parts for action has just begun.

In his excellent book, *Leading Minds*, Howard Gardner quotes political commentator Michael Korda: "Great leaders are almost always great simplifiers who cut through argument, debate, and doubt to offer a solution everyone can understand and remember—straightforward but potent messages."[3] Recall the discussion in chapters five and six about the importance of clear speech and concise writing as elements in the leadership toolkit. Note now that neither is possible without clear thinking between the ears of the leader. In an interview for *McKinsey Quarterly*, five years after he became CEO of Procter and Gamble and succeeded in turning that mammoth consumer-products company around, Alan G. Lafley said that the need "to communicate at a Sesame Street level of simplicity" was one of the most important discoveries he made when he took the helm of a company where he had worked for twenty-five years.[4] Keeping it simple, not simplistic, is a sign of a well-functioning, uncluttered mind.

You sometimes hear it said that "the wish is father to the thought." True enough. So indulge yourself in large-hearted wishing as you search for thoughts that will translate into programs and policies that will engage your troops and inspire them to move. Large-hearted wishing is another way of saying "magnanimity." The leader is a magnanimous person—generous, open-minded as well as open-hearted, creative—who sees solutions before others do because he or she has grasped an idea. If ideas are to have their intended consequences, there must be a lot of thought at work paving the way to progress. Where will the ideas originate if not in the mind of the leader and the collaborating minds surrounding him or her? When a leader or leadership group stops thinking about problems, their potential (power) for solving problems is zero.

*Thunderthinkers* is the term a friend of mine uses to flatter (as well as amuse) any small group gathered to put their heads together in search of a solution to a given problem. He points out that cognition is one thing and "smarts" are something else again. Moreover, you can be "book smart" or "street smart," depending on your orientation toward the ivory tower or to an experiential, on-the-ground assessment of reality. You can be bookish or an activist in developing your approach to sizing up a situation. Whichever way you lean, whatever approach you prefer, you would be wise to avoid either extreme of the dilemma articulated by one observer of the human condition who said, "The trouble with the world is that the people who do all the thinking never act, and those who do all the acting never think!"

## THINKING IS SEEING

Both thought and action are essential. Balance brings them together in the effective leader. Such a person will have learned that there is an etymological link between the words *theory* and *theater*. Each derives from the Greek word for "eye." Theories and theaters are designed to focus the attention of the viewer. The trained leadership eye will "see" in the dual sense of (1) understanding and (2) identifying the problem to be solved, the objective to be sought, and the action to be taken. Without action, there will be no leadership. Without thought, action may be impulsive and quite wide of the mark.

No matter how we cut it, there is no escaping the necessity of thought being part of the leadership equation. But thought is not disembodied; it can only take place between the ears of the thinker. Hence the importance of thinking—cogent, clear, consistent thinking—in the practice of leadership.

Just as an exasperated college student might sometimes plea, "Teach me how to write!" you might be wondering who or what is going to teach you how to think. Algebra was supposed to do that. So was philosophy. Crossword puzzles may have made a minor contribution. Scrabble can be a helpful exercise toward this end. How about the study of foreign languages and the assimilation of the rules of grammar? Did playing chess make you a better negotiator? And how about the syllogism? The what?

The syllogism is a form of inferential thinking. *Infer* is a good word for leaders to understand, internalize, and apply. Inferential thinking considers the options, reads the connections, discovers the possibilities. But you cannot think unless you first have something in your mind to think about. Logical thinking is taught in many colleges in a course called Logic. I've often thought of a course in logic as the vestibule to philosophy—to deeper, systematic reflection on the meaning not only of life but of all reality.

Logical progress from something already known—a proposition—toward a conclusion, is known as syllogistic thinking. Here's an example of a really simple syllogism that I remember from my first logic class many years ago (notice the logical progression of the argument): Every dog is an animal; every greyhound is a dog; therefore every greyhound is an animal. One, two, three—there it is. The third proposition flows logically from the first two.

Fallacies (the word means "false") are also products of thought. They can be detected by any clear thinker; they will always be avoided by the honest thinker. Since honesty is at the top of the list of the qualities people want to see in their leaders, those who would be leaders have to take great care to avoid fallacious thinking in themselves and be able to spot it in the arguments of others.

People look to leaders for new ways of thinking. It is not unusual to hear expressions of the need to "think outside the box." There's a certain realism in the cartoon complaint where one fellow says to another, "They stick us in a cubicle and expect us to think outside the box!" The work environment should be conducive to reflection and creative thinking, although not everyone needs quiet in order to be productive. I once knew a reporter at the *Washington Post*, for example, who was so used to the noisy atmosphere surrounding his desk in the newsroom that, when given time off to write a book at home, he "just couldn't find the starter button" in the quiet of his home. So he went into the office every day during his sabbatical just to be able to get himself in gear to write and make progress on the book.

If you are not a reflective person, you are unlikely to be able to "see the big picture," as leaders are expected to be able to do. Nor will you be able to discern shifting patterns of thought or behavior in others. Nor will you notice the shifts in values that precede shifts in cultures.

## BRAINPOWER—NEITHER MUSCLE NOR BRAWN

The leader is the organization's quarterback who has to be good at "reading" defensive patterns in order to move the ball toward the goal in the air or on the ground. This is an application of brainpower, not muscle; it requires thinking, not brawn.

To switch for a moment to another sport, consider Connie Mack (1862–1956), the "grand old man of baseball," a founder of the American League and longtime manager of the Philadelphia Athletics. In his playing days, he was first and foremost a catcher. A recent biography describes his catching as "first class." He had the ability to get inside a hitter's head and a feel for what a pitcher should throw in a given situation. Instincts, 'baseball smarts,' are not a matter of intelligence or schooling. They cannot be taught. A player has them or he doesn't. The great catchers, measured by their leadership on the field, their handling of pitchers, and their calling of a game, have them. Connie Mack had them.[5]

And Connie Mack became one of the game's greatest managers. He had baseball intuition and instincts, but he also had an understanding of human nature.

> Mack understood the need to handle each man as an individual. He studied the situation and adopted the method he thought would work. Some managers were by nature mild and easygoing, no matter what. Others were always gruff and pugnacious. Mack was Jekyll and Hyde, sometimes in the same bawling-out session. He might light onto the object of his displeasure with a cutting tongue-lashing and when he saw the player's face bathed in remorse, quickly switch to a gentle hand on the shoulder and a paternal concern for the player's welfare and future.[6]

Mack gave his players a lot of freedom and responsibility to figure out on the field ways to win. "Many of his methods were similar to those that later brought great acclaim to Thomas Watson for his management innovation at IBM. In every office at IBM, Watson would post a one-word sign: THINK. Connie Mack posted the same sign in the mind of each of his players. He didn't do their thinking for them. He focused on his objectives, told his men what he wanted to accomplish, and suggested ways they might succeed. He then left it to them to carry out the mission."[7]

"One bold idea. That's all it takes." This is the introduction to a request for proposals issued by an initiative funded in 2008 by the Bill and Melinda Gates Foundation called "Grand Challenges Explorations." The program wants to "reward innovative ideas in global health" and invites proposals from all disciplines—"anyone can apply." The proposal encourages "unorthodox thinking," which, it notes, is "essential to overcoming the most persistent challenges in global health." This is another reminder that ideas do indeed have consequences and that new ideas are needed to meet the challenges presented by new problems in any area of human life. That's why thinking belongs in the leader's toolkit.

Younger persons, the potential leaders I have in mind as I write this book, have to be honest with themselves and, as they might measure their weight and monitor their physical exercise, they have to assess the extent to which they are exercising their minds. Passive televiewing, light reading, and underutilization of their library cards (or electronic bookseller accounts) are danger signs. The danger is possible erosion on the I.Q. scale and certain reduction of skill in problem solving. This means diminishment of leadership potential. And potential, of course, means power.

What, then, should be done? Become better informed first by reading widely (specialized journals and magazines) and deeply (really good books). Next, become engaged in good exchanges with other minds both directly, through regular conversations and small-group discussions, and vicariously, by watching televised panel discussions and interviews. If your television tastes are all sports and no business or politics, you are most likely going to be an observer of the passing parade, not a leader. You may not even notice that the parade is passing through your neighborhood!

All of this attention to the life of the mind not only helps you to stay informed and know what is going on, it gets your intellectual engine running and makes the generation of ideas become first, second, and third nature to you. You become, through observation and study—admittedly, hard work—a better problem solver. And, if it happens that there is no problem waiting to be solved, you are ready and cleared for takeoff on a creative imagination flight-path studded with new and exciting ideas. Thinking will make it so!

The "Corner Office" column in the Sunday Business section of the *New York Times* invited Dany Levy, founder and editorial director of DailyCandy.com, a website and e-mail newsletter focused on shopping and culture, to respond to this question: "If you were to teach a business school course, what would it be?" She replied, "I'd love to teach a course called 'The Idea,' which is basically, so you want to start a company, how's it going to work? Let's figure it out—just a very practical plan, but not a business plan, because I feel like business plans now feel weighty and outdated. . . . [It used to be that] the longer your business plan was, the more promising it was going to be. And now it's . . . the shorter your business plan is, the more succinct and to the point it is, the better. You want people to get why your business is going to work pretty quickly."[8] Getting to the point, or getting to the "why" of anything, is, as I stressed in chapter six, highly desirable in the practice of leadership. And to have the benefit of a course called "The Idea," is itself a great idea. But that course will go nowhere unless the participants can think.

In another "Corner Office" interview, Jacqueline Kosecoff, CEO of Prescription Solutions, a pharmacy benefit management company with over 10 million customers, was asked about her "approach to leadership." She replied, "I think a good leader has to do three things. It's almost like a three-act play. The first act is coming up with the concept for a product or service to offer. And then you have to make sure that the entire team believes in that concept and understands it. The second job is execution. . . . The third act is measurement: 'What are the metrics against which we are going to measure our success?'"[9] Note the importance of the concept, the idea. Concepts depend on disciplined and creative thinking.

As I suggested above, algebra might have prepared the way for improved thinking and the study of logic will surely help. How about calculus? Maybe it's too late for that, but it is never too late to explore new ideas. Ask yourself, better still, ask your friends in an informal setting, how they would respond if a venture capitalist expressed a willingness to put a hefty sum—say, $50 million—into a new idea if the idea was really good. I've done that in the business school classroom and am still waiting for the really good idea. I don't have the venture capitalist standing by either, so nothing has yet been lost, which is not to say that nothing productive can emerge from conversations along these lines. Keep thinking!

One of the many things a good leader has to be good at is generating options. I had a very intelligent student at Georgetown who joined a consulting company after graduation and was assigned a couple of years later to the task of recruiting other bright young men and women to join the firm. He dropped in for a visit one day while recruiting in Washington, DC. This was long before every collegiate ear was connected to a cell phone; in fact it was back in the day when banks of telephones lined airport concourse walls and the plexiglass phone booth was still standing on street corners. I asked him what kind of consulting problems he posed to potential recruits so that he could get a feel for their likely success in handling professional assignments. He used public pay phones as an example.

"The phone company is your client," he would tell them. "They want some advice on how to make their phones more user-friendly for left-handed people." The phones, of course, were rigged in favor of right-handed people—they could hold the receiver in their left, drop the coins in with their right, and have the right hand free to jot down notes while on the call. The bright young men and women would typically begin with an estimate of the ratio of right- to left-handed people in the general population—say, about four to one. They would often suggest rigging eight phones on a given bank for right-handed people and the remaining two in a bank of ten for left-handed users. Some would suggest a variety of intricate ambidextrous design adjustments for all phones. And when I asked my friend what he wanted to hear when he asked that question, he told me that he would like to have someone say, "Let's survey left-handed people and find out what they want."

That is always a good way to begin to attack a problem. Find out what those most likely to benefit from a solution would like to have happen. But that is just the beginning. The generation of options never ends. Creative minds will always come up with new ways of doing things. Those who do the creative thinking will influence others. If they are both creative and persuasive, they can lead.

## CORE VALUES

When I work with young people in an academic setting, I always take care to let them know that I regard and respect each one as the world's leading expert on his or her own opinion. Opinions are fine; they must however be articulated, explained, and, in some cases, defended. If the idea is clearly indefensible in the company of their peers, or in comparison with community standards and the wisdom of the ages, the "expert" might be inclined to reconsider. All this requires serious thought. In fact, thinking abut values—your own and the values of those whom you would lead—is step number one in the leadership process. Clear and serious thought is the firm foundation needed to make step one a sure-footed move.

You might pause here for a moment and jot down your three core values. In a few days, or perhaps within a week, upon further reflection, you may want to revise your list. That's fine; reflection has a way of making that happen. In any case, jot them down before reading further. And notice, by the way, that something is going on between your ears as you prepare your list. You are thinking.

Whenever this exercise takes place, certain values usually emerge. Honesty and integrity are always there. Persistence, sometimes called determination, has a way of surfacing, especially for those who look to persons from the world of sports as model leaders. Compassion, some think of it as empathy, often makes the list, as does loyalty—even in this era in American business where that value appears to be on the decline.

Here are some other values that are usually mentioned in the "go-round" within a group that is asked to identify core personal values: justice, fairness, veracity, excellence, commitment, service, passion, family, respect, courage, love, and the dignity of the human person (some will specify that as the value of human life). Some will say they value open-mindedness.

The issue of relativity surfaces whenever the question of core values is asked in terms of "What would you go to the wall for? On what values or principles would you stake your life? What is nonnegotiable?" And this is where an understanding of commitment finds its place in the sun.

Discussion of "values you would die for" and "values you would live for" can result in the identification of different values. If the values are the same, the thought process that produces the answers may be different. Whatever the process and the values it identifies, this exercise—individually or in groups—can be a powerful experience.

Thinking about these things is stimulated by insistence on a clear definition of what a given value means. Further thought is required to rank one's values in priority order and reduce the list to three.

Typically, I ask for discussion of core values in the opening session of a seminar on leadership and then expect to have each person's list of three at the beginning of the second week. Some thought is then to be given to the alignment of those core values with the vocational or occupational goals the person has in mind for the future, and then to the embodiment of any or all of those goals in the life of a model leader. With the goals specified and the model leader identified, participants in my seminar then have the rest of the semester to work both the values and the model behavior into a term paper on some aspect of effective leadership.

The idea, of course, is to become better able to exercise effective leadership in your own time and your own way. Although a lot about leadership can be learned from others, the thoughtful leader is an original, not an imitation. And without thought on the part of the leader, the leadership process will not begin.

It is very much in your own employment self-interest at any time in your career, but particularly in the early stages, to keep yourself in constant companionship with good ideas. In the introduction to the revised edition (2003) of his 1989 book, *On Becoming a Leader*, Warren Bennis wrote, "The New Economy was fueled by intellectual capital, as the economy of the twenty-first century will be. The days when a company's most important assets are buildings and equipment are gone forever. Ideas are now the acknowledged engine and currency of the global economy. For leaders, and would-be leaders, the take-home lesson of the New Economy is that power follows ideas, not position."[10]

You won't become a leader if you don't have solid, creative ideas. You won't remain a leader if you cannot communicate those ideas to potential followers. And you won't have an organization to lead unless you and those who comprise the organization have something lively going on between the ears—all the time. That goes by the name of awareness.

At the end of his book, *Leading Minds*, which I referenced earlier, Howard Gardner makes a plea for something he considers essential for "a leadership that is responsible as well as effective." He calls it "*consciousness about the issues and paradoxes of leadership.*"[11] He thinks that those who would lead should be "intimately aware of a number of issues and paradoxes." I list them here; you can regard them as food for further thought as you continue to ponder the importance of thinking as a component of the leadership toolkit.

- The tension between the need for technical expertise— which requires sophisticated thinking—and the necessity for broad-based communication skills, so that you can reach the "unschooled mind"

- The need for stories that can speak to many individuals and help them achieve a more satisfying individual and group identity

- The potential of such stories either to broaden or to fragment a sense of community

- The realization that more comprehensive knowledge may well be distributed across members of a group, but that it is much easier to deal with a single authorized leader

- The knowledge that all leaders are limited in what they can accomplish, that all leaders experience failure as well as triumph, and that nearly all leaders eventually encounter obstacles that they cannot overcome

- The alternative possibilities of an audience that is manipulated by a leader, an audience that influences the leader, and an audience that cooperatively molds a message in conjunction with the leader

- The need to aid leaders or share their burdens, rather than try to exploit or undermine their authority

- The choice between leadership that is direct (a leader speaking to her audiences) or indirect (a leader achieving effects either through symbolic products or through the education of political leaders), and the possibility of combining both direct and indirect strands in a synergistically effective manner

- The tension between a rational approach and one that is founded on spiritual dimensions, and the desirability of synthesizing these complementary stories

Now let's turn to remembrance.

**NOTES:**

1. "Taking the Ted out of Turner Broadcasting," *Business Week* (May 4, 2009): 58.

2. Richard M. Weaver, *Ideas Have Consequences* (Chicago, IL: University of Chicago Press, 1948).

3. Howard Gardner, *Leading Minds: An Anatomy of Leadership* (New York: Basic Books, 1995), 259.

4. Rajat Gupta and Jim Wendler, "Leading Change: An Interview with the CEO of P&G," *McKinsey Quarterly* (July 2005); online version can be accessed at http://www.mckinseyquarterly.com/Organizatin/Change_Management/Leading_change.

5. Norman L. Macht, *Connie Mack and the Early Years of Baseball* (Lincoln: University of Nebraska Press, 2007), 41–42.

6. Ibid., 283.

7. Ibid.

8. Adam Bryant, "In Praise of All That Grunt Work," *New York Times* (May 31, 2009): BU2.

9. Adam Bryant, "The Divine, Too, Is in the Details," *New York Times* (June 21, 2009): BU2.

10. Warren Bennis, *On Becoming a Leader* (New York: Basic Books, revised edition, 2003), xii.

11. Howard Gardner, *Leading Minds*, 305 (emphasis in the original).

# CHAPTER NINE

## LEADERS REMEMBER

I was president of the University of Scranton when Gerald Ford was president of the United States. His good friend from law school days at Yale was the former Pennsylvania Governor William W. Scranton, a friend of mine and of the university that bore his famous family name.

Bill Scranton stopped by my office one day in January 1976 and asked, "Would you like to have Gerry Ford as your commencement speaker next June?" That sounded like a great idea, so I said yes and Governor Scranton made the contact. President Ford agreed to join us for graduation. It occurred to me that presidential schedules are subject to unexpected changes and cancellations, so it might be wise to make arrangements for a substitute speaker, if the need arose. So I called the recently elected junior senator from Delaware, Joseph R. Biden Jr., who spent the first decade of his life in Scranton, and told him that we would like to give him an honorary degree at commencement and that the president was scheduled to speak. "If for any reason, he has to cancel, would you be willing to stand in and speak to the graduating class?" I asked Senator Biden. "That would be a pleasure," he said.

The White House called Senator Biden and invited him to fly up with the President on the day of commencement. All was set. Then, a few months later, just a day or two after the Indiana Primary (which President Ford lost), I received a call from his appointments secretary who said, "It's just not in the cards now. We can't come. We have to be in Oregon that weekend for the Oregon primary. The president sends regrets."

So I called Senator Biden to tell him he was on. He made it to Scranton without the benefit of Air Force One, gave a great commencement address, and enjoyed the opportunity to catch up again with some boyhood friends.

Two years later, former President Ford (he lost the presidency to Jimmy Carter) came to Scranton to address a large Chamber of Commerce Dinner. At a reception beforehand, he walked up to me, shook hands, smiled and said, "I owe you one."

Richard J. Daley was mayor of Chicago from 1955 until his death in 1976. While in office, he asked Jesuit Father Robert Mulligan, an administrator at Loyola University of Chicago, for assistance in gaining admission and scholarship assistance for the son of a Chicago police officer who had been killed in the line of duty. The request was granted. Four years later, Mayor Daley saw Father Mulligan at a funeral and went out of his way to say hello and thank him for the favor.

Leaders remember—big things or small. A good memory is a useful leadership tool.

Senator John F. Kennedy once remarked, "The modern politician—although not all of them I should make clear—knows well that what he says but never writes can almost always be denied; but that what he writes and never remembers may someday come back to haunt him."[1] A good memory is useful for self-defense as well as positive advancement in politics and many other walks of life.

A college president I knew always carried a note-pad in his pocket. His was a jot-it-down style of leadership in the sense that he would never forget a suggestion that was offered, a reference given, a number to be called, a book to be bought, a contact to be made. Those items were noted whenever they entered his ear or crossed his mind; the notepad produced an unending stream of entries for his "to do" list every day. He always remembered.

Memory, of course, can play tricks. It is important to realize, before the fact, that emotions can distort memory. You may not actually have heard what was spoken, or read what was on the page, when your emotion-rattled eyes and ears received a message. Emotional turmoil can blur vision and alter the acoustics. If the message is distorted, the memory will be also. But let's for the moment assume an emotional calm; let's simply note the importance of remembering (memorizing in some cases, but remembering in general) in order to lead.

## MEMORY AND PRESENCE

There is a little-noticed but highly important connection between memory and physical presence. What I want to say here may appear to be indirect and a bit involuted, but bear with me as I try to establish the link. Presence is, of course, central to leadership.

There is a biblical understanding of *remembering* that means simply to make present again, to relive an event. This is rooted in the Hebrew Bible where to forget is to obliterate and to remember is to keep a relationship very much alive. (The Lord "forgets" our sins and "remembers" his promises, his covenant, with us.) There is probably no connection, but this prompts me to wonder whether this biblical sense might be the foundation of our modern usage of "remembrance" as gift. Interesting isn't it, that we call a gift a present? You present it, of course, to the other, but in doing so you make yourself present in a special way. We sometimes speak of giving a birthday "remembrance" to another person. Maybe—maybe not. But the point to ponder is the bringing-to-life-again dimension of the scriptural sense of remembering, and the relevance of this to leadership.

Leaders can "remember" in compelling and creative ways that have nothing to do with recall of what may have been noted mentally, nor with memorization of poems and speeches, nor with the "he never forgets a name" quality we so admire in certain leaders. In the United States, we have an annual Memorial Day celebration when the deeds of those who fought and died in our wars are made present again in a celebratory way in parades and pageants, in music and visual art. By invoking words and images from the past in order to frame present challenges, leaders can draw from the pool of memory in order to inspire and prepare the people for future progress.

The point I want to make here by associating remembering with presence in the context of leadership is developed nicely in an unusual book, *Leadership Presence*.[2] This book looks to the stage—to dramatic on-stage experience—to discover characteristics that can enhance the quality of leadership. You've often heard references to an actor's stage presence. Well, reflection on the link of remembering to presence opens the door to further consideration of how what happens on the stage can be used to improve the quality of leadership.

It is more than simply speaking well—strong projection, declamation. It has to do with a leader's bearing, how one establishes oneself in the midst of others. The actor must be (1) present to him- or herself ("get into the part"), (2) present to those on stage, and thus connected with self and fellow actors, and (3) connected to the audience.[3] In this context, the actor enjoys what is clearly an influential presence, an interactive influence on self, the other actors, and the audience. And, of course, influence has everything to do with leadership.

Here is how that point is made in *Leadership Presence*: "Being present is fundamental to the work of an actor. The worst insult you can give an actor is that he 'phoned in' his performance, that he wasn't present, that he simply reeled off his lines and hit his marks. Being fully present is the first requirement of acting—be there, in the moment, alive, energized. From that quality springs all else in the theater. So it should come as no surprise that actors spend a large amount of time training to be completely focused and concentrated in the moment."[4]

I've served on thirty or forty governing and advisory boards—for schools, colleges, hospitals, businesses, associations, foundations, civic and church-related organizations—and I've observed many CEOs in action in their respective chairs and perches of leadership. Some have been quite effective; others not. It is only recently, however, that I began to notice that the most effective tended to be truly present to their boards and to the constituencies they were serving. The least effective tended to "phone in" their reports even though they were physically present in the room. When their formal presentation (note again the link to "presence") came to an end, the "any questions?" conclusion registered with the hearers more as a threat than an invitation to dialogue. A full meeting day (or overnight) could pass without a greeting, handshake, or coffee-break personal comment from the leader to a board member. If "being present is fundamental to the work of an actor," it is all the more fundamental to the work of a leader.

The good ones can and will "work the room" without slighting anyone and never—repeat, *never*—exercising that insulting and infuriating over-your-shoulder search to see if someone "more important" is elsewhere in the room waiting to be met. As the authors of *Leadership Presence* put it, "Being present means more than just physical presence, important as that is. It means being present *in the moment*—focused totally and completely on what is happening right here and right now. It means, when you're with people, giving them your full attention, so that they will feel recognized and motivated. When you're not present to the people you lead, it weakens their willingness to commit."[5]

If your mind is somewhere else, if you are text-messaging while others are speaking, if you answer my question before I finish asking it, you are A.W.O.L., not present, not leading. To put it simply, if you hope to lead, you cannot be both aloof and effective.

Not infrequently, the reason why you might hold yourself aloof from some is the simple reason that you do not like them. You don't have to like everyone you are there to lead. Like them or not, you have to acknowledge their presence, by being present to them. You might not only dislike some others, you might fear some of them and thus want to hold your distance. Another possibility is that you do not respect them; you may judge them to be intellectually inferior to you. Whatever the reason, it is an obstacle to be overcome in order that you might lead. Absent any reason, this may be an indication of narcissism; your self-enclosure leaves you not unwilling but simply unaware of your need to acknowledge the worth of others and your need to be present to them.

Belle Halpern and Kathy Lubar, the authors of *Leadership Presence*, wrote their book after years of performance experience in the theater as well as extensive experience in teaching presence to leaders in a variety of organizational settings. Their PRES model of Leadership Presence has four parts: (1) being present, (2) reaching out, (3) expressiveness, and (4) self-knowing.[6] These touch on both a state of mind (or what I've been calling a leadering attitude) and behavior patterns associated with good leadership.

What Halpern and Lubar call "Leadership Presence"—the incorporation of dramatic techniques into the leadership toolkit—relates to everything you read earlier in chapter five, "Leaders Speak." In fact, you might recognize now that something essential was missing in the last PowerPoint presentation you observed where the speaker clicked with the slides but not with the audience. He or she kept turning to the screen (and away from you), read what you were perfectly capable of reading for yourself, and clicked to the next slide before you had time to jot down some points that may have been of interest to you. Moreover, most PowerPoint presenters pace back and forth, to and fro, without maintaining eye contact with the audience, and they often send messages in body language that you interpret—even though they may not intend it—to mean that they can hardly wait for the last slide to say "The End," thus permitting them to leave a stage that they never realized they were on!

As I've been writing this chapter, I've recalled the wisdom of the reply, given by executive-search consultant Gerry Roche, to a question from a Wharton School MBA student when he gave a lecture there a decade or so ago: "What do you recommend that I study if I want to become a CEO?" Roche, whom *Business Week* once described as "the high priest of headhunting," replied, "Study human nature."[7] The study of human nature might be a good title for a business school course on leadership! If you get that right, you'll remember most of what you really need to know to be a successful leader.

"What's the most important leadership lesson you've learned?" asked Adam Bryant in his interview with Clarence Otis Jr., CEO of Darden Restaurants, the holding company that owns the chains Red Lobster, Olive Garden, and Capital Grille. Otis replied, "It's one that I learned early on, and it kept getting reinforced and cemented over time with a number of different leaders. It's the notion that leaders really think about others first. They think about the people who are on the team, trying to help them get the job done. They think about the people who they're trying to do a job for. Your thoughts are always there first, and you think about what's the appropriate response for whatever that audience is, and you think last about 'what does this mean for me?'"[8]

And to the follow-up question, "Anything in your background that, looking back, prepared you for the act of building a team?" the Darden CEO replied, "The thing that prepared me the most was theater, which I did a lot of growing up—in high school, during college, law school and even for a couple of years after law school. I would say that probably is the starkest lesson in how reliant you are on others, because you're there in front of an audience. It's all live, and everybody's got to know their lines and know their cues and know their movement, and so you're totally dependent on other people doing that."

Thinking of yourself and your team as being "onstage," even when there is no audience anywhere in sight, is a good way to stay energized and to generate a sense of vitality in an organization. This is not make-believe. It is all about presence. And presence, in the context of leadership, is all about remembering.

Leadership, as I've indicated earlier in this book, is the art of inducing others to follow. It is a personal relationship, not a position. Its success depends on the character of the leadering person in that relationship. It begins with an artist—not a president, not a CEO, not a prelate. It begins with a person skilled in the art of leading. And if that person is not effectively present to those who would be led, leadership will simply not happen.

## THE MEMORY IS IN THE MUSCLES

Once you learn how to ride a bicycle, your can always ride a bike. That's because your muscles remember. The same can be said for your basic golf swing, or your ground strokes in tennis. That's why it is important to get them right from the very beginning; it is difficult to "undo" the incorrect motions that have worked their way into your muscle memory.

All of this is relevant to leadership. Consider what Daniel Goleman and his colleagues call our "emotional memory banks."[9] Their book, *Primal Leadership* builds on Goleman's earlier work on emotional intelligence and deals with the importance of "gut" reactions in the practice of business leadership. They have great respect for the role of intuition in leadership and acknowledge that intuition is the product of wisdom gathered over the years in the experience of living. "Why should an intuitive sense have any place in business today, amid the plethora of hard data available to leaders? Because attuning to our feelings, according to neurological research, helps us find the meaning in data, and so leads to better decisions. Our emotional memory banks thus enable us to judge information efficiently. Emotions, science now tells us, are part of rationality, not opposed to it."[10]

Here's what the neurological research tells us:

> With the eagerness of a constant learner, the brain soaks up life's lessons to better prepare us for the next time we face a similar challenge, uncertainty, or decision point.
>
> Because this kind of learning goes on largely in a deep zone of the brain outside the reach of words (in the basal ganglia, a primitive part of the brain atop the spinal cord), leaders need to learn to trust their intuitive sense to access their life wisdom. The circuitry involved in puzzling decisions, in fact, includes not just the basal ganglia, but also the amygdale, where the brain stores the emotions associated with memories. When it comes to drawing on a lifetime of silent learning as we face decision points again and again, it's not the verbal part of the brain that delivers the best course of action—it's the part that wields our feelings.
>
> Every day that a leader spends in a given business or career, his brain automatically extracts the decision rules that underlie one turn of events or another, or the operating cause-and-effect sequences. As the brain continually learns in this tacit mode, a leader accumulates the wisdom from a life's on-the-job experi-

ence. This wisdom increases throughout a leader's career, even as the abilities to pick up new technical skills may wane.[11]

Several phrases here deserve attention—"emotional memory banks," "the brain soaks up life's lessons," "a lifetime of silent learning," "on-the-job experience." If these ideas and images get the attention they deserve now in the minds of those who would be leaders, they will find expression in future decisions that come "from the gut" and are powered by memory muscle that lies below the level of consciousness. This is an important but underappreciated dimension of what I mean when I say that effective leaders are skilled at remembering.

Whenever I see reference made to the importance of intuition in the practice of leadership, I engage in some mental meandering back to the origins of a word that the young and their bill-paying elders know all too well, namely, tuition. How can the young be so painfully aware of the tollgate to educational progress that goes by the name of tuition, and oblivious to the role of intuition in effective leadership?

*Tuition*, I've always assumed, has something to do with *tutor* and *tutelage*, words that relate to protection and direction, perhaps even to strength. I'm insufficiently expert to provide a "tutorial" on this point, but it seems to me that *intuit*, *intuitive*, and *intuition* all have a lot to do with getting a closer look, gaining some depth of understanding, grasping a lesson that could easily be missed by the inexperienced and untrained mind. Hence, the need for tutors and the tuition that gives seekers access to their services. The tutor is a special presence. The experience shared and wisdom gained bring the remembered past into present consciousness. And the remembering leader is able to see what others often miss because the remembering leader is able to intuit what others cannot see.

Now that you have seen that there is a partnership between presence and remembering in the practice of leadership, just remember to be fully present at all times to those whom you would lead.

But don't let this deeper meaning of remembering distract you from the front-line, popular meaning of the word—mental retention, not forgetting. If you are forgetful, you can't be relied upon to lead.

When Arizona governor Janet Napolitano, was nominated by President Barack Obama to head the Department of Homeland Security, *the New York Times* reported from Phoenix that "the cautious, deliberative nature of a governor whose ability to vacuum up and retain information as disparate as the minutiae of fiscal audits and the lyrics from 'West Side

Story' is legend here."[12] And the story went on to say, "She is a 51-year-old self-described nerd who, despite a less-than-electrifying public persona, privately quotes lines from Monty Python movies, extols the virtues of Arizona's professional sports teams and startles aides with a near photographic memory. She has not met a briefing book she could not absorb and makes time to read two books, one fiction and one nonfiction, simultaneously." So, as I've said, leaders read. Remember this, too: leaders remember.

Recall the leadering attitudes discussed in an earlier chapter. Add the intuitive, compassionate dimension of leadership mentioned here. Be sure to notice that leaders feel. They have to feel in order to lead. They have to be in touch with their feelings before they can decide, and that's the theme—decision making—that we will explore in the next chapter.

## NOTES:

1. Speech at the Women's National Press Club Luncheon, Washington, DC, February 23, 1956.
2. Belle Linda Halpern and Kathy Lubar, *Leadership Presence: Dramatic Techniques to Reach Out, Motivate, and Inspire* (New York: Gotham Books, 2003).
3. I learned these three points in a conversation I once had with Helen Hayes, often referred to as the "First Lady of the American Theater." We were having dinner at The Catholic University of America with her friend, the legendary Dominican Father Gilbert Hartke, who founded the drama department at CUA many years earlier and had invited his friend Helen Hayes to perform there in the title role of *Good Morning, Miss Dove* to launch a fund-raising campaign to get the money needed to construct a new theater on campus. When the new Hartke Theater opened, Miss Hayes returned to play the role of Mary Tyrone in Eugene O'Neill's *Long Day's Journey into Night*. She told me many years later that her "greatest moment in theater" occurred one night during that run on the Hartke stage. "You have to get completely into your role," she said, and "the others in the cast have to get into theirs. Then you and they have to come together as one, and all of you, thus connected, have to connect with the audience." She smiled as she said, "It never happens, but it did happen once for me and it was on the stage of the Hartke Theater."
4. Ibid., 19.
5. Ibid., 18, emphasis in the original.
6. Ibid., 9.
7. Personal conversation with the author.
8. "Ensemble Acting, in Business," the "Corner Office" feature in *New York Times* (Sunday, June 7, 2009): BU2.

9. Daniel Goleman, Richard Boyatzis, and Annie McKee, *Primal Leadership: Learning to Lead with Emotional Intelligence* (Boston: Harvard Business School Press, paperback, 2004), 42.

10. Ibid.

11. Ibid., 44.

12. "For Homeland Security Nominee, Good Leadership Is in the Details," *New York Times* (January 15, 2009); online at www.nytimes.com/2009/01/15/us/politics/15napolitano.html.

# CHAPTER TEN

# LEADERS DECIDE

It is possible, perhaps even probable, that my life was saved by virtue of a decision made by President Harry S Truman in the summer of 1945.

I was then in the army in basic infantry training at Camp Wheeler in Georgia. President Truman made the decision to drop the atomic bomb on the cities of Hiroshima and Nagasaki in Japan. That decision ended the war for all practical purposes; the Japanese immediately surrendered.

I was being trained in Georgia that summer for eventual jungle warfare in the South Pacific with a view to the invasion of Japan. Military intelligence estimated that the war would continue through 1946 and end with victory on the Japanese mainland and cost heavy American casualties, perhaps a quarter of a million men, along the way. I could have been one of those casualties. The Japanese surrender altered the equation of my military career. Instead of going to the South Pacific, I spent 1946 in Germany with a regiment of the 82nd Airborne Division assigned as strategic reserve and honor guard for USFET (U.S. Forces in the European Theater) headquarters in Frankfurt, Germany. No one ever shot at me; I fired weapons only on the practice range. But it occurred to me many years later that I could have been killed had Truman not made that fateful decision.

Was it the right decision militarily? Probably it was. Was it right morally? I don't think so. Truman did not make the decision lightly, I'm sure. We had at that time only two atomic bombs. I would have favored a "demonstration drop" out in the ocean in the presence of the Japanese authorities to show them how unimaginably lethal this weapon was. Would they have surrendered? Who knows? And what if it had been a dud? But the decision was made, knowing that innocent human beings would be killed and radioactive fallout would poison the atmosphere and the survivors. Let's take a moment to consider the implications.

In 1945, *Time* magazine ran a cover story about this world-shaking event, an event that wounded us so profoundly that it has remained to trouble us, mind and soul, ever since. The incident, which was reported in the August 20, 1945 issue of the magazine, marked both an end and a beginning—the end of World War II and the beginning of the Atomic Age.

This report was published, as were all *Time* stories in those days, without attribution of authorship. I learned years later that a young (and then relatively unknown) *Time* staffer by the name of James Agee wrote the piece under a very tight deadline. The overarching headline was "Victory." The first subhead was "The Peace." The second subhead was "The Bomb."

*Time* was covering a big story that week, perhaps the biggest of the century. Agee saw the "controlled splitting of the atom," which produced the bomb used to attack Hiroshima and Nagasaki and thus bring to an end the greatest conflict in human history, as an event so enormous that in comparison "the war itself shrank to minor significance." To Agee's eye, "Humanity, already profoundly perplexed and disunified, was brought inescapably into a new age in which all thoughts and things were split—and far from controlled."

*Time* readers, still dizzy with the thrill of victory, could hardly have seen, as Agee did, the potential for both good and evil that the atomic bomb represented. That potential bordered "on the infinite—with this further, terrible split in the fact: that upon a people already so nearly drowned in materialism even in peacetime, the good uses of this power might easily bring disaster as prodigious as the evil. . . . When the bomb split open the universe . . . it also revealed the oldest, simplest, commonest, most neglected and most important of facts: that each man is eternally and above all else responsible for his own soul, and in the terrible words of the Psalmist, that no man may deliver his brother, nor make agreement unto God for him."

Then Agee made a shattering observation that rings every bit as true today as it did that memorable August. Here are the words he wrote—words that were available to any reader of the nation's most popular newsmagazine in 1945, and that have gone largely unheeded for more than half a century: "Man's fate has forever been shaped between the hands of reason and spirit, now in collaboration, again in conflict. Now reason and spirit meet on final ground. If either or anything is to survive, they must find a way to create an indissoluble partnership."

These powerful words were perceptive and prophetic. They appeared just before the baby boomers were born. They explain, I think, the cause of the "split" that has been troubling us for well over a half a century. We have not yet forged the "indissoluble partnership" between reason and spirit (reason that produced the bomb and spirit that must control the use of nuclear power); we are even more adrift now than we were then on a sea of materialism. We may, however, be beginning to notice what Agee saw when the bomb split open the universe, namely, that each of us is responsible for his or her own soul. This, of course, means responsible decision making.

Harry Truman made the fateful decision to use atomic power against human beings. I doubt that he had more than a slight hint of its implications. Most leaders do not have to make decisions of this importance, but all leaders have to decide.

## AN INFORMED DECISION-MAKING PROCESS

I remember asking a Jesuit friend, Father Raymond Baumhart, who was then at the midpoint of a long and successful presidency of Loyola University in Chicago, what a president did. (I was being asked to consider becoming a university president at that time.) He said, "You make decisions; that's what you do every day." "Where do you find satisfaction in your work?" I asked. "In making decisions."

Noel Tichy and Warren Bennis say that judgment is "the essence of effective leadership."[1] They open their book, *Judgment*, with that assertion and go on to say that judgment is "a contextually informed decision-making process encompassing three domains: people, strategy, and crisis. Within each domain, leadership judgments follow a three-phase process: preparation, the call, and execution. Good leadership judgment is supported by contextual knowledge of one's self, social network, organization, and stakeholders."

For any reader who may have missed their point, Tichy and Bennis insist early on that "judgment is the core, the nucleus, of leadership."[2]

Back in chapter eight, the importance of thinking was stressed—not intelligence alone, but intelligence at work. Every decision involves the exercise of judgment and, as Tichy and Bennis put it, "Good judgment depends on how you think as well as what you know." An incisive thinker is likely to make good judgments.

*Incision* is a word familiar to surgeons. *Recision* crops up in conversations in the military and insurance underwriting. Just as an incision is a cut the surgeon makes to begin an operation, a recision is a cutoff, the cancellation of a policy or order. There is knife-like sharpness in a good decision. Indecision, on the other hand, connotes delay, confusion, and the misapplication of blunt instruments.

Leaders must be decisive. The more incisive their thinking, the better their decisions will be. There is no place at all for indecision in the leadership toolkit, which is not to say that there is no place for thoughtful ethical reflection. Chapter twelve will consider the ethical leader. Let me simply note here that decisiveness is not impulsiveness. An absence of caution mixed with an absence of empathy can turn decisiveness into impulsiveness and, in the process, run a high risk of insulting—even hurting—others in the organization.

Former U.S. Secretary of State Henry Kissinger once observed, "High office teaches decision making, not substance. It consumes intellectual capital; it does not create it. Most high officials leave office with the perceptions and insights with which they entered; they learn how to make decisions but not what decisions to make."[3] Kissinger also believed that "the highest task of a public servant is to take his or her society from where it is to where it has never been [and this requires] the courage to face complexity [and] the character to act when the outcome is still ambiguous."[4]

The courage to act is a prerequisite for leadership; every action presupposes a decision. The direction of the action depends on the value orientation of the one who acts. And it is the values that a leader has internalized that propel that leader's principled activity.

Early in his administration, President Barack Obama had to come to terms with a question that was debated during the 2008 presidential campaign, namely, the alleged torture of prisoners in the detention center at Guantanamo Bay.

In mid-April, 2009, Obama met with top advisers who were divided on whether or not to release four top-secret memos that gave detailed accounts of interrogation methods used by the Central Intelligence Agency. They described harsh tactics that had been approved by lawyers in the Bush administration. The present and former CIA directors along with Obama's top counterterrorism adviser opposed the release. The Attorney General, Director of National Intelligence, and White House counsel favored release, as did the Secretary of Defense and the Chairman of the Joint Chiefs of Staff. Here is how the *Washington Post* described the April 15, 2009 meeting that produced the President's decision: "Seated in Chief of Staff Rahm

Emmanuel's West Wing office with about a dozen of his political, legal and security appointees, Obama requested a mini-debate in which one official was chosen to argue for releasing the memos and another was assigned to argue against doing so. When it ended, Obama dictated on the spot a draft of his announcement that the documents would be released, while most of the officials watched, according to an official who was present. The disclosure happened the next day."[5]

The "mini-debate" idea is a good one. This method relates to what I call group decision making in the Jesuit tradition. It has sixteenth-century origins in the person and "way of proceeding" of St. Ignatius Loyola, founder in 1540 of the Society of Jesus, the Jesuit order. It may seem like a long leap from the sixteenth century to the twenty-first, and back again, from a select group of White House advisers to a small band of companions planning how to establish what eventually became the Jesuit order, but bear with me as I try to explain. And note the relevance of this centuries-old practice to making sound decisions today and for decades to come.

## AN IGNATIAN APPROACH TO DECISION MAKING

I once spoke to an international gathering of Jesuit business school deans and faculty on the topic, "Education for Business in the Jesuit Tradition." This was a group of committed Jesuits and lay colleagues from all over the world; they met for several days at Sanata Dharma University, a Jesuit institution in the university city of Yogyakarta, Indonesia. Their focus was on discovering the defining characteristics of Jesuit business schools.

Unlikely as the prospect seemed when I first considered what I might say to this group, my presentation dealt with decision making in the Jesuit tradition. I thought there was much in the tradition that could be translated into decision-making processes not just in the schools themselves, but in the secular business organizations where their graduates would eventually work. It proved to be a stimulating topic for discussion. The paper I gave on that occasion was translated into many languages for local consumption back on the campuses from which these business educators came.[6]

## COLLABORATIVE LEADERSHIP

I began by pointing out that two questions found in the preface of a book published that year (1995) by the American Management Association had special relevance for the conversation we were opening up. These were good questions for anyone to consider who is interested in fitting his or her spirituality (in our case, Ignatian spirituality) into workplace decision making. The book, *Transforming the Way We Work: The Power of the Collaborative Workplace* by Edward M. Marshall,[7] was certainly not a spiritual tract, but here are the useful questions Marshall raises in his preface: "What would the world of work be like if we all truly respected one another? How effective would our workplaces be if we all knew how to collaborate?"[8]

Later in the book,[9] the essence of Marshall's message is summarized in these words:

> The new realities in business require a new type of leadership. Command-and-control no longer applies. Collaborative leadership, however, requires a significant shift in our relationships in the workplace. Since leadership is no longer a position but a function, and since everyone can be a leader, the responsibility for leading the organization shifts to the entire workforce. The traditional roles and responsibilities of leadership also change— from commanding to coaching, from telling to engaging, and from delegating to others to working with others. Our behaviors must change as we learn how to function in an environment of consensus formation, conflict resolution, and full responsibility.

A bell went off in my mind when I first read those words. I wanted to reflect on them and ponder their implications not only for practical workplace living, but also for how Jesuit schools prepare men and women for careers in business.

I've been a member of the Jesuit order since 1950. I learned very early on that there is a theme in Jesuit spirituality that bears directly on the way one can search out God's will. It goes by the name of discernment— discernment of spirits. It has profound relevance for decision making in business. There is nothing secret or spooky about it; it is a centuries-old "way of proceeding," a tested method for sorting things out so that you can make your way through the human predicament with some degree of confidence that you are following God's will in a particular set of circumstances. Discernment is a characteristically Jesuit way of "testing the spirits," as in the advice found in 1 John 4:1: "Beloved, do not trust every spirit but test the spirits to see whether they belong to God, because many false prophets have gone out into the world." Or, to put "discernment of spirits" in the language of 1 John 4:6, "This is how we know the spirit of truth and the spirit of deceit."

Since this is part of me—part of my own personal spirituality—I was able to lay it out there in Indonesia and want to do that again here in these pages. As readers consider the applicability of all this to their own lives and to choices in the workplace, they will find themselves discovering a link between faith and work.

In his own words at the beginning of his *Autobiography* (written as a third-person narrative), Ignatius of Loyola describes himself as a young adult: "Up to the age of twenty-six he was a man given over to the vanities of the world, and took special delight in the exercise of arms, with a great and vain desire for winning fame." An early biographer (Polanco, d. 1574)[10] tells us that "Iñigo's education was more in keeping with the spirit of the world than of God; for from his early years, without entering into other training in letters beyond that of reading and writing, he began to follow the court as a page; then he served as a gentleman of the Duke of Najera and as a soldier till the age of twenty-six when he made a change of life." This same biographer lists a few disciplinary lapses that would have had "Iñigo" tossed out of any modern Jesuit college or university if he were enrolled in one today: "Up to the time [of his conversion], although very much attached to the faith, he did not live in keeping with his belief or guard himself from sins; he was particularly careless about gambling, affairs with women, brawls, and the use of arms; this, however, was through force of habit. But all this made it possible also to perceive many natural virtues in him."

A modern biographer notes this: "As to what concerns the religious life of the Loyolas, we may say that it was, more or less, that of the people of Spain at that time. A profound and sincere faith and a substantial fidelity to religious practices was accompanied by moral lapses, which they themselves found no difficulty in admitting."[11]

Ignatius was seriously wounded by the French at Pamplona in May of 1521. A cannon ball shattered his right leg and wounded his left. Immediate medical attention was ineffective; he was sent home to the castle of his ancestors. The bones would not heal properly, so he chose (for reasons of vanity) to undergo repeat surgery.

During a long recuperation period, he had his "first reasoning," his first reflective experience "of the things of God." It happened this way. The only books available in the house of Loyola to help him pass the time were a four-volume *Life of Christ* and another book containing selections from the lives of the saints. He read these, reflected at intervals as he worked his way through them, and noticed that his reflections were accompanied by feelings of warmth and attraction toward the person of Christ and the generous deeds of the saints. An alternative pastime was daydreaming, turning over in his imagination, as he recounts it in the *Autobiography*, "what he would do in the service of a certain lady, the means he would take so he could go to the country where she lived, the verses, the words he would say to her, the deeds of arms he would do in her service."[12]

This reflective imagining gave him an immediate feeling of pleasure that invariably dissolved into a feeling of dryness and discontent. He then found himself doing a sort of "archaeology" on his contrasting moods, desires, and feelings. When he cut under them, he recognized that what was happening within him, in his interior life (as the spiritual writers would put it), was a struggle between two competing forces or spirits—one drawing him toward good, the other toward evil. His *Autobiography* mentions that "this was the first reflection he made on the things of God." Later on, when he was putting together his book of *Spiritual Exercises* (a retreat manual), it was "from this experience within him that he began to draw light on what pertained to the diversity of spirits."[13] Notice the focus on what was being experienced "within"—an emphasis on human feelings.

As I mentioned at the end of chapter three, I once helped a young woman at an important decision point in her life by encouraging her to focus on her feelings and deepest desires. I gave her an Ignatian idea from a non-Ignatian source, an ancient Hindu text: "You are what your deep driving desire is/ As your desire is, so is your will/ As your will is, so is your deed/ As your deed is, so is your destiny."[14] Ignatius would remind a person that love is shown in deeds, not words, and that one's deeply felt desires are the place to begin looking for the direction in which God might be calling a person to do great deeds. (You will find much more about the principles of Ignatian leadership in the appendix to this book.)

## GROUP DECISION MAKING

With all that as background (including the pre-decision mini-debate among White House advisers), let me begin to outline the method of group decision making, of choosing a course of action, that grew out of these Ignatian insights. It is traceable to the earliest deliberations of Ignatius and his first followers concerning the establishment of what is now known as the Jesuit order, and it is avowedly religious (although it clearly has secular significance). Ignatius grew in his faith experience of God, as I mentioned, by taking an "archaeological" approach to his moods and feelings. He would also have his facts lined up before attempting a decision. Ignatian discernment includes judgment of fact and assessment of feeling. You have to have the data before you decide.

Here's how it works. If a choice is to be made or an action taken, the relevant facts should be laid out first. This means having the necessary data and information in hand. On the basis of the available information, appropriate judgments of fact are made. Does this in fact add up? Does it all compute? Do we have adequate and correct information?

After judgments of fact comes the question: What now shall we do? Options—each representing a plausible choice, each representing a relative good—are raised. Then the "goods" are weighed and measured against the feelings stirred in the decision maker in the face of any particular option.

Given a certain state of soul—tranquility, for example, or anxiety, or dejection—Ignatius would have anyone interested in this method examine the origin of that feeling. Is the Spirit of God trying to alert me to something? Or perhaps the origin of the mood is me; the feeling is no deeper than my own selfish preference for the inertia of the status quo, and the anxiety is, in fact, resistance to change. Or, perhaps an altogether different force can be operative—a diabolical influence referred to by Ignatius as the "evil spirit" and the "deadly enemy of our human nature." Ignatius had a tendency to see life as a struggle between the forces of good and the forces of evil. He saw God in all good things, but he was a realist and also took careful account of the reality of evil in the world. Ignatius had a healthy respect for what he saw as an adversarial relationship between divine and diabolical activity. We tend to ignore this in our contemporary, secular, business-decision processes, but we do so at our peril.

Christians are advised by the evangelist John: "Beloved, do not trust every spirit but test the spirits to see whether they belong to God, because many false prophets have gone out into the world" (1 John 4:1). Believers are also aware that the "Spirit of Yahweh" is active throughout biblical history. For instance, the Holy Spirit inspires ("in-spirits") the Judges (Judges 3:10; 6:34; 11:29) and Saul (1 Samuel 11:6); the examples could be multiplied.

Acknowledging, then, the presence of divine activity in the world and a divine will for men and women, and acknowledging as well the possibility of divine communication to human persons (inspiration or "in-spir-iting"), believers, following the promptings not only of divine revelation but of logic and self-interest as well, consider it wise to count God in on their decision-making processes here and now. This calls for more than just a quick invocation or prayer of petition; the decision-making process has to be laced with a quest for God's will.

Ignatius and his first followers did this relative to the structure, purpose, and organization of their "company," the formal grouping of a committed band of brothers into what gained papal approval as the Company or Society of Jesus. What shape was this new enterprise to take? They processed the question in a structured, prayerful way and came up with an answer that produced not just acceptance, but peace in the heart of all participants in the decision.

Based on that early experience, which is documented elsewhere,[15] the Jesuit procedure would have each participant in the group decision-making process ask (note the relevance of group decision making to the "collaborative workplace"): How do I *feel* about the issue? What is the origin of that particular feeling? Is it from God, or not from God? (The not-from-God feelings can be from self (from ignorance, obstinacy, indigestion), from other persons (whose position on this particular issue may be "not from God"), or from diabolical sources.

To sort out all the elements, not only of the issue to be decided but also of the sources of my feelings related to that issue, is a subtle exercise. Even those who know the theory of spiritual discernment back off from the practice because of an unwillingness or inability to meet the four prerequisite demands. To discern or decide well, one must be (1) ready to move in any direction that God wants, therefore radically free; (2) open to sharing all that God has given him or her, therefore radically generous; (3) willing to suffer if God's will requires it, therefore radically patient; and (4) questing for union with God in prayer, therefore radically spiritual.

I realize this discussion is moving into higher altitudes and thinner air than most of us are accustomed to, but there is clarity ahead and even a few practical conclusions will soon be within reach. Jesuits would agree with former House Speaker Sam Rayburn's famous remark that "when two people always agree about everything, it just goes to show that one of them is doing all the thinking!" We respect that. We also know that if union is to be achieved, it can only come out of difference. The point of the process I am outlining here is, in fact, to provide a method for moving from difference to consensus amicably and prayerfully. It is part of the Jesuit tradition. What a transformation (revolution?) that would mean for the typical workplace! And what a unique and attractive opportunity this way of proceeding offers to those who are willing to give it a try.

It is true, of course, that group discernment grows out of a faith-based communal process. It is not simply a matter of reflective common sense and informed prudence. Central to this method is the isolation of pros from cons, and the uninhibited expression of arguments, both pro and con, by each of the participants. Each is expected to disclose how he or she thinks (judges) the situation to be. An inclination "pro" will not hold up if it rests on factually inaccurate or false data. "Is it true or false?" is a question of intelligence or understanding.

Each participant is also expected to disclose how he or she *feels* about both sides of the issue. "Is it good or bad?" is very much a question of feeling. And this is where discernment, the sorting out of feelings, comes in. (This is what the early Jesuits did as they were deciding how best to design the very organization that would define them as Jesuits!) Seeing something good on either side of a question is not insincerity or make-believe; any question important enough to become a policy issue certainly has two sides. But honesty requires that an effort be made to determine why you *feel* one way or another about a proposed option. Disordered affections (as Ignatius would call them) can sabotage the work of intelligence and distort accurate judgments of fact.

Is there a place for conflict and positive persuasion anywhere in the process? Yes. But the appropriate place is in the initial phase of the process where the issue for discernment, the question to be decided, is formulated. Once the process is on the tracks, the discussion of positive and negative arguments is to be separated. Contrary to what some might suspect, this saves time instead of wasting it. When debate (proper to the formulation stage) displaces dialogue (proper to the discernment process), ears and minds close, points are tallied, and a win–lose fulcrum falls into place, making the process vulnerable to the loudest voice, the greatest threat, or the highest emotion. Repair meetings are needed, which often fail to prevent unwise decisions. The Jesuit method is totally civilized, basically religious (although adaptable to secular settings), and properly nonviolent. What's more, it works!

How does the group know it has reached a good decision? What confirmation does it have that the divine will has been perceived and followed in this particular case? The Jesuit tradition puts the premium on peace as the confirmatory factor. Am I at peace with this decision? Am I at ease now, especially if what I antecedently regarded as the best course of action is not the one chosen by the group consensus? Or am I uneasy?

It is my personal view that a group is well on its way toward good decision making if everyone in the group feels free to express, in the presence of the others, any unease he or she may feel about the issue before them, which is much easier if subjective reactive feelings have been shared very early in the process. After the decision is made, the disappearance of that unease is, I think, sufficient confirmation that God's will is working in the group. No vote was taken. No disgruntled minority remains. Group unity is substantially enhanced.

Another useful norm is the consistency or inconsistency of the decision with the statement of purpose that constitutes the corporate vision of the group (a mission or goal statement). If the decision is consistent with the shared vision, you have another confirmatory factor in place. Let me just note in passing the obvious mischief waiting to break out if any participant in the process does not really share—in the sense of buying into—the vision of the group. Anyone who remains uncommitted to the vision (the declared purpose or mission) of the organization or group has no rightful place in deciding the future of that organization or group. This is a common problem in organizational life.

What is the relevance of all this to lay men and women in business or other areas of the world of work? This is another way of asking what the relevance of religious faith is to business or professional practice. If this kind of decision making has no relevance in the workplace, one has to ask whether what we do in weekend worship can spill over into our Monday-through-Friday responsibilities. It should, of course, but does it?

Recall that the workplace setting is changing. Social and economic forces are "transforming the way we work," as the AMA book title cited earlier puts it. A new respect is emerging for "the power of the collaborative workplace," as that same publication's subtitle suggests. Who can say that spiritual forces are not also at play, along with the social and economic, to prompt these workplace developments? I would never concede that there is no place for faith-based decision making in corporate America today. Indeed, more of this sort of thing may be precisely what corporate America needs. To the extent that Jesuits and their lay collaborators apply this decision-making approach to themselves in their schools and teach it to their students, the probabilities increase of seeing the method spill over into secular decision-making circles.

Men and women of faith cannot remain faithful while ignoring the invariant God when they shrewdly examine "all the variables" in a decision-making process. But how, you ask, can they do this without looking silly, wasting time, or converting the enterprise into a monastery?

First, look at your charter, mission statement, articles of incorporation, brand name, motto, or slogan. Is there room for the admission that your organization, like your nation, operates "under God"? If so, reaffirm that fact and determine not to hide it at the policy-making table. If not, then at least acknowledge the power and presence of the group as larger than the power and presence of any one participant (including the boss), and expect more from the group than could come from the individual.

Next, have a little "quiet time" before and during decision-making meetings. In many cases it would be a good idea for top management or group leaders to take a few days off for a communications workshop or a management retreat to dissolve interpersonal tensions, reduce anxiety levels, and open members of the decision-making group to the possibility of exchanging feelings and subjective views. Mutual trust is a sine qua non for good group decisions.

Then allow for full participation in the preparation of agenda with provision for strong advocacy of a position early in the meeting process. Make careful provision for the accumulation and assimilation of all necessary information.

Provide opportunities for all elements of unease to surface, followed by a "quiet time" when each can reflect on the possible sources of his or her own unease.

Then segment the meeting into time "pro" and time "con" with respect to every major issue (as President Obama did in the White House meeting mentioned earlier). In each of these meeting segments, all participants must speak, if only to agree with a point already made.

Whoever chairs the process then tries to "read a consensus" and tests it against the group. If there is no clear consensus, the chair can probe for areas of consensus. At this juncture, some open debate may be useful. As a last resort, the group can decide by vote. Confirmatory procedures will evolve as the group gains experience with the process.

This method is well suited to what psychologist Kenneth Kenniston and others began in the 1960s to call "the post-modern style." "A focus on process rather than on program," says Kenniston, "is perhaps the prime characteristic of the post-modern style, reflecting a world where flux and change are more apparent than direction, purpose or future."[16] Men and women in business tend to drive directly toward program decisions as the target or "output" of group meetings. Too little attention is paid to process on the way to the program, or even to process as an end or program in itself. As a consequence, valuable human interaction is plowed under by neatly cut programs to which the group is unevenly committed. The prognosis for subsequent success in executing such programs is not bright.

The output of a good discernment process is clarity. The direction of an ongoing decision-making group is from clarity to clarity. In this sense, planning is iterative and, therefore, unmistakably human, not inhumanly mechanical.

What I attempted to do in Indonesia and want to repeat here is to emphasize that awareness of divine activity in the midst of a group serves to enhance both the humanity (the process begins with the feelings) and the *quality* of a group's decisions. By making a little more room for God in their day-to-day world, organizational men and women will maximize their enlightened and clarified self-interest. Their actions will demonstrate that the word of the Lord, as received from Isaiah (65:1–3) is to be taken seriously: "I was ready to be approached by those who did not consult me, ready to be found by those who did not seek me. I said, 'I am here, I am here,' to a nation that did not invoke my name. Each day I stretched out my hand to a rebellious people who went by evil ways, following their own whims, a people who provoked me to my face incessantly."

Inner peace can be found through a discernment process that leads to decisions that embody clarity. Full respect must be given, however, to the preconditions: freedom, generosity, patience, and a desire to find union with God in prayer. No believer should ever forget that the outstretched hand of God is always there to help.

Even if an individual or group falls short in meeting the preconditions, much can be learned from attempting and participating in the process. It will reveal how leadership as function can replace leadership as command-and-control position, once the latter is seen by all to be anachronistic. (And that day is surely already here!)

Before any major decision is made, the decider, in the Jesuit tradition, will want to ask how he or she *feels* when considering the options. Once sources of the feeling are identified and clarified, the decider will be better able to choose, and in making the decision, more likely to find his or her will aligned with the will of God. Even if alignment with God's will is not a major concern for you in approaching a decision that will affect you in the workplace, tuning into your feelings before you decide is still a good idea.

Washington-based executive search consultant Jonathan E. McBride says in a "Manager's Journal" essay for the *Wall Street Journal* (December 9, 1985), that when he is asked to counsel a promising candidate for a position, he often finds himself saying, "If your head says 'go' and your heart says 'no'—don't do it; if your heart says 'go' and your head says 'no'—give it a whirl. You can usually find facts to support your feelings; you can't really massage your feelings around to support the facts." When I asked Jon McBride about the relevance of what I've laid out in this chapter to a specific decision of taking or not taking a particular job opportunity, he said that it is always wise to start with the feelings. "Career decisions will be more successful and more rewarding," he told me, "when the candidate's head and heart both embrace a job-changing decision."

I would add this characteristically Jesuit perspective to that comment: the believer can count on finding God there at the intersection of head and heart.

Throughout his spiritual teaching, Ignatius of Loyola stresses the principle of adaptation. By that he means that God works with respect for the freedom of each individual, with regard for the history, temperament, and talents of each man or woman. It relates well to what is referenced earlier in this book as adaptive—as opposed to technical—leadership. Ignatian spirituality, then, is about encounter not performance, about freedom not manipulation, about individual choice not group pressure. Consequently, Ignatian spirituality is open to ecumenical participation, enculturation, and interreligious dialogue. It can also find a home in business decision making.

## NOTES:

1. Noel M. Tichy and Warren G. Bennis, *Judgment: How Winning Leaders Make Great Calls* (New York: Portfolio, 2007), 1.

2. Ibid., 5.

3. Quoted in Michiko Kakutani, "The Deciders and How They Decide," *New York Times* (May 8, 2009): C21.

4. From Kissinger's introduction to Peter W. Rodman, *Presidential Command* (New York: Alfred A. Knopf, 2009), viii.

5. R. Jeffrey Smith, Michael D. Shear and Walter Pincus, "In Obama's Inner Circle, Debate over Memos' Release Was Intense," *Washington Post* (April 24, 2009).

6. What follows here draws upon chapter six, "Discernment: A Spirituality of Choice," in my book *Jesuit Saturdays: Sharing the Ignatian Spirit with Friends and Colleagues* (Chicago, IL: Loyola Press, revised edition, 2008).

7. (New York: American Management Association, 1995).

8. Ibid., v.

9. Ibid., 86.

10. Quoted in Cándido de Dalmases, S.J., *Ignatius of Loyola, Founder of the Jesuits* (St. Louis, MO: Institute of Jesuit Sources, 1985), 32, 33.

11. Ibid., 23.

12. *Autobiography*, 23.

13. Cited in Cándido de Dalmases, S.J., *Ignatius of Loyola, Founder of the Jesuits* (St. Louis, MO: Institute of Jesuit Sources, 1985), 44.

14. These words are from one of the Upanishads, ancient Indian philosophical treatises; this saying appeared on a bookmark and no precise reference was given.

15. Cf. John C. Futrell, S.J., *Making an Apostolic Community of Love* (St Louis: Institute of Jesuit Sources, 1970).

16. *Young Radicals: Notes on Committed Youth* (New York: Harcourt Brace, 1968), 275.

# CHAPTER ELEVEN

# LEADERS EFFECT CHANGE

In 1973, I became dean of arts and sciences at Loyola University in New Orleans. Loyola is separated from Tulane University by a property line; the two campuses are contiguous. In those days (it may still be the case, I just don't know), there was a modest amount of cross-registration and informal cooperation between the two institutions. So, since I was new to higher education administration, and the Tulane dean, Joe Cronin, had been on the job for eighteen years, I thought it would be not just courteous, but wise, for me to walk over and get acquainted with my counterpart.

It was a pleasant meeting. In what some might regard as a sudden burst of humility on my part, I asked the Tulane dean if he had any advice to offer to help me get off to a good start. "You will soon learn," said this veteran academic administrator, "that it is easier to move a cemetery than to move a liberal arts faculty."

How right he was!

Most people resist change and prefer to live in the immediate past. Psychologists might nuance that observation by saying that it is loss, not change that people fear. What they have, they know. The familiar is, by definition, in hand; it is a possession. To let go amounts to a loss. Rarely do they regard it as good riddance; more often than not they see it as loss. Since leaders are in the business of bringing about change, they have to be sensitive to the perception of loss on the part of those whom they are trying to lead.

James J. Schiro, chairman of Zurich Financial Services is quoted in the "Corner Office" feature of the Sunday Business section of the *New York Times* as saying, "People don't like change, but they can manage change. They can't handle uncertainty. I think it is the job of leaders to eliminate uncertainty."[1] We live in an uncertain world, but that does not condemn us to a state of hesitation and indecision. Uncertainty, like change, can be managed. Obstacles can be overcome. Decisions can be made, indeed must be made if progress is going to be achieved.

Leadership is about getting people to tackle tough problems. That is the view of Ronald Heifetz whose work has been nicely summarized by Sharon Daloz Parks[2] whose own writing on leadership is cited elsewhere in this book. Tough problems abound not only in higher education but in virtually every corner of organizational life where leadership operates. Just ask any leader!

Art Hauptman is a veteran observer of change in higher education. (It is interesting to note, by the way, that *Change* is the name of a fine magazine that has been serving the higher education community in the United States since the 1960s.) Hauptman has written wisely and often about strategic change in higher education. On one such occasion, he defined a *strategic response* as "a decision controlled by institutional officials that (1) requires changing a major policy, program, or practice and (2) involves some risk."[3]

Note first that when it comes to bringing about change, institutional officials (management and trustees) have control; next, something major is at stake, and third, a certain degree of risk is involved. The risk is inescapable, as is the responsibility on the part of officials to bring about the change.

We've seen in chapter eight that clear and critical thinking belongs in the leadership toolkit. Just as strategic planning should go before any major change, strategic thinking should precede the plan. Strategic thinking begins with this question: What sets us apart? That's another way of asking about comparative advantage. Your comparative advantage could be nothing more than your location and your people (where you operate and who runs the operation), but they are uniquely yours and they set you apart from the rest of the pack. What to do with what is uniquely yours is for leaders to decide, but not without consulting others. Such decisions will almost always involve change. I say "almost" because there will be times when the leader has to resist change, stand fast in the face of opposition, even stand down if principle requires it. But that would be the exception, not the rule. Leadership is indeed about change, even though it might not be all about change.

Thinking strategically is second nature to the experienced leader. And, as Tom Ricks has observed, *strategy* "is a grand-sounding word" that is frequently misused by laymen as a synonym for tactics. In fact, strategy has a very different and quite simple meaning that flows from just one short set of questions: Who are we, and what are we ultimately trying to do here? How will we do it, and what resources and means will we employ in doing it? The four answers give rise to one's strategy. Ideally, one's tactics will then follow from them—that is, this is who we are, this is the outcome we wish to achieve, this is how we aim to do it, and this is what we will use to do it.[4]

Knowing who you are, knowing your immediate goal, knowing how you are going to get there , and identifying the resources you will need—all this begins with strategy and points to tactics. Leaders bring strategy, which is the product of vision, into partnership with tactics, which relate to immediate objectives. Strategy is a long-term consideration; tactics are short-term steps. Working together they produce progress. Only by working together can they overcome resistance to change.

Change involves process. It takes time. It presupposes vision, of course, and requires clear and persistent communication. To say that change takes time is another way of saying that it requires patience in the persons who initiate, manage, and are affected by the process.

The best book I've encountered on the relationship of change to leadership is *Leading Change*.[5] It is organized around an eight-stage change process.[6] Each stage involves a leadership responsibility. I will first describe the eight stages and then comment on their relevance to other tools in the book you are holding in your hand.

The initial stage is establishing a sense of urgency. Next, the leader has to form a *guiding coalition*—a group with enough power to lead the change. Third, there must be the identification of a vision to propel the effort, accompanied by strategies for achieving the vision. Communication comes next; it is in this fourth stage that a seemingly endless repetition, by word and example, of the vision and strategies begins. Stage five is what construction workers would call "clearing and grubbing"—getting rid of obstacles, eliminating whatever would undermine the change vision. Sixth, there should be periodic pauses to celebrate the "wins" along the way, not to declare victory or encourage complacency, just to recognize and reward where recognition might be due. The seventh stage can be a "decade-long process" that consolidates the gains while avoiding triumphalism and facilitating still more change. Finally, the new ways of doing things must be "anchored" in the culture.

Let's examine that process, stage by stage.

*URGENCY.* This is not a call for a pressure-cooker work environment, or running an assembly line through the executive suite, or adopting a metrics-driven performance schedule. It is an on-your-toes, heads-up, wide-awake posture that amounts to an organizational refusal to become complacent. You don't have to be ill in order to get better. So why presume, when you are healthy and things are going very well, that they couldn't be going better? And since "going better" means better for all (clients, customers, workplace associates, shareholders, and all other stakeholders, including the community within which you operate), how can you not want to see that happen? Once a decision for change has been made, a sense of urgency must accompany it all the way through every stage of implementation.

*GUIDING COALITION.* Recall the center-of-the-circle location, as opposed to the top-of-the-pyramid imagery mentioned earlier when I discussed the geometry of leadership. Think now of a sawed-off pyramid and notice that there is plenty of room there, on a platform near the top, for a leadership team, what John Kotter, whose eight stages we are reviewing here, would call a guiding coalition. Leadership is indeed all about change. That change must be guided by a leadership coalition, a group that has the power to lead the change. We're not talking here about a king and his court, a ruler with a few advisers. This is a team of leaders who trust one another, share a vision, and have sufficient authority to make things happen.

Kotter lists four key characteristics as essential if the guiding coalition is to be effective: (1) position power—all key positions in the organization are included, no one capable of blocking progress is left out; (2) expertise—the required competencies needed to get the job done are represented; (3) credibility—all members of the team have good reputations and are respected throughout the organization; and (4) leadership—the group has "enough proven leaders to be able to drive the change process."[7] Kotter adds this: "Two types of individuals should be avoided at all costs when putting together a guiding coalition. The first have egos that fill up a room, leaving no space for anybody else. The second are what I call snakes, people who create enough mistrust to kill teamwork."[8]

What do you do if these two types occupy some of those key positions that have to be part of the coalition? You've got a major problem that has to be solved by transfer or termination before the process of change can begin. This is one of the toughest challenges leaders have to face. Failure to meet this challenge is the reason so much hoped-for change never happens.

VISION. "Without a vision, the people perish," says the book of Proverbs (29:18). The wisdom of that ancient assertion is indisputable. The question then becomes this: Where does the vision originate and how is it translated into a plan for change? It originates in the mind of the leader or the collective mind of the leadership group. It won't emerge unless there is imagination at work between the ears of those who would lead. They then have to reduce the vision to strategy on the way to fashioning a strategic plan.

Individuals throughout the organization will rally around a clear vision—presuming, of course, that it is also the right vision (ethically and strategically correct). The right vision will unify and motivate the people. And remember that without a vision, the people will wander off into purposeless make-work activity. Eventually, they—or, more accurately, their organization—will perish. If the vision is really clear, down-the-line managers and individual associates (we used to call them employees) can figure out for themselves what needs to be done in a given situation.

Effective visions, says Kotter, will be imaginable, desirable, feasible, focused, flexible, and communicable.[9]

COMMUNICATION. All the ink I devoted in chapters five and six to providing a place in the leadership toolkit for speaking and writing will have been spilled in vain if those who would lead do not train themselves to become effective communicators. Who else can be counted on to communicate the vision?

John Kotter's propensity to produce numbered stages and lists of principles works well for his readers on this important point. There are seven principles that he offers to facilitate effective communication of a vision: (1) keep it simple; (2) use metaphors, analogies, and examples; (3) use many different forums; (4) repeat, repeat, and repeat once more; (5) walk the talk, lead by example; (6) explicitly address seeming inconsistencies; and (7) listen and be listened to.[10]

ELIMINATING THE OBSTACLES. This stage of the change process relates to the empowerment of people throughout the organization. The barriers to empowerment, as Kotter sees them, are the realities in any given organization that tend to box people in. These are (1) structural barriers,

(2) lack of the needed skills, (3) inadequate information systems, and (4) troublesome supervisors—people who refuse to get with the program but possess enough power to slow it down, even sabotage it.[11]

How do you deal with the particularly difficult person who is clearly blocking progress? Kotter is good on this point:

> From what I've seen, the best solution to this kind of problem is usually honest dialogue. Here's the story with the industry, the company, our vision, the assistance we need from you, and the time frame in which we need all this. What can we do to help you help us? If the situation really is hopeless, and the person needs to be replaced, that fact often becomes clear early in this dialogue. If the person wants to help but feels blocked, the discussion can identify solutions. If the person wants to help but is incapable of doing so, the clearer expectations and timetable can eventually make his or her removal less contentious. The basic fairness of this approach helps overcome guilt. The rational and thoughtful dialogue also helps minimize the risk that good short-term results will suddenly turn bad or that [the dissenter] will be able to launch a successful political counterattack.[12]

It would be all so easy if we lived in a friction-free world with no ill will, incompetence, or mean-spiritedness, and no unreasonable demands. But we don't, and never will. So relational skills, patience, persuasion, and a fair measure of luck will always be needed to keep the change process moving forward.

*SHORT-TERM WINS.* Failure to celebrate small wins along the way represents lost opportunities to recharge the batteries that fuel the progress. Moreover, failure to celebrate is risky. You risk losing momentum. But when you do give recognition to short-term wins, you also run the risk of letting the celebration get out of hand, producing a complacency capable of impeding further progress. The point of giving public recognition and modest rewards is to shore up what might otherwise become sagging spirits, thus keeping all shoulders to the wheel and all eyes focused on the distance not yet covered. Instead of tooting your horn at a decibel level that registers as hyperbole, try the quiet background music of encouragement as accompaniment to continuing progress.

"The primary purpose of the first six phases of the transformation process is to build up sufficient momentum to blast through the dysfunctional granite walls found in so many organizations. When we ignore any of these steps, we put all our efforts at risk."[13] Dysfunctional granite wall? Count your blessings if you haven't encountered them; recommit yourself to an understanding of leadership as "the art of inducing others to follow" if you want to get under, over, around, or through them.

*CONSOLIDATING GAINS.* Recognizing that change takes time and that many glitches can stall the process, leadership has to view what has been achieved thus far as if it were a ball of consolidated gains that must keep rolling. It won't roll unless "the guiding coalition uses the credibility afforded by short-term wins to tackle additional and bigger change projects." It won't roll unless "additional people are brought in, promoted, and developed to help with all the changes;" unless "senior people focus on maintaining clarity of shared purpose for the overall effort and keeping urgency levels up;" unless "lower ranks in the hierarchy both provide leadership for specific projects and manage those projects;" and unless "unnecessary interdependencies" are eliminated.[14] Interdependencies are those permission points and reporting centers that have a way of multiplying in organizational life. Keep them to a necessary minimum; otherwise the quicksand effect will soon be felt.

*ANCHORING.* The final stage of the change process involves "anchoring" the change—the new way of doing things—in the organization's culture. A culture, as I explain in chapter twelve, is a set of shared meanings and values. Everyone buys in. The values are shared. Their meaning is clear. Cultures are defined by dominant values. Cultures influence behavior. So, for all practical purposes, nothing will have changed unless the change is anchored in the culture.

## NOT SO FAST

Most of what I have presented so far in this chapter comes from Boston, from the Harvard Business School; it is the work of John Kotter, whose book is published by the Harvard Business School Press. A qualifying perspective, not contradictory, just qualifying, comes from Palo Alto, from Stanford Business Books—*Change the Way You Lead Change: Leadership Strategies That REALLY Work.*[15] (Notice the not-so-modest subtitle.) What's going on here? The authors, David Herold and Donald Fedor, have their academic home in the College of Management at Georgia Tech. Their book states that

> the majority of other books, articles, and seminars on organiza-
> tional change [like Kotter's] focus their attention addressing
> HOW to implement change, that is, the change *process*. The rec-
> ommended process "dos" and "don'ts" of change implementa-
> tion are the result of many years of practitioner and research
> observations about things that tend, in general, to help or hinder
> change implementation. . . . For example, we've all heard about
> the need for a change vision; the importance of communication;
> the need to motivate people to change by means of creating a
> "burning platform"; and the importance of involving others, cel-
> ebrating victories, and reinforcing the appropriate behaviors.
> These recommendations are based on a great deal of evidence
> that if leaders do not effectively communicate, motivate, in-
> volve, or reinforce, the results of change efforts will often be
> disappointing. Surely, if leaders all followed these prescriptions,
> most changes would turn out well. But they don't. Why?[16]

Herold and Fedor find that "change is never a straightforward, stepwise, linear, or easily prescribed process. Rather, it is messy and com-plicated, and its outcomes are easily swayed by a host of factors, making prediction of success difficult at best."[17] The root causes of the failed change efforts their research analyzed were not related to problems with the change process. "Rather, they were often systemic or situational factors that doomed the planned changes no matter how much attention was paid to process."[18]

> While some disappointing change efforts could be diagnosed as
> suffering from "communication," "vision," or "sense of ur-
> gency" issues, more often than not, the lists of most recom-
> mended change steps did not map onto leaders' lists of root
> causes for failed changes. These recommendations could not ex-
> plain failures due to pursuit of bad change ideas; failures due to
> the inadequacy of those asked to lead change; failures attribut-
> able to the behaviors of those expected to implement the
> changes; failures attributable to cultural and intra-organizational
> factors; or failures attributable to factors in the organization's
> environment.[19]

They are saying, in effect, that the proposed change isn't going to happen if it is not, first and foremost, a good idea. Nor will it happen if it is not in the hands of able leaders. Moreover, there are cultural and environmental considerations outside the organization that could prevent an otherwise good change-idea from surviving long enough to become a viable program or project, a really new way of doing things that becomes rooted in the organization's culture.

There are no guarantees. Even the best leaders are not immune to bad luck. Those who address the challenge of change (as all leaders must) would do well to carry an adequate supply of what is called (as noted back in chapter one) humbition—a practical blend of humility and ambition.

In more technical language, Herold and Fedor put it this way: "Slowly, we came to understand that successful changes require leaders to develop better ways of analyzing (1) *what* they think they want or need to change, (2) what they know about *themselves* and the *others* who will be asked to lead and make the behavioral adjustments implied in the change, and (3) what they know about the *context* in which the change is to occur, especially about what other changes are taking place. Only then can change leaders develop a strategy for *how* they will go about it, when they will do what, and how fast they can move."[20]

If you can pull this off, you are a "savvy change leader" in the estimation of these authors. Their book will introduce you to famous examples of the savvy and not-so-savvy, who either established themselves at the top or fell from the ranks of corporate leadership in recent years.

## PULLING UP THE ANCHOR

The importance of anchoring a change in the corporate culture was discussed above. You cannot assume, however, that subsequent change will never be necessary. When and if it is, how do you go about lifting the anchor to allow for new and necessary change? The *McKinsey Quarterly*, the online journal of McKinsey & Co., addressed this question in a 2009 article, "The Crisis: Mobilizing Boards for Change."[21] The board must become involved; but how? Those who chair the boards must lead the way.

The process of anchoring leads to anchored thinking. Board procedures become anchored also. There are fixed patterns to meetings, agendas, and even to the time allocated for discussion of policy matters on the meeting agenda. An annual off-site meeting that encourages freewheeling discussion is not a solution, if that meeting won't happen for another six or nine months. The rhythm of the normal monthly or quarterly board meeting has to be disturbed; otherwise, anchored thinking will rule the organizational roost.

What to do? The solution is to explicitly change the way the board interacts. The chairman should insist that members articulate what they have thought but have not had the confidence to express. These conversations will often be more conceptual than rote, and participants will have to take the risk of "saying something stupid." Chairmen will need to muster up the courage to drive relentlessly the discussions that will take most boards into deep and frightening waters. Long-cherished assumptions, existing plans, or defined ambitions may go down the drain.[22]

McKinsey recommends the Edward de Bono "six thinking hats" technique to force board members into new conversations. Each "hat" represents a different way of approaching a problem. Visit their Web site (www.debonoconsulting.com) and you will learn that white-hat thinking focuses on data, facts, and known or needed information; black-hat thinking centers on difficulties and potential problems; red-hat thinking focuses on feelings, hunches, and intuition; green-hat thinking features creativity—possibilities, new ideas; yellow-hat thinking centers on values and benefits; and blue-hat thinking deals with forcing the thinking process to include next steps and action plans.

Members of the board have to say which hat they are wearing. As the discussion proceeds, the chair or facilitator has to keep an eye on those hats that are being over- or underused. This is a leadership role for board chairs. In effect, they are pulling up the anchor and preparing the way for still another change process to begin.

## THE WEATHER OUTSIDE

Throughout this chapter, the emphasis has fallen on change within an organization and the virtual certainty that there will be resistance from within. Not to be overlooked, of course, is resistance from without—the expected opposition that new initiatives (typically expansionary) will trigger once word gets out that an institution is on the grow. I can still hear an angry neighborhood community activist at an open meeting in the late 1960s shouting at an official of the mammoth Johns Hopkins Medical Center in East Baltimore, "Fix your boundaries; set your perimeter! No more expansion into our neighborhood! We won't let you do it!"

That was an exercise of leadership on the part of the activist and a test of leadership for the Hopkins official. Those exchanges continue to happen all the time. Take Fordham University in New York for a recent example. Their main campus is an oasis in the Bronx; they also have a compact Lincoln Center campus in mid-town Manhattan. The *New York Times* reported on January 23, 2009 that Fordham wanted to expand at Lincoln Center. "For more than a decade," said the news report, "Fordham University officials have been trying to figure out how to address overcrowding at their Manhattan campus and fill the coffers of their relatively small endowment. They thought the answers to both could be found in one of their most valuable assets: the Manhattan real estate." The story continues,

> So for four years, Fordham officials have been trying to win support from community groups and city officials for plans to turn their four-building site into a far denser 12-building campus in the same space between Amsterdam and Columbus Avenues and 60th and 62nd Streets. Fordham uses the site for various graduate programs . . . .
>
> The completed campus next to Lincoln Center would have three million square feet of classrooms, libraries and dormitories. It would also include two lots that Fordham would sell to luxury apartment developers, using the profits to bolster the endowment.
>
> After going back and forth with the Department of City Planning on its proposal, the school received permission on Nov. 17 to move ahead and seek approval from various government agencies. The university has begun the uniform land-use review procedure, which includes public hearings and votes by several layers of public officials. It hopes to start construction later this year, saying the project could take 25 years to complete.
>
> But Fordham has already suffered a setback: At a raucous meeting on Wednesday night, Community Board 7 rejected the plan 31 to 0. The meeting was punctuated by shouts of disapproval from more than 150 neighbors, many of whom waved signs with slogans like "No to the Fordham Fortress."[23]

What's a Fordham leader to do? That, of course, is the question confronting Fordham's president and his leadership team. The Board 7 vote was just advisory. It didn't stop the proposal from moving up the line. But the overwhelming opposition is daunting. The City Councilwoman who represents the neighborhood called for changes in the plan and added, "We like Fordham, but the project is too big. We'll keep talking."

The talk will continue. How long? No one can say. But however long this talk turns out to be, it will tell a tale of option generation on the side of the University, and resistance from the community, which, if not overcome by Fordham's powers of persuasion, will bring home a leadership trophy for the Lincoln Center neighborhood.

It turns out that Fordham gets to keep the trophy; the project is moving forward. But much discussion and more persuasion will pave this road to progress.

Those who like to play with words can take the title of this chapter, "Leaders Effect Change," as a definition of leadership. That's what leaders do. They bring about change. But this chapter title could be interpreted to mean that all of us, including neighbors, are leaders. Some are in better positions than others, but all of us are capable of coming up with a new idea, a new way of doing things. That new idea could become step one is a process of change. But if that idea is incapable of carrying the day, change will not occur.

This takes us back to the eight-stage process outlined above. It will not begin unless a sense of urgency is felt individually and collectively.

Perhaps the needed urgency will emerge from a sense of ethics, which is a "science of the ought." Our next chapter focuses on the ethical leader without whose sense of "oughtness" the urgency for change will not surface. At least it will not emerge as a platform for leadership. The ethics of those who occupy that platform will always be questioned by those who resist change. Both resisters and innovators will have to have their ethical ducks in line if what is right is ever going to come to be. Leaders can make that happen.

## NOTES:

1. "The C.E.O., Now Playing on YouTube," *New York Times* (May 10, 2009): BU2.

2. *Leadership Can Be Taught: A Bold Approach for a Complex World* (Boston: Harvard Business School Press, 2005).

3. Arthur M. Hauptman, "Strategic Responses to Financial Challenges," pamphlet published by the Association of Governing Boards of Universities and Colleges (1998), 3.

4. Tomas E. Ricks, *Fiasco: The American Military Adventure in Iraq* (New York: Penguin, 2006), 127.

5. John P. Kotter, *Leading Change* (Boston: Harvard Business School Press, 1996).

6. Ibid., 21.

7. Ibid., 57.

8. Ibid., 59.

9. Ibid., 72.

10. Ibid., 89–100.

11. Ibid., 101–14.

12. Ibid., 113–14.

13. Ibid., 130.

14. Ibid., 143.

15. David M. Herold and Donald B. Fedor, *Change the Way You Lead Change* (Stanford, CA: Stanford University Press, 2008).

16. Ibid., 126.

17. Ibid., xiii.

18. Ibid., x.

19. Ibid., xi.

20. Ibid.

21. Andrew Campbell and Stuart Sinclair, "The Crisis: Mobilizing Boards for Change(www.mckinseyquarterly.com/article_print.aspx?L2=39&L3=3&ar=2300,2/6/2009).

22. Ibid. 3.

23. Christine Haughney, "Fordham Seeks to Build on Manhattan Campus," *New York Times* (January 23, 2009): online version at www.nytimes.com/2009/01/23/nyregion/23fordham.html.

# CHAPTER TWELVE

# THE ETHICAL LEADER

Every ethical leader was once a developing child. To discuss ethical leadership intelligently, therefore, it helps to consider the formation of character in children and then the development of that character in young adulthood and beyond.

In his book *Leading Quietly: An Unorthodox Guide to Doing the Right Thing*,[1] Joseph L. Badaracco Jr. quotes a major computer company executive, who was mistreated as a child, as saying, "In life, I have found that there are basically two ways a child develops into a principled and ethical adult: by having a positive adult role model to emulate or by seeing the ugly side of human nature and disdaining it."[2] Another observer, former Secretary for Health, Education, and Welfare, John Gardner, says young people do not assimilate values by learning definitions, "They learn attitudes, habits and ways of judging. They learn these in intensely personal transactions with their immediate family or associates. They learn them in the routines and crises of living, but they also learn them through songs, stories, drama and games. They do not learn ethical principles; they emulate ethical (or unethical) people."[3]

These views echo the time-honored saying that values are "caught not taught," and, as I'll explain a bit more fully below, just as the common cold is often caught at school, not at home, values too are usually communicated by interaction with peers, a point not to be overlooked in considering how character is formed.

For many years, Stephen R. Covey's *The Seven Habits of Highly Effective People*[4] dominated the bestseller lists. Largely forgotten is that book's original subtitle: *Restoring the Character Ethic*. Restoration of the character ethic is a good way to think about the formation of an ethical leader, particularly in a book aimed at younger readers on their way to assuming leadership responsibilities.

How is character developed? To the extent that character formation is influenced by images (on computer and movie screens), sound (in words and music), and print (good reading for both pleasure and education), those three influences—image, sound, and print—have to be kept in mind by those trying to understand the situation, and they must be held in balance by those who would be leaders. Several additional key points should be borne in mind as we examine character formation: (1) parental influence is essential; (2) peer influence has far more weight than most of us realize; and (3) there are enemies abroad who will damage a developing character for economic gain.

If a child never sees a parent reading anything but a newspaper, that child is unlikely to become a reader. If there are no books around the house and in the hands of parents, there will be no books in the hands of children. If parents neglect reading to their children before the child is able to read, those not read to (nor exposed to the warmth of being held in the arms and lap of a reading parent) are—there's no other word for it—neglected children.

If exposure to children's books is not part of the dawning of awareness in a young mind, not only will the engine of intellect get off to a slow start, but watching television passively will fill the hours and dull a child's natural potential for experiencing that magic moment "when the lines . . . separated into words," as the first-person narrator puts it—describing herself as a child learning how to read while sitting in her father's lap each evening after dinner—in Harper Lee's *To Kill a Mockingbird*.

Neglect of the printed word will contribute to vocabulary deficits, raise barriers to written composition, and lead to deprivation of childhood enjoyment of stories told and heard. Parents are the ones who tell bedtime stories; parents should be the ones who form story-telling circles with participating children right there in the middle of the circle.

Finally, creative schools and cooperating parents will be open, at the middle- and upper-school levels, to things like joint book reports. Books assigned in school to be read at home by students will be read as well by parents so that the parent can meet his or her "assignment" of submitting (not for grade, just for meeting a participation requirement) a report on a book that will, presumably, have been read and discussed beforehand between parent and child. Now there's an opportunity for meeting the nothing-to-talk-about-with-your-kids challenge! Bonding triggered by the binding of a good book is worth a try.

Peer influence is so important it merits more thought than I'm qualified to offer and more space than this chapter could reasonably provide. Psychologists will acknowledge that parents are vital in shaping positive environmental influences on their children (as complement to the genetic endowment they provide), but empirical studies offer a lot of evidence that says the influence of peers is even more important. The environmental influence that really shapes a child's character and personality is his or her peer group, hence the importance of wise choices in the selection of schools, playmates, and friends, not to mention the importance of examining the values embodied in films, fashion, music, magazines, and lingo that enjoy peer-group popularity. Once that examination gets underway, you will find yourself on an analytical path that will have you following the dollars back to the source of those films, songs, and fashions. And when the Internet is factored in with the other media, you will be astounded at the amount of money being generated from the exploitation of the immaturity and peer-dependency of children and adolescents.

What can be done about that? This question raises in my mind the issue of creativity versus censorship and the need for good leadership on the creativity side. Not to be overlooked is participation in school sports, school plays, and similar types of leisure activity. We simply have to find a way to engage the creative potential of children, adolescents, and young adults to, first, build a demand for good, positive, and healthy fare from all the media; and, second, to engage the creative potential of persons of all ages—artists, writers, entrepreneurs, composers, producers, performers— in the production of works that celebrate love and courage instead of exploiting sex and violence. Will this be easy? Of course not. Is it possible? Maybe. Will it happen? Not unless there is some leadership on the part of those who say they want something better, boycott the other stuff, and buy (that is, view and enjoy) only what is good, true, and beautiful.

It is obvious that children have to learn what is good or bad for them in the consumption of food and drink; so too, they have to be encouraged to internalize the values that will prompt them to consume only appropriate imagery, whatever the medium conveying that imagery may be. Good reading will help to raise their standards; the right friends will reinforce their resolve to maintain those standards. If that happens, they are on their way to the leadership level.

There is a good book by Michael Koehler with the attractive title, *Coaching Character at Home: Strategies for Raising Responsible Teens.*[5] Another book worth looking into is Roberta Richin's *Connecting Character to Conduct: Helping Students Do the Right Things.*[6] This study says schools "are uniquely equipped to engage parents and other stakeholders in helping students use guiding, universal principles for individual and group decision making."

What a person does in secret tells you a lot about that person's character. Character development is the key strategy to pursue in your search for a balance in your children's preferences between and among images, printed words, and appealing sounds. Strong character will help a child shun secrecy for openness. Such a child will, without worrying about getting caught or getting away with it, just go ahead and do the right thing. But you have to be the right person (a question of character) if you are going to do the right thing (a question of conduct). Your "parent–education partnership" is a joint venture aimed at bringing character and conduct together in companionship for success in the practice of life.

Assuming that the foundation has been laid in childhood and adolescence, and assuming that character is there in the teens and twenty-somethings who are on their way to positions of leadership influence, more must now be said about what it takes to be an ethical leader.

To set the stage for what follows, let me turn to Robert Bolt's introduction to his 1960 play, *A Man for All Seasons*. The protagonist is Thomas More (1478–1535), who, as Chancellor of England, was executed for refusing—on the grounds of religious conviction—to violate his conscience. Bolt, an agnostic, was impressed with More's character and troubled by what appeared to him to be an absence of character in post–World War II England and the United States, where, as Bolt saw it, "both socially and individually it is with us as it is with our cities—an accelerating flight to the periphery leaving a center which is empty when the hours of business are over."[7] So Robert Bolt chose to do his part in filling up the "empty center" he observed in citizens of the United States and Britain by dramatizing for their entertainment the life of Thomas More.

The problem that prompted Bolt to write is still with us. There is a cultural and educational challenge here that relates directly to leadership development. Core values are central to leadership. Leaders must internalize values and have the courage to act on them. The right values are the stuff of good character (just as standing up for those values is the stuff of good drama). Cultures are defined by dominant values. It takes leadership to displace bad values (greed, for instance) and substitute good values (compassion, for example) in their place. Think of the political culture, the Wall Street culture, entertainment culture, corporate culture, youth culture, sports culture, the culture of science and technology. If society is to be served (some might say, saved), the dominant value shaping each of these areas of human interaction must be good, wholesome, and positive.

## PRINCIPLES ARE INTERNALIZED VALUES

For a simple, down-to-earth, practical illustration of articulating a dominant value, translating that value into a principle, and allowing that principle to influence a culture, I would refer the reader to a summer camp in Westport, in upstate New York, on the shore of Lake Champlain. Camp Dudley has been there since 1885. Founded by the YMCA, it is now an independent corporation, governed by a board of trustees, and operates as a nondenominational Christian camp for boys, ages 7 to 15, under a motto that expresses the dominant value and thus defines the culture of this camp. The motto is this: "The Other Fellow First."

I spend a long weekend at Dudley every summer as a guest chaplain—one of a number of guest clergy, male and female, of different denominations—to lead a noon Sunday interfaith chapel service in an outdoor "chapel" of long log "benches" on a tree-lined slope running down to a bluff that overlooks the lake. There is a platform there equipped with lectern, microphone, organ, and chairs for readers, cantors, and the leader of prayer (who is also the chapel speaker).

Some years ago, my visit to Dudley coincided with Parents' Weekend. Soon after arriving on Friday afternoon, I happened to meet a couple from New York City who had come to visit their eight-year-old son. He was experiencing his first extended absence from home. His parents mentioned that their boy had been having a few adjustment problems in his Upper East Side private elementary school and they were anxious to see how he was getting along at camp. A few minutes later the youngster, a bit overweight, came waddling up to greet his parents. He was introduced to me and just to make a bit of ice-breaking conversation I asked, "What do you like best about Camp Dudley?" His immediate response: "Nobody here makes fun of you."

That response says a lot about culture shaping behavior. It also suggests the wisdom of encapsulating the organization's central value in a motto ("The Other Fellow First") that conveys the organization's culture.

Principles are internalized values and values define cultures. Before providing a general overview of "old" ethical principles, I want to say a few words about culture.

A culture is a set of shared meanings, principles, and values.[8] Values, as I indicated, define cultures. Where values are widely shared and the sharing bonds together, with common ties, those who hold the same values, you have an identifiable culture. There are as many different cultures as there are distinct sets of shared meanings, principles, and values. This is not to say that everyone in a given culture is the same. No, you have diversity of age, wealth, class, intelligence, education, and responsibility in a given culture where diverse people are unified by a shared belief system, a set of agreed-upon principles, a collection of common values. They literally have a lot in common and thus differ from other people in other settings who hold a lot of other things in common. You notice it in law firms, hospitals, colleges, corporations—wherever people comment on the special "culture" that characterizes the place.

Willa Cather said, in a tribute to Nebraska, written in 1923 upon completion of her novel *A Lost Lady*:

> We must face the fact that the splendid story of the pioneers is finished, and that no new story worthy to take its place has yet begun. . . . The generation now in the driver's seat hates to make anything, wants to live and die in an automobile, scudding past those acres where the old men used to follow the corn-rows up and down. They want to buy everything ready-made: clothes, food, education, music, pleasure. Will the third generation—the full-blooded joyous ones just coming over the hill—be fooled? Will it believe that to live easily is to live happily?[9]

Subsequent generations have been fooled. Perhaps each generation has to learn for itself, but the experience of previous generations can help the young identify and understand the values that will eventually constitute the sets of shared meanings in new, and, one might hope, better cultures.

Jesuit prep schools today say they are educating "men and women for others." The U.S. Army invites you to "be all that you can be." Hewlett-Packard wants to do things "the H-P way." "Cornellcares.com" is one medical center's Web address offering innovative tools, strategies, and advice related to geriatric mental health. The Web address expresses a value wrapped in a slogan: "Cornell cares." And so it goes throughout the world of slogan communication here on earth and out in Cyberspace.

The old corporate culture in America was characterized by values like freedom, individualism, competition, loyalty, thrift, stability, fidelity to contract, efficiency, self-reliance, power, and profit. If not controlled (regulated) by self, or by social norms, or by public law, pursuit of some of these values could be fueled by unworthy values like greed and the desire to dominate (rather than a desire to serve), and thus propel a person or a firm into unethical territory.

The new (or newer, or most recent) corporate culture is defined by many but not all of these same values, although they are interpreted now somewhat differently. And there are some new values emerging in the new corporate context.

Where the old corporate culture (say, fifty years ago) would tolerate an employer's not looking much beyond the interests of a firm's shareholders, the new corporate culture has grown comfortable with the notion of "stakeholders" and sees an ethical connection between the firm and not only its shareholders, but all others who have a stake in what that firm does: employees, suppliers, customers, the broader community, and the physical environment—to name a few. The outlook is more communitarian, more attentive to the dictates of the common good. There was some of this in the past, a "social compact" between employer and employee that was somewhat paternalistic and relatively free of both the deregulation and foreign competition that have caused much of the present economic dislocation in America. But the dominant value of the old corporate culture was individualism, not regard for the other, and certainly not communitarianism—a concept both explained and praised by George Lodge to classes of not readily receptive business executives in the Advanced Management Program at the Harvard Business School in the 1970s.[10] There is a good deal of evidence now that individualism is again on the rise. Greed's ugly head has risen high above the surface once again in corporate America.

There are also some encouraging signs, however, that communitarian concerns are influencing the decisions of some major corporations that want to balance corporate self-interest with community concerns. Note, for example, what William Clay Ford Jr., then chairman of Ford Motor Company, told Jeffrey Garten in an undated interview for Garten's 2001 book *The Mind of the C.E.O.*: "At the end of the [twentieth] century, many of the great ideological issues are off the table. It's now a question of what consumers are going to be demanding, rather than what business leaders are envisioning. Consumers want a safer, cleaner, more equitable world, and they'll buy from companies that display those characteristics. I believe that companies that are responsive to those needs—assuming they have great products and services, of course—will have a commanding market position."[11]

Mr. Ford had his words thrown back at him in a full-page "open letter" advertisement that ran in the *New York Times* on December 2, 2004, under the heading "Gas guzzling is un-American." Signed by Michael Brune, Executive Director, Rainforest Action Network, the letter read in part, "When you took the helm, you announced Ford Motor Company's 'Cleaner, Safer, Sooner' campaign and raised our hopes that a self-avowed 'life-long environmentalist' was now running America's flagship automaker. We believed you then, but four years later the facts tell a very different story. Ford has ranked dead last among all major automakers in overall fuel efficiency every year since you became CEO. Since the oil crisis of the 1970s, the EPA has ranked your company last in overall fuel efficiency for 20 out of the last 30 years. Ford's fleet today gets fewer miles per gallon on average than the Model-T did 80 years ago."

The letter ends on this accusatory note: "In October 2000, you said that your vision was 'to achieve new levels of success as a business, and clear leadership in resolving social and environmental issues.' Mr. Ford, if this is your best, then your best won't do. America deserves better."

It would have been just about inconceivable in 1950 to imagine airplanes, office buildings, restaurants, and college residence halls that are smoke-free. In the same way, no one then gave a thought to picking up after their dogs in the interest of neighborhood aesthetics (not to mention sanitation). Increased sensitivity over environmental and health concerns is just one small piece of evidence of a value shift away from mindless individualism toward a more enlightened communitarian outlook.

## THE OLD ETHICAL PRINCIPLES

In any case, here, in brief outline, are what I call "old ethical principles" that can, I believe, surface in individual and community consciousness to meet the ethical challenges of our new corporate culture. Bear in mind that although principles can be neglected, they, unlike laws, cannot be broken. They are always there, waiting to be applied, although they can be permitted to lie dormant. Principles have no loopholes.

I've identified ten classic ethical principles and invite the reader to come up with his or her own understanding of each one. You are the world's leading expert on your own opinion. It is important that you articulate your own opinion on these matters so that you can assess how widely shared, in your present or future workplace, are your values and the understandings you have of these classic principles. Remember, a culture is a set of shared meanings and values. How widely shared are your meanings and values relative to these ten principles?

1. Integrity. I think of integrity in terms of wholeness, solidity of character, honesty, trustworthiness, and responsibility. What would you add or subtract from that list?

2. Veracity. This, to me, involves telling the truth in all circumstances; it also includes accountability and transparency.

3. Fairness. By this, of course, I mean justice, treating equals equally, giving to everyone his or her due.

4. Human Dignity. This bedrock principle of all ethics—personal and organizational—acknowledges a person's inherent worth. It prompts respectful recognition of another's value simply for being human.

5. Participation (in this case, workplace participation). This principle respects another's right not to be ignored on the job or shut out from decision making within the organization.

6. Commitment. What I have in mind here is that a committed person can be counted on for dependability, reliability, fidelity, and loyalty.

7. Social Responsibility. This points to an obligation to look to the interests of the broader community and to treat the community as a stakeholder in what the corporation or organization does.

8. The Common Good. This operates as an antidote to individualism; it aligns one's personal interests with the community's well-being. This may indeed be the most difficult of all these principles around which to form an organizational consensus relating to the common good of the

corporation and then relating that understanding to an understanding of the broader common good outside the organization.

9. Subsidiarity. This might best be understood in terms of delegation and decentralization, keeping decision making close to the ground. It means that no decision should be taken at a higher level that can be made as effectively and efficiently at a lower level in the organization. This could be viewed as a "principle of respect for proper autonomy." It could also be understood in terms of Saul Alinsky's "Iron Rule" for his Industrial Areas Foundation: "Never, never do for others what they can do for themselves."

10. Love. I see this as a principle, an internalized conviction that prompts a willingness to sacrifice one's time, convenience, and a share of one's ideas and material goods for the good of others.

Some of these would coincide with what William Faulkner, in his famous acceptance speech upon receiving the Nobel Prize in Literature, called "the old verities." By these he meant "truths of the heart, the universal truths lacking which any story is ephemeral and doomed." Specifically, he was thinking of "love and honor and pity and pride and compassion and sacrifice."[12] Even those in my set of ten that are not quite so grand are, nonetheless, principles—lofty, but not so far above the fray that they cannot be applied on the ground in business decision making. Their application will, by the way, prove that Oliver Wendell Holmes Jr. was clever, but not necessarily correct when he remarked in 1897 that "a man is usually more careful of his money than of his principles."

## THE CORNER OFFICE

It is a commonplace to note that the search for business, organizational, or corporate ethics will lead directly to the corner office, to the executive suite, to the person and character of the CEO. And that raises a question I will not explore here, namely, the presence or absence of a direct connection between the personal morality in the private life of the CEO, on the one hand, and, on the other, the organizational morality in the public moral person of a corporation, institution, or organized collection of the many persons, who, working under the leadership of a CEO, try to achieve an organizational purpose.

I prescind from the question of whether a man who, for example, is unfaithful to his wife can lead an ethical organization, or whether a woman who habitually lies to a friend can lead her organization to a high and consistent level of ethical integrity. It is easy to judge, but it's hard to measure the correlation between the personal character of the leader and the institutional integrity of the organization. I do not attempt anything along those lines here, but it is a question that I regard as worthy of careful consideration and study, all the more so after the March 2005 forced resignation of the Boeing Company's CEO, Harry C. Stonecipher, who, when confronted by his board, admitted to having a consensual "personal relationship" with a female Boeing executive.

Boeing's code of ethical business conduct, applicable to all employees, makes no mention of sexual misconduct, but states, "Employees must not engage in conduct or activity that may raise questions as to the company's honesty, impartiality, or reputation or otherwise cause embarrassment to the company."[13] Stonecipher, who had come out of retirement fifteen months earlier to restore the company's credibility after several widely publicized ethical scandals, did not protest the board's action, saying that it acted "fairly," and that he had "used poor judgment."[14] Part of the poor judgment, according to one observer, was his decision "to detail his actions and desires in a series of very explicit e-mails to the woman in question."[15]

Around the same time, Holland & Knight, the second largest law firm in Florida and the fifteenth largest in the United States, drew embarrassing headlines when the *St. Petersburg Times* disclosed that the firm had promoted Douglas A. Wright, one of its tax lawyers, to chief operating partner in the 1,250-lawyer Tampa office knowing that an internal investigation had found him guilty a year earlier of sexual harassment. Nine female lawyers in that office had accused him of harassing them. When the story became public, he resigned the new position but retained his partnership.

In a 2003 "Ideas & Trends" essay in the *New York Times*, Geoffrey Nunberg acknowledges that America "does have a culture of the corporation," but "it is increasingly detached from the values that are touchstones in our personal dealings. Few people nowadays perceive the historical connection between 'private sector' and 'private life.'"[16] The private lives of those who hold executive responsibility in the private sector reflect personal character and—although there are no scientific studies to support this conclusion—probably do influence corporate behavior for good or ill.

In her opening remarks to the jury in the famous Martha Stewart trial of 2004, Assistant U.S. Attorney Karen Patton Seymour said, "Ladies and gentlemen, lying to federal agents, obstructing justice, committing perjury, fabricating evidence, and cheating investors in the stock market—these are serious crimes." Indeed they are. And although her organization—Martha Stewart Living Omnimedia, Inc.—was not on trial, the faults and failures of Martha Stewart raised questions about the ethics of the organization she headed, questions the organization seems to have been able to handle to the satisfaction of shareholders and outside observers.

Around that same time, Paul Krugman's (*New York Times*) February 8, 2004 review of two books "about C.E.O.'s who looted their companies and the financial press that covered up for them," opened with these words:

> Eighteen months ago, American capitalism seemed to be in crisis. Stocks had plunged, and some of the nation's most celebrated business leaders had been exposed as phonies if not crooks. Now the economy is growing, and the Dow's been back above 10,000. So is it safe to buy stocks again? After you read Roger Lowenstein's *Origins of the Crash* [*The Great Bubble and Its Undoing*: Penguin Press] and Maggie Mahar's *Bull!* [*A History of the Boom, 1982–1999*: HarperBusiness] you'll have serious doubts. Both tell the story, from different angles, of how ordinary investors got suckered into supporting the lifestyles of the rich and shameless. And you have to wonder whether anything has really changed.

Krugman's review goes on to say, "Lowenstein's title may convey the impression that his book is mainly about stock prices. It isn't: it's about the epidemic of corruption that spread through corporate America in the 1990s, though that epidemic was in part both an effect and a cause of the bull market. A better title might have been *Executives Gone Wild*."

Do these executives have integrity? Hardly. Do their organizations embody high levels of ethics? Not likely. Part of the problem in the case of errant CEOs, is a lack of oversight on the part of governing boards, and where wrongdoing occurred at lower ranks of executive responsibility, the problem is a failure of higher-ups to monitor what was going on below them.

After describing, in *Origins of the Crash*, the problems that triggered several of the major corporate scandals, Roger Lowenstein writes,

"It is fair to wonder why directors went along with such abuses, and the answer has its roots in the distinct culture of America's boardrooms."[17] Elements of that culture are (1) the twinning of the positions of chairman and CEO in one person ("think how inappropriate would the description President and Chief Justice sound, or Head Coach and Quarterback," Lowenstein says); (2) the "fraternal" character of boardrooms (Lowenstein calls them "modern oases of gentility"); (3) long tenure; (4) interlocking directorships (so that the watchers were also being watched by those they were overseeing); (5) use of compensation consultants whose recommended salary hikes for the CEO would boost the average against which outside directors, who were also CEOs, would have their compensation compared; and (6) an accepted boardroom etiquette where, in Warren Buffet's words, to stand up and criticize the CEO felt like "belching" at the table.[18]

## CULTURE AND TRUST

It all comes down to culture and trust. What is the dominant value that defines the culture, not just of the boardroom but of the entire organization? How widely is it shared throughout the organization? How trustworthy are the leaders in an organization? How trustworthy are they perceived to be by those they lead in that organization? How fully encompassing is the trust that generates the energy and purifies the air of the organization that has a claim on the time, talent, and commitment of all who work there? Trust is something of an elusive concept. The enemy of trust is secrecy. What is the substance, the texture, the fabric of a trusting relationship in business?

Competence—being very good at what you do—is part of that relationship, as are integrity, veracity, dependability, and availability. Cooperation and honesty are two important strands in the relationship. Both competence and cooperation are integral to the relationship of trust, and that relationship is strengthened by integrity, veracity, dependability, availability, and honesty.

How can this reality, this kind of trust, become part of the life of a corporation? It begins with persons and it has to begin with the small things—the courtesies, the reliabilities, the acknowledgments, and a genuine institutional humility. In the person of the CEO—the occupant of the corner office—there must be what the philosopher Dennis Goulet has called "availability, accountability, and vulnerability." Any executive who has been there will understand what he means by vulnerability. Any effective

CEO will agree that availability and accountability belong in the successful executive's toolkit.

Two additional considerations might be helpful. You cannot afford to wait until trust is lost to begin thinking about the maintenance and preservation of trust in your organization. Preventive measures in preserving organizational trust are always less costly and more effective than waiting for a crisis to arise and then deciding to deal with it.

The other consideration is captured in the term "trust bank," coined by Al Golin over forty years ago. He is author of *Trust or Consequences: Build Trust Today or Lose Your Market Tomorrow*.[19] "Just as you wouldn't go without health insurance because you're physically fit, you shouldn't go without a trust bank just because your organization has good values," says Golin. And what is a trust bank? "As the name implies, a trust bank involves making deposits of good deeds into an account over time that can be drawn upon in times of need."[20] This suggests that the organization should be doing "good deeds" for its employees, its clients or customers, and in its surrounding community. Organizational generosity can build organizational trust.

Put yourself in any present or future workplace environment and think for a moment of all your associates in that place, all those who work in your organization. And think of them within the framework of trust. Recognize that your organization cannot operate without social trust, without the social collaboration of human beings. "The way you create trust," says Kenneth Dunn, dean of the business school at Carnegie Mellon, "is to have complete transparency of your decisions."[21]

Sir Geoffrey Chandler, former director of Shell International, pointed out in a letter to the editor of *The Economist* (February 5, 2005) that there is a "prevailing public distrust of companies arising from the perception that profit precedes principle, rather than being based upon it." "Capitalism," he continues, "the most effective mechanism the world has so far known for providing goods and services and creating wealth, is under threat not from without, but from itself and from its lack of underlying principles."

Trust is one way of summarizing the principles of business ethics. You have to identify the principles, understand them, and internalize them. If they are not part of the makeup of persons who populate the corporation, the corporation will not be a principled organization. If your organizational workplace is a caring community built on a foundation of mutual trust, you will be conducting your affairs at an ethical altitude far above the minimalist horizons of "corporate compliance." You will also be a happier human being.

If you want to be an ethical leader in business, give some thought to this question: What is the purpose of business? "To maximize profits" is no answer; "to optimize profits" is not helpful either. Neither explains the deeper purpose of business activity. Nor is it fully satisfying to express "purpose" in terms of maximizing the long-term viability of the firm. If you are in business as owner, manager, or worker somewhere down the line, you are doing for others on condition of receipt of something of fair value in return. Essentially, business involves exchanges. Persons in business relate to other persons whose needs, preferences, and desires are met, to some degree of satisfaction, by the product or service the business is organized to provide—at a price. To meet that need, preference, or desire is the purpose of business. To do so at a price (and thus differentiate the activity from voluntarism or altruism) means receiving in exchange sufficient remuneration to cover the costs (including risk) of providing the service or product. This enables the provider to receive the income necessary to meet his or her own legitimate needs, preferences, and desires. Otherwise, the business system, the network of relationships where need and satisfaction meet as question and answer, could not attract and hold you the provider; you would have to find some other way to "make a living."

Why you choose business to occupy your reimbursable time, instead of earning income in other ways, is a good question. The answer will surely point to service and include the needs of others.

The business organization is there to meet, on the buyer's side, a human need for product or service. For the seller, business generates necessary income. The business context, with all its market intermediaries, enables the needs of both buyer and seller to be met in a reliable, predictable, organized fashion. This makes it possible for society to get on with the daily dynamic of life. Business organizes the material basis for human existence and well-being. Business is thus seen as foundational to the construction of a community's material relationships. If you are in business, you should take proper credit for the fact that you are fostering a human good that would not be achieved without you and the others who form the business community. Your purpose for being in business has a whole lot more to it than making money. As food is necessary for life; profit is necessary for the health of a business. But who would recommend that you stuff yourself full of food at every opportunity?

If you are a leader in business (or any other kind of organizational life), your purpose is to help create a culture within which your associates can lead a balanced life. You have an opportunity quite literally to make life richer for others.

Need, preference, and desire are graded considerations in the provision of goods and services by organized business activity. If you grant priority to need over both preference and desire, you might say that provision to meet material human need is the immediate and fundamental purpose of business. Meeting preferences, not basic needs, accounts for most of the volume of business activity and is, of course, a worthy purpose. But when business aims to satisfy unreasonable and even harmful desire, or worse, promotes and stimulates personally and socially harmful desire, the purpose of business is perverted. If the organization's product or service is hurting people, you have a choice: change things or get out. Otherwise you shrink into a person of diminished integrity if you remain on that job.

Unreasonable desire can be at work on the supply side of the exchange too. Where greed, far removed from need or legitimate preference, drives the income motivation of the provider—the seller—the business mechanism is abused for unreasonable personal gain. Society is not only ill-served but seriously injured by abuses on either side of the exchange. If you notice this happening in or around your organization, that should probably be enough to send you packing.

Another purpose of business is to provide employment—an organized environment within which individuals can, on a regular and stable basis, provide service to others and earn income for personal and family support. It would be difficult to exaggerate the value to society of providing economic security to working persons and those who depend on them. We look to business to do just that, although no one expects any one business organization to provide uninterrupted employment for all its workers all their working lives.

These considerations provide a broader context for understanding why it is a good thing to release your human potential in full-time business activity and a privilege to be a business leader.

There is real significance in the human action of making available, through fair exchanges, the goods and services people need, prefer, and in some cases simply desire. There is meaning in the managerial and entrepreneurial function of making employment available for others—helping them to be more active and productive human beings.Business firms are organized, as I said, to serve the material needs of the human community; working there can easily be viewed as just a job. But it can also be viewed as a privileged opportunity to serve others in the human community. Doing it right is doing it ethically. And doing it as a servant leader, as we shall see in the next chapter, is doing it better.

## NOTES:

1. (Boston: Harvard Business School Press, 2002).
2. Ibid., 98.
3. John Gardner, *Self-Renewal* (New York: Harper Colophon, 1963).
4. (New York: Simon & Schuster, 1989).
5. (Notre Dame, IN: Ave Maria Press, 2003).
6. (Alexandria, VA: Association for Supervision and Curriculum Development, 2000).
7. Robert Bolt, *A Man for All Seasons* (New York: Random House, 1960), xii.
8. I like Bernard Lonergan's definition of culture: "A culture is a set of shared meanings and values informing a common way of life, and there are as many cultures as there are distinct sets of meanings and values." *Method in Theology* (St. Louis, MO: Herder & Herder, 1972), 301. Much of what follows in this chapter is drawn from my book *The Power of Principles: Ethics in the New Corporate Culture* (Maryknoll, NY: Orbis, 2006).
9. Quoted in Henry Steele Commager, *The American Mind*, (New Haven, CT: Yale University Press, 1950), 154.
10. See George C. Lodge, *The New American Ideology* (New York: New York University Press, paperback, 1986), 15–21.
11. Jeffrey E. Garten, *The Mind of the C.E.O.* (New York: Perseus Basic, paperback, 2002), 140.
12. Given in Stockholm, December 10, 1950.
13. Boeing, *Ethical Business Conduct Guidelines* (undated), 5.
14. *Wall Street Journal* (March 8, 2005): 1.
15. Alan Murray, "Indiscreet E-Mail Claims a Fresh Casualty," *Wall Street Journal* (March 9, 2005): A2.
16. "Initiating Mission-Critical Jargon Reduction," *New York Times* (August 3, 2003).
17. Roger Lowenstein, *Origins of the Crash: The Great Bubble and Its Undoing* (New York: Penguin, 2004), 42.
18. Ibid., 43.
19. (New York: American Management Association, 2003).
20. See "Q&A with Al Golin," *The Public Relations Strategist* (Fall 2003): 28–29.
21. *Business Week* (March 29, 2004): 91.

# CHAPTER THIRTEEN

# THE SERVANT-LEADER

Earlier in this book, I asked you to begin thinking of the kind of leader you would like to be. This applies to any reader, but it has particular importance for young people who are potential leaders, those who have their core values in place and have begun to observe, even imitate, qualities possessed by one or several model leaders. For some, the model leader may become a mentor; if that's the case for you, you are indeed fortunate. For all, some imitable model of effective leadership should be there in your mind and heart (yes, the heart, since emotion is an important component of leadership) to accompany you on the way toward the top in organizational life. (And don't forget that "the top" should really be "the center of the circle.")

I always encourage students to imagine themselves as servant-leaders of the future. You encountered the term *servant-leader* in earlier chapters of this book in your reflections on what I call the geometry of leadership. The notion of servant leadership originated with Robert Greenleaf, whose book bearing that title is a classic. He was inspired, he says, by the character Leo in Hermann Hesse's novel *The Journey to the East*.[1] In the novel, Leo is a guide on a mythical journey. Early in the journey, the guide refers to "the law of service" and says, "He who wishes to live long must serve, but he who wishes to rule does not live long."[2]

As the story unfolds, the guide disappears and the group loses its way. Leo emerges again toward the end of the story, not as guide, but as leader and titular head of the Order that sponsored the journey. It turns out that he was in fact the leader while he was in service to the group as their guide.

Robert Greenleaf was a vice president of AT&T when he first read *The Journey to the East*. He was also a student of organizations and a consultant to businesses large and small. He carried with him into his practice of management and consulting the image of Leo, the servant leader, and over the years Greenleaf came to this conclusion:

> A fresh critical look is being taken at the issues of power and authority, and people are beginning to learn, however haltingly, to relate to one another in less coercive and more creatively supporting ways. A new moral principle is emerging, which holds that the only authority deserving one's allegiance is that which is freely and knowingly granted by the led to the leader in response to, and in proportion to, the clearly evident servant stature of the leader. Those who choose to follow this principle will not casually accept the authority of existing institutions. Rather they will freely respond only to individuals who are chosen as leaders because they are proven and trusted as servants. To the extent that this principle prevails in the future, the only truly viable institutions will be those that are predominantly servant led.[3]

In his book, Greenleaf runs individuals and institutions through the servant-leader filter. He covers businesses, foundations, churches, universities, and some other not-for-profit organizations. He gives a lot of attention to trustees as servants. His view on the distinction between oversight and management of organizations will be controversial, but, correctly understood, his point about more direct involvement by trustees (or, in the case of business, directors) in managing the organization's affairs is not all that wide of the mark. I've served on many boards—universities, schools, hospitals, insurance companies, a bank, a presidential commission, and a lot of community-based not-for-profit organizations—and I know that, generally speaking, boards are insufficiently alert and active in meeting their oversight responsibilities. The on-the-scene CEO and his or her chief financial officer tend to control the flow of information and both the formulation and implementation of on-the-ground policies.

## BEWARE THE TOP OF THE PYRAMID

Greenleaf's book cobbles together articles and papers prepared for delivery to various audiences, and he is annoyingly anonymous when it comes to identifying the organizations he is discussing. In his chapter "Servant Leadership in Business," for example, he mentions that the statements that comprise the chapter were delivered, "one to a general audience and two addressed to specific businesses," but he does not identify the businesses. I learned from a friend, who works full time for the Greenleaf Center for Servant Leadership in Indiana, that it is quite likely that the businesses were the Olga Company and either Delta Airlines or Royal Dutch Shell. I can't say for sure.

Since 1950, I've been a member of the Society of Jesus (the Jesuits) and, in 1961, was ordained a priest of the Roman Catholic Church. Knowing that, please now read along with me the following paragraphs from *Servant Leadership*.

> To be a lone chief atop a pyramid is *abnormal and corrupting.* None of us is perfect by ourselves, and all of us need the help and correcting influence of close colleagues. When someone is moved atop a pyramid, that person no longer has colleagues, only subordinates. Even the frankest and bravest of subordinates do not talk with their boss in the same way that they talk with colleagues who are equals, and normal communications patterns become warped. . . . The pyramidal structure weakens informal links, dries up channels of honest reaction and feedback, and creates limiting chief–subordinate relationships that, at the top, can seriously penalize the whole organization.
>
> A self-protective *image of omniscience* often evolves from these warped and filtered communications. This in time defeats any leader by causing a distortion of judgment, for judgment is often best sharpened through interaction with others who are free to challenge and criticize.[4]

Abnormal and corrupting? Greenleaf is not saying that this has to be the way; he is simply suggesting that there is a high probability that the lone chief at the top will be out of touch and thus less effective as a leader. Given my background as a Catholic priest, I naturally thought of the pope when I first read the words I've just quoted, and I winced at the scenario Greenleaf lays out. It prompted me to reflect on the organizational structure of my church. I accept that structure, of course, but I recognize that it is staffed by human beings and that they are subject to the weaknesses, foibles, and failings that Greenleaf observed in his study of organizations.

When Pope Benedict XVI occasionally finds himself in a public relations jam, as happened early in his pontificate with both the Muslim and the Jewish communities, and five years later when new allegations regarding the clergy sex-abuse scandal emerged in Europe, both misunderstanding and possible offense might have been prevented by closer collaboration on the part of the pope with a good editor, or pre-pronouncement consultation with advisers who are invited and encouraged to say what they think. There is nothing in the hierarchical structure of the Church to prevent this, but it will not happen unless the pope wants it to happen.

In Catholic circles, whenever an ordinary priest is "elevated" from the ranks and made a bishop, he is likely to receive a congratulatory note from a priest friend who reminds him that he'll never have another bad meal, nor will he ever hear the truth again! The humor carries with it a hint of truth. Those called to serve as bishops have to remember that they walk on feet of clay and rely on the power of prayer and sacraments to protect them from the dangers of earthly ambition and corrosive pride.

Some bishops view themselves a "little popes," and, failing to understand the shepherding nature of their episcopal role, they attempt to rule rather than lead the "flock" that has been entrusted to their care. That simply doesn't work, and it is regrettable that the bishop is often the last to notice.

Insensitive presidential leadership in higher education is by no means restricted to Catholic colleges and universities, but the Catholic setting probably influenced the choice of words of a frustrated academic vice president in a Catholic university who described once for me his priest–president as being afflicted with a "bad case of the infallibles."

I surely don't want to give the impression that I'm out to beat up on the Catholic clergy; I just want to acknowledge that those of us who love and live in a hierarchical church should welcome the self-imposed discipline of servant leadership as protection against the temptation to forget an important principle articulated by Jesus, our Leader, who described himself as coming among us "not to be served, but to serve, and the give his life as a ransom for many" (Matthew 20:28).

## THE IMPORTANCE OF STAYING IN TOUCH

Extensive research on leadership styles in business has produced this sobering conclusion: "The higher up the ladder a leader climbs, the less accurate his self-assessment is likely to be. The problem is an acute lack of feedback."[5]

Straight across the hierarchical board, not just in religion, but also in business, the military, the corporation, and virtually every other form of organizational life, there is a clear and constant danger of the leader being out of touch. That means being cut off from needed information and honest criticism. And in complex organizations, it is rare that one person has thorough knowledge of all the complicated parts of the whole. Every leader needs expert advice and, it goes without saying, he or she has to be humble enough to accept it.

The *Wall Street Journal* offered the following unorthodox advice in 2008 in an article on leadership: "Don't put one person in charge."[6] Here are the opening paragraphs:

> It's a common corporate approach to a problem. Build a team of experts from different parts of the company and ask them to find a solution. But these teams could be a lot more effective if companies took one radical step: share leadership.
>
> This concept, of course, flies in the face of the traditional idea of how companies should operate—one person in charge, and the others follow. But in a team of specialists, one expert usually doesn't have the know-how to understand all the facets of the job at hand. Instead, a better approach is to share the top duties, so the person in charge at any moment is the one with the key knowledge, skills and abilities for the aspect of the job at hand. When that changes, a new expert should step to the fore.

It is interesting to note, by the way, that this unorthodox approach still seems to prefer that someone, at any given moment, is in charge. The article acknowledges that shared leadership faces big hurdles in companies accustomed to top-down, command-and-control, central authority. Nonetheless, "companies usually hamstring the group right from the start by appointing one team member to lead the crew."

Some readers of the *Houston Chronicle* were surely surprised to find servant leadership as the recommended solution to corporate arrogance seen by that newspaper as the cause of the economic meltdown troubling the nation at the end of 2008. "The American public has had it with arrogant leadership," said the *Chronicle*, which then suggested that businesses take "a quick U-turn from the greed-is-good model and beat a retreat to the tried and true, the ancient and honorable notion of servant leadership."[7] The editorial mentioned Robert Greenleaf and tied his seminal 1970 essay back to its ancient roots.

For the sake of the national economy, the concept of servant leadership deserves a closer look today.

Humbition is a leadership quality that I mentioned back in chapter one. If you have that, you will always want to listen and you will welcome constructive criticism. Indeed you may even find yourself asking for it from time to time, and doing so in an un-intimidating way without giving any impression that you might be fishing for praise.

Kent M. Keith makes the case for servant leadership in a book[8] bearing that title (*The Case for Servant Leadership*) that quotes Peter M. Senge, a Greenleaf admirer and author of *The Fifth Discipline*:

> I believe that the book *Servant Leadership*, and in particular the essay, "The Servant as Leader," which starts the book off, is the most singular and useful statement on leadership that I have read in the past twenty years. Despite the virtual tidal wave of books on leadership during the last few years, there is something different about Bob Greenleaf's essay, something both simpler and more profound. . . . For many years, I simply told people not to waste their time reading all the other managerial leadership books. "If you are really serious about the deeper territory of true leadership," I would say, "read Greenleaf."[9]

And I would add, "Try service." By that I mean, make time in your schedule at every stage of your busy life—not just in your student years—for voluntary community service. Sometimes called "the rent you pay for your citizenship," community service is an opportunity to pay your dues for membership in the human community. Be a giver, not a taker; a sharer, not a grabber. Try service.

## A Time to Serve

My generation (which was labeled "The Greatest Generation" by Tom Brokaw, largely because of its World War II military experience), tended to use the word service with reference to time spent in the military. "When I was in the service . . ." "Where were you in the service?" "He was a buddy of mine in the service."

The generation of Americans who were kids during the Great Depression and in uniform during the Second World War, tended to equate service with time in the military. As returning veterans, many went to college under the G.I. Bill of Rights and moved into positions of influence and responsibility in civilian life. They built the great economic machine that produced the affluence of the postwar years. They became the "movers and shakers" in American life in the second half of the twentieth century. But not all that they produced was unqualifiedly good.

Early in the twenty-first century, an editorial in *America* magazine declared that "consumerism, greed and self-centeredness have surely contributed to the economic morass in which we find ourselves."[10] The magazine called for a new emergence of civilian service that could become so marked as to justify naming the teens and twenty-somethings of today "Generation S"—successor to Generations X and Y mentioned earlier in this book. The editorial quotes the late Albert Schweitzer, Nobel Prize-winner, Scripture scholar, and physician who served the poor in Gabon, West Africa, as offering this advice many years ago to a group of college students in the United States: "I do not know what your destiny will be, but one thing I know; the only ones among you who will really be happy are those who have sought and found how to serve."

One of my Jesuit friends, Fr. Tim Brown, remarked to me recently that there is a current in our contemporary culture that "discourages commitment in general while inspiring an impossible quest for a life free of suffering and sacrifice."

Instead of encouraging the young to "dream the impossible dream" (as the song in *Man of LaMancha* phrased it) in order to get moving in the direction of great achievement, our contemporary culture is inviting the young to experience frustration by setting out on an "impossible quest" for a life free of sacrifice. It just isn't there. The opportunity to serve will always be there, however. Service involves sacrifice to some extent. It also offers an assurance of happiness to those willing to take that route. The easy life is not the happy life; the life of service is.

An editorial version of servant leadership was taken by *Time* magazine in publishing the cover story (September 11, 2007), "A Time to Serve." It contributed some creative ideas to the policy debates that fueled the primary campaign leading up to the 2008 presidential election. *Time* offered a ten-point program that is still there, embalmed in print, waiting to be tried. The successful candidate, Barack Obama, no stranger to community service, would do well to factor that plan into his ambitious policy agenda. He aspires to be a servant leader himself; he can "model the way" of servant leadership for others holding positions of responsibility in both the public and private sectors. His first step in that direction was outspoken support for a 2009 Congressional initiative that increased funding for AmeriCorps that swelled the ranks in this national volunteer service enterprise from 75,000 to 250,000.

## CHARACTERISTICS OF SERVANT LEADERSHIP

Larry Spears is executive director of the Greenleaf Center in Indianapolis, Indiana. He understands servant leadership; his center is dedicated to the "keeper-of-the-flame" mission of explaining it and facilitating the adoption of servant-leadership principles in contemporary organizational life. In his introduction to a book of essays on Greenleaf's contribution, Spears identifies the following ten characteristics of servant leadership:[11]

LISTENING. This involves "a deep commitment to listening intently to others." Servant leaders are able to get at and clarify the will of a group because they "listen receptively."

EMPATHY. This means accepting and recognizing people for "their special and unique spirits," assuming the "good intentions of co-workers," and becoming "skilled empathetic listeners."

HEALING. Quoting Greenleaf, Spears writes: "There is something subtle communicated to one who is being served and led if, implicit in the compact between servant-leader and led, is the understanding that the search for wholeness is something they share." A leader's ability to heal is "a powerful force for transformation and integration."

AWARENESS. Being acutely aware of what is happening around him or her, as well as being in possession of a refined sense of self-awareness, is a necessity for any leader. It can be unsettling at times to see yourself as you really are and to see the problems that loom large around you, but this can be managed if the leader is also emotionally well-balanced and has him- or herself comfortably in hand.

PERSUASION. Positional authority does not confer leadership; the ability to persuade does. "Servant-leaders seek to convince others, rather than coerce compliance." Leaders are consensus builders.

CONCEPTUALIZATION. This is the visionary function. Leaders "must think beyond day-to-day realities." "Servant-leaders must seek a delicate balance between conceptualization and day-to-day focus."

FORESIGHT. "Foresight is a characteristic that enables servant-leaders to understand the lessons from the past, the realities of the present, and the likely consequence of a decision for the future. It is deeply rooted within the intuitive mind." If you unpack the first of those two sentences, you will have a training agenda for the would-be leader, namely, (1) to read history (and thus become familiar with "the lessons from the past"), (2) to stay current with developments in the news (in other words, to stay abreast of "the realities of the present"), and (3) to cultivate a capacity for reflection by pondering "the likely consequence of a decision for the future." Attention to all three of these points will lead to a mastery of both the art and the science of intuition—an essential quality of leadership.

STEWARDSHIP. When applied to leadership, the idea of stewardship means that the leader is not an owner, but more like a manager who holds both position and property in trust for the good of others. The leader is entrusted with the care of resources—human, natural, and forged or fabricated—that constitute the organization. The leader guides the use of all these resources with an eye to the common good. Stewardship involves a commitment to the service of others.

COMMITMENT TO THE GROWTH OF PEOPLE. "Servant-leaders believe that people have an intrinsic value beyond their tangible contributions as workers. As such, servant-leaders are deeply committed to the personal, professional, and spiritual growth of each and every individual within the institution." Admittedly, this sounds idealistic, but not to be missed is the link between this kind of commitment of leader to led, wherever it exists, and the loyalty and productivity that will come from followers fortunate enough to experience this kind of leadership.

BUILDING COMMUNITY. "Servant-leadership suggests that true community can be created among those who work in businesses and other institutions. Greenleaf said: 'All that is needed to rebuild community as a viable life form for large numbers of people is for enough servant-leaders to show the way, not by mass movements, but by each servant-leader demonstrating his [or her] own unlimited ability for a quite specific community-related group.'"

These ten characteristics summarize the idea and the movement that originated in the mind of Robert Greenleaf many years ago. If understood and internalized by would-be leaders today, they can shape the future of leadership across the board in organizational life.

There is a book with a curious title—*The Art of Woo* (I'll explain it in just a moment)—that offers no evidence of familiarity with Greenleaf's work or with the idea of servant leadership. Yet it belongs in the hands of any would-be servant-leader. *Woo* is an acronym for "winning others over." "So what is woo?" ask Richard Shell and Mario Moussa in their introduction:[12] "It is relationship-based persuasion, a strategic process for getting people's attention, pitching your ideas, and obtaining approval for your plans and projects. It is, in short, one of the most important skills in the repertoire of any entrepreneur, employee, or professional manager whose work requires them to rely on influence and persuasion rather than coercion and force." The authors are professors at the Wharton School of the University of Pennsylvania and co-direct the "Strategic Persuasion Workshop" that is housed there.

I've made the point repeatedly in this book that leadership equates with influence and requires persuasion. Command-and-control is dead. Coercion and force have no place in the leadership toolkit; strategic persuasion clearly does. As Larry Spears put it in summarizing Robert Greenleaf's philosophy of leadership, "Servant-leaders seek to convince others, rather than coerce compliance." The "art of woo" helps show the way.

## NOTES:

1. Translated by Hilda Rosner (New York: First Noonday, paperback, 1957).

2. Ibid., 34.

3. Robert K. Greenleaf, *Servant Leadership: A Journey into the Nature of Legitimate Power and Greatness*, (Mahwah, NJ: Paulist Press, 1977), 23–24.

4. Ibid., 76.

5. Daniel Goleman, Richard Boyatzis, and Annie McKee, *Primal Leadership: Learning to Lead with Emotional Intelligence* (Boston: Harvard Business School Press, paperback, 2004), 92.

6. Craig L. Pearce, "Follow the Leaders: You've created a team to solve a problem. Here's some advice: Don't put one person in Charge," *Wall Street Journal* (July 7, 2008): R8.

7. "Servants First: America's business and political titans face an alienated public. It's time for servant leadership," *Houston Chronicle* (December 13, 2008): Sec. 8, p. 8.

8. (Westfield, IN: Greenleaf Center for Servant Leadership, 2008).

9. Ibid., 34.

10. "Generation S," *America* (March 2, 2009): 5.

11. Larry Spears, "Servant Leadership and the Greenleaf Legacy," in Larry C. Spears, ed., *Reflections on Leadership: How Robert K. Greenleaf's Theory of Servant Leadership Influenced Today's Top Management Thinkers* (New York: John Wiley & Sons, 1995), 4–7.

12. G. Richard Shell and Mario Moussa, *The Art of Woo: Using Strategic Persuasion to Sell Your Ideas* (New York: Penguin, 2007), 1.

# APPENDIX

# PRINCIPLES OF IGNATIAN LEADERSHIP

COMPILED BY

## WILLIAM J. BYRON, S.J.,
### AND
## JAMES L. CONNOR, S.J.

# CONTENTS

# INTRODUCTION

This Appendix identifies and explains principles of Ignatian leadership. They are directly connected to the person and life of St. Ignatius of Loyola (1491–1556), founder of the Society of Jesus, the Jesuit Order. They have broad applicability beyond Jesuit organizational life. They apply to leadership in any organization, including leadership in completely secular settings.

But be forewarned. These principles are unapologetically Christian and, when considered in the context of American capitalism, completely countercultural. They can, however, be relevant and practical as part of the leadership toolkit those who are graduates of Jesuit schools, or are influenced by Ignatian spirituality, can carry with them into leadership positions in the twenty-first-century world of business and organizational life. Easy? By no means. Necessary? Yes—if the system is to deliver on its promise of enhancing human life and advancing the common good.

Our primary motivation in assembling the material for this appendix is to encourage those who are responsible for the alumni associations of Jesuit schools, colleges, and universities to invite their graduates—men and women with leadership potential—to form local groups for leadership training, small groups for once-a-month prayer, reflection, and discussion that will enable them to internalize these Ignatian principles and then apply them wherever they happen to be in the world of work and organizational life. For the most part, that application will take place in secular settings, but the origin of these principles is spiritual. It is Ignatian and Jesuit, and thus of particular relevance to graduates of Jesuit schools whose education was rooted in these same faith-based principles.

To begin at the beginning, therefore, we offer here a summary of the life of Ignatius and the order he founded.

## IGNATIUS OF LOYOLA AND THE ORIGINS OF THE SOCIETY OF JESUS

- Iñigo Lopez de Loyola was born in the Basque country of Spain in 1491. Loyola was the name of his ancestors' family house and farmland in northern Spain. Iñigo was his given name; it was later changed to Ignatius. He and his brothers were, in various capacities, in service to the kings of Castile.

- He was seriously wounded by the French at Pamplona in May of 1521 when a cannonball shattered his right leg and wounded his left. During a long recuperation, the future saint had what he describes as his first reasoning, his first reflective experience of the things of God.

- In his third-person autobiography, Ignatius writes, "Up to his twenty-sixth year he was a man given over to the vanities of the world, and took a special delight in the exercise of arms, with a great and vain desire of winning glory." While recuperating, he read from the only two books available—a life of Christ and stories about the saints. He also daydreamed of performing exploits of chivalry to attract the attention of a beautiful noblewoman. He noticed that his reading and his daydreams left him with different feelings. He experienced enthusiasm (consolation) after reading about Christ and the saints, but he felt disconsolate and empty (desolation) in the wake of his daydreams. From this reflective experience, he subsequently developed the practice of what is called "discernment of spirits."

- Upon recovery, he made his way in 1522 to the Benedictine Monastery at Montserrat in Spain, sought out a confessor, and unburdened his soul in a general confession. Then, during a "Knight's Vigil," he hung up his sword and dagger—emblems of a swashbuckling past—at the famous Shrine of the Black Madonna.

- Ignatius spent the next eleven months in prayer in the nearby village of Manresa, where he experienced interior trials as well as divine illuminations. At Manresa, he underwent a spiritual transformation, an experience he would later draw upon in producing his *Spiritual Exercises*, a handbook intended to serve as an outline for a month-long period of prayer and reflection. (Subsequent references in this appendix to the *Book of Spiritual Exercises* will be noted as SpEx with the relevant section number.) Near Manresa, on the banks of the River Cardoner, Ignatius received an illumination that gave him an awareness of the loving presence of God in all things.

• After Manresa, he began referring to himself as "the pilgrim." In 1523, Ignatius made a pilgrimage to Jerusalem to visit the places made holy by the presence of Christ—the Holy Sepulchre, the river Jordan, Bethlehem, and the Mount of Olives.

• At age 33, he began to study grammar with children in Barcelona, so that he could move on to higher studies subsequently in Paris. As one historian put it, "He applied his untrained mind for two laborious years to the mastery of Latin declensions and conjugations" (William V. Bangert, S.J., *A History of the Society of Jesus* (St. Louis, MO: Institute of Jesuit Sources, second edition, 1986), 11–12).

• While pursuing university studies in Alcalá in 1526, he was twice imprisoned by the Inquisition over issues of clothing and preaching, and was jailed again in 1527 in Salamanca when the orthodoxy of his *Book of Spiritual Exercises* and his spiritual teaching were questioned. He was cleared but decided to get out of Spain and head for Paris to further his studies.

• Beginning in 1528, Ignatius spent seven years in Paris studying grammar, philosophy, and theology. It was there, especially at the University of Paris, where, after lengthy preparation, he began giving the *Spiritual Exercises* to his first companions. Gradually, the small band of brothers formed what was to become the Society of Jesus.

• On August 15, 1534, Ignatius and six of his early followers (Peter Faber, Francis Xavier, Simón Rodríguez, Diego Laínez, Alonso Salmerón, and Nicolás Bobadilla) walked from the Latin Quarter of Paris to the chapel of St. Denis on the slope of Montmartre, where Faber, the only priest among them, celebrated Mass and all seven pronounced the vows of poverty, chastity, and a commitment to go on pilgrimage to the Holy Land, failing that, to offer themselves in service to the pope. Three others from the University of Paris—Claude Le Jay, Paschase Broët, and Jean Codure—subsequently joined the group that began to identify itself as the Company of Jesus.

• Ignatius was ordained a priest in Venice on June 24, 1537.

• In a wayside chapel in the village of La Storta in November 1537, while enroute to Rome, Ignatius, accompanied by Faber and Lainez, experienced a vision of God the Father looking upon Christ his Son carrying the Cross. Both looked on Ignatius with love and Ignatius heard the Son say to him, "My desire is that you become my servant." He also heard the Father say, "I shall be propitious to you in Rome."

• In Rome, on September 27, 1540, Pope Paul III gave formal approval to the establishment of the Society of Jesus as a fully canonical religious order.

**********************

The Jesuit Order, founded on Ignatian principles, has numbered outstanding leaders in its own ranks. But the point we want to emphasize here is that, through their educational ministries, the Jesuits have produced notable lay leaders throughout the world who, if they draw on the Ignatian foundations of their Jesuit education, have something quite special to offer. That special something can quite literally set them apart.

As this appendix will demonstrate, Ignatian principles are countercultural; they are grounded in the Gospel of Jesus Christ and stand in opposition to the dominant values of secular culture. Ignatius would identify those dominant secular values as "riches, honor, [and] pride" (SpEx No. 142). The countercultural values he recommends are "poverty, insults, [and] humility" (SpEx No. 146). These will be explained in subsequent sections of this appendix.

The challenge this appendix proposes to meet is to translate authentic Ignatian principles into practical guidelines for effective leadership in contemporary secular culture.

We view ourselves as opening a door; we welcome the reader to step inside. And we remind those who have been touched in any way by Ignatian influences earlier in their lives that Ignatius referred to himself in his early post-conversion years as a pilgrim. May his pilgrimage and yours converge on the path to leadership in a world that needs you more than we can say.

**WJB AND JLC**

# ONE

## FIRST PRINCIPLE AND FOUNDATION

*You are created to praise, reverence, and serve God your Lord, and by this means to save your soul.*

*The other things on the face of the earth are created for you to help you in attaining the end for which you are created.*

*Hence, you are to make use of them in so far as they help you in the attainment of your end, and you must rid yourself of them in so far as they prove a hindrance to you.*

*Therefore, you should make yourself indifferent to all created things, as far as you are allowed free choice and are not under any prohibition. Consequently, as far as you are concerned, you should not prefer health to sickness, riches to poverty, honor to dishonor, a long life to a short life. The same holds for all other things.*

*Your one desire and choice should be what is more conducive to the end for which you are created.*

These several short paragraphs at the beginning of his book of *Spiritual Exercises* constitute what Ignatius of Loyola calls the "First Principle and Foundation" (SpEx No. 23). These words can serve as a personal mission statement for those who see life and faith from an Ignatian and Jesuit perspective. They emphasize God's intent that all humans pursue a single ultimate end in life, namely, loving service. They further stress that all other created things are meant to be a means toward this ultimate goal.

> **THE FIRST PRINCIPLE AND FOUNDATION PROVIDES YOU WITH THESE LEADERSHIP LESSONS:**
>
> *If you keep in mind an awareness of your ultimate purpose, you will choose wisely and lead well. If you are properly "indifferent," that is, free of disordered attachments to created things, your freedom and sense of purpose will provide clear direction for your leadership.*

# Two

## Generosity

> *Dear Lord, teach me to be generous; teach me to serve you as you deserve to be served; to give and not to count the cost; to fight and not to heed the wounds; to toil and not to seek for rest; to labor and not to ask for any reward, save that of knowing that I am doing your will, O God.*
>
> [These words do not appear in the text of the *Spiritual Exercises*; their exact origin is unknown.]

It takes spiritual maturity to catch the Ignatian vision, to see, for example, the "Principle and Foundation" as a basis for living, as a focus that helps one find God and God's love in all things. It takes additional spiritual maturity to be willing to make this famous Ignatian prayer for generosity (presented above) your own.

### THE PRAYER FOR GENEROSITY OFFERS
### THIS LEADERSHIP LESSON:

*Selfless service in accordance with the will of God is an essential characteristic of Ignatian leadership.*

# THREE

## *AD MAIOREM DEI GLORIAM*

---

### *A.M.D.G.*

---

Ignatius of Loyola understood the "greater glory of God" to involve a greater, more generous, and selfless service to others. And, for Ignatius, the help of souls meant the help of bodies too, because he sent his men into hospitals for the care of the poor, into cities for the protection of prostitutes and marginalized people, as well as into classrooms for the religious instruction of unsophisticated children.

Ignatius had a tendency to see life as a struggle between the forces of good and the forces of evil. He was a mystic who saw the world from God's point of view. He founded his religious order, the Jesuits, for like-minded men called, as *he* was, to be contemplatives in action. Ignatius and his first companions committed themselves "to travel anywhere in the world where there is hope of God's greater glory and the good of souls."

The initials *A.M.D.G.* and that phrase, *God's greater glory*, appear on the logo or coat of arms, of many Jesuit institutions and organizations.

THE JESUIT MOTTO—*AD MAIOREM DEI GLORIAM*—
SUGGESTS THE FOLLOWING LEADERSHIP LESSON:

*Ignatian leadership keeps looking higher—to the greater good of others and to the greater glory of God.*

# FOUR

## MAGIS

> *Those who wish to give greater proof of their love, and to distinguish themselves in the service of the eternal King and the Lord of all, will not only offer themselves entirely for the work, but will act against their sensuality and carnal and worldly love, and make offerings of greater value and of more importance in words such as these:*
>
> > *Eternal Lord of all things, in the presence of Thy infinite goodness, and of Thy glorious mother, and of all the saints of Thy heavenly court, this is the offering of myself which I make with Thy favor and help. I protest that it is my earnest desire and my deliberate choice, provided only it is for Thy greater service and praise, to imitate Thee in bearing all wrongs and all abuse and all poverty, both actual and spiritual, should Thy most holy majesty deign to choose and admit me to such a state and way of life. (SpEx No. 98)*

A key meditation in the *Spiritual Exercises* is a prayerful engagement of the imagination that invites the one making the exercises to consider "The Call of an Earthly King" (SpEx No. 91) and to compare it with the call and reign of Christ the King (SpEx No. 95).

Note the words *greater* and *more* in the text; they are the foundation for the Jesuit theme of the *magis*—the fuller stretch, the higher reach, the extra effort. The *magis* resides in the human heart. It frames the Ignatian vision. It focuses any properly Ignatian initiative.

---

THE *MAGIS* THEME SUPPORTS THE FOLLOWING
IGNATIAN LEADERSHIP LESSON:

**Whatever the initiative, the objective is always
to move toward the better and the more.**

---

# FIVE

## INCARNATION

> *This will consist in calling to mind the history of the subject I have to contemplate. Here it will be how the Three Divine Persons look down upon the whole expanse or circuit of all the earth, filled with human beings. Since They see that all are going down to hell, They decree in Their eternity that the Second Person should become man to save the human race* (SpEx No. 102).

There is an Ignatian perspective here, quite literally, a point of view—it is from all eternity. The Ignatian outlook is comprehensive and universal—seeing *"those on the face of the earth, in such great diversity in dress and in manner of acting. Some are white, some black; some at peace, and some at war; some weeping, some laughing; some well, some sick; some coming into the world, and some dying . . . . I will see and consider the Three Divine Persons seated on the royal dais or throne of the Divine Majesty. They look down upon the whole surface of the earth, and behold all nations in great blindness, going down to death and descending into hell* (SpEx No. 106). *I will also hear what the Divine Persons say, that is, 'Let us work the redemption of the human race'"* (SpEx No. 107).

*I will think over what I ought to say to the Three Divine Persons, or to the eternal Word incarnate. . . . According to the light I have received, I will beg for grace to follow and imitate more closely our Lord, who has just become man for me"* (SpEx No. 109).

The contemplation on the Incarnation provides a specifically Ignatian worldview. All things human belong in the Ignatian vision. The Ignatian eye sees the world in the light of eternity, sees all creation as good, and sees participation in the work of redemption as the Jesuit vocation.

---

**THE INCARNATIONAL WORLDVIEW OF ST. IGNATIUS POINTS TO THIS LEADERSHIP LESSON:**

*Accept the fact of human solidarity and acknowledge the importance of excluding no place and no person from any effort to improve the human condition.*

---

# SIX

## POVERTY, INSULTS, HUMILITY

*Consider how the Lord of all the world chooses so many persons, apostles, disciples, and the like. He sends them throughout the whole world, to spread his doctrine among people of every state and condition.*

*Consider the address which Christ our Lord makes to all his servants and friends whom he is sending on this expedition. He recommends that they endeavor to aid all persons, by attracting them, first, to the most perfect spiritual poverty and also, if the Divine Majesty should be served and should wish to choose them for it, even to no less a degree of actual poverty; and second, by attracting them to a desire for reproaches and contempt, since from these results humility.*

*In this way there will be three steps: the first, poverty in opposition to riches; the second, reproaches or contempt in opposition to honor from the world; and the third, humility in opposition to pride. Then from these three steps they should induce people to all the other virtues.*

In the *Book of Spiritual Exercises*, there is a special Meditation on Two Standards, *"the one of Christ, our Supreme Commander and Lord, the other of Lucifer, the mortal enemy of our human nature."* The above paragraphs, excerpted from that meditation, pertain to the Standard of Christ (SpEx 145–46). Ignatius states that *"Christ calls and desires all persons to come under his standard,"* and then invites the retreatant, in an exercise of the imagination, to place him- or herself in the presence of Christ and listen.

---

**THE STANDARD OF CHRIST OFFERS THIS COUNTERCULTURAL IGNATIAN PRINCIPLE OF LEADERSHIP:**

*The three steps to genuine success are poverty as opposed to riches; insults or contempt as opposed to the honor of this world; humility as opposed to pride. "From these three steps let them lead men to all other virtues"* (SpEx 146).

---

In 2008, Jesuit Cardinal Carlos Martini said that delivery of the Spiritual Exercises, particularly the proclamation of the Standard of Christ, is "the service that the Society of Jesus is called to perform for the Church today." To the completely secular eye, that will be seen as no service at all. To the eye of faith, acceptance of the genuine Ignatian vision and values will be seen as a form of liberation that frees a person to become an effective leader.

# SEVEN

# THE CROSS

> *Whoever wishes to serve as a soldier of God beneath the banner of the cross in our Society, which we desire to be designated by the name of Jesus, and to serve the Lord alone and his vicar on earth, should keep in mind that once he has made a solemn vow of perpetual chastity he is a member of a community founded chiefly for this purpose: to strive especially for the progress of souls in Christian life and doctrine and for the propagation of the faith by the ministry of the word, by spiritual exercises and works of charity, and specifically by the education of children and unlettered persons in Christianity.*

There is a famous phrase—*beneath the banner of the cross*—in the Formula of the Institute of the Society of Jesus, approved in 1540 by Pope Paul III, thus marking the formal establishment of the Society of Jesus. That phrase (quoted above) has special meaning for all Jesuits and special relevance in the tradition of Ignatian spirituality.

THE LEADERSHIP PRINCIPLE TO BE DERIVED FROM THIS
PORTION OF THE IGNATIAN AND JESUIT HERITAGE MIGHT
BEST BE COMMUNICATED IN THESE WORDS OF
MAHATMA GANDHI:

*"There comes a time when an individual becomes irresistible and his action becomes all-pervasive in its effects. This is when he reduces himself to zero"* (Gandhi the Man: The Story of His Transformation, 150).

# EIGHT

# THE EXAMEN

(See SpEx No. 43): the examen is an essential and daily component of Ignatian prayer.

---

### Steps in Making the Ignatian Examen

1.      We begin by quieting ourselves. Become aware of God's goodness, the gifts of life and love. Be thankful. Recall that without faith, the eye of love, the human world seems too evil for God to be good, for a good God to exist.

2.      Pray for the grace to see clearly, to understand accurately, and to respond generously to the guidance God is giving us in our daily history.

3.      Review in memory the history of the day (week, month, and so on) in order to be shown concrete instances of the presence and guidance of God and, perhaps, of the activity and influence of evil. These can be detected by paying attention to strong feelings we experienced that may have accompanied or arisen from situations and encounters.

4.      Evaluate these instances in which we have either collaborated with God or yielded to the influence of evil in some way. Express gratitude and regret.

5.      Plan and decide how to collaborate more effectively with God and how, with God's assistance, to avoid or overcome the influence of evil in the future.

Conclude with an "Our Father."

---

(This exercise, which is recommended to be made at mid-day and in the evening before retiring, involves five steps: (1) thanksgiving, (2) request for enlightenment, (3) review of failings (as well as moments of grace), (4) request for pardon, and (5) resolve to mend my ways.

---

**THE LEADERSHIP LESSON TO BE DERIVED**
**FROM THE PRACTICE OF THE EXAMEN IS THIS:**

*Gratitude keeps the leader grounded in God's presence; the daily examen, opening with an expression of gratitude, cultivates awareness of one's call to faithful service.*

---

# NINE

## PRESUPPOSITION

*It is necessary to suppose that every good Christian is more ready to put a good interpretation on another's statement than to condemn it as false. If an orthodox construction cannot be put on a proposition, the one who made it should be asked how he understands it. If he is in error, he should be corrected with all kindness. If this does not suffice, all appropriate means should be used to bring him to a correct interpretation, and so defend the proposition from error.*

This famous presupposition, stated early in the *Book of Spiritual Exercises* (SpEx No. 22), is a guiding principle for all effective leadership. It leads to a predisposition that shapes the character of a good leader.

**THE LEADERSHIP LESSON TO BE LEARNED
FROM THE PRESUPPOSITION IS THIS:**

*Think positively and listen receptively when others speak. Error on the part of another is not to be presumed, although once detected, error is to be corrected with kindness.*

# TEN

# DISCERNMENT OF SPIRITS

> Ignatius offers *"rules for understanding to some extent the different movements produced in the soul and for recognizing those that are good, to admit them, and those that are bad, to reject them"* (SpEx No. 313).

In dealing with persons leading a seriously sinful life, the *evil* spirit will "fill their imagination with sensual delights and gratifications, the more readily to keep them in their vices and increase the number of their sins. With such persons, the *good* spirit . . . will rouse the sting of conscience and fill them with remorse" (SpEx No. 314).

"In the case of those who . . . seek to rise in the service of God to greater perfection, . . . it is characteristic of the *evil* spirit to harass with anxiety, to afflict with sadness, to raise obstacles backed by fallacious reasonings that disturb the soul. Thus he [the evil spirit] seeks to prevent the soul from advancing. It is characteristic of the *good* spirit, however, to give courage and strength, consolations, tears, inspirations, and peace. This he [the good spirit] does by making all easy, by removing all obstacles so that the soul goes forward in doing good" (SpEx No. 315).

First, you have to locate yourself (are you on the slippery slope to sin or the upward path to virtue?); then you identify the source (good or evil spirit) of the feeling or mood you are experiencing. If you are on a downward moral slope, the feeling of delight is coming from the evil spirit; a feeling of remorse is from the good spirit. If you are on the moral upside, sadness and anxiety have their source in the evil spirit; a sense of peace is from the good spirit.

Note especially that good and evil spirits are at work in the world. The "push" or "pull" within you can be from God or not from God. You have to discern the origin of a particular "movement" or feeling, and in order to do that you have to give yourself a fair reading of where you stand before God. Are you moving away, on the downward slope—or trying to let yourself be drawn toward God, moving in the right direction? Beware of anxiety and discouragement when you are doing your best to move toward God; they are from the evil spirit! Heed the pangs of conscience when you are on the down side; the good spirit is trying to get through to you.

---

**THE LEADERSHIP LESSON TO BE LEARNED FROM AN AWARENESS OF THESE "MOVEMENTS" OF YOUR SOUL IS THIS:**

*Leaders decide; deciding is essential to leadership. But leaders first have to discern accurately in order to decide well. Hence they must first locate themselves (self-awareness) and be sufficiently "quiet" to detect the movements of competing spirits in a world where both good and evil spirits are at work.*

---

# ELEVEN

# CONSOLATION

> *I call it consolation when an interior movement is aroused in the soul, by which it [the soul] is inflamed with love of its Creator and Lord, and as a consequence, can love no creature on the face of the earth for its own sake, but only in the Creator of them all. It is likewise consolation when one sheds tears that move [him or her] to the love of God, whether it be because of sorrow for sins, or because of the sufferings of Christ our Lord, or for any other reason that is immediately directed to the praise and service of God. Finally, I call consolation every increase of faith, hope, and love, and all interior joy that invites and attracts to what is heavenly and to the salvation of one's soul by filling it with peace and quiet in Christ our Lord* (SpEx No. 316).

*Consolation* is a feeling, a movement within the soul. Ask yourself how you are feeling, and consolation, as described by Ignatius, may well describe your feeling. If that's the case, great! Presumably, the source of the consolation that Ignatius describes is God. "In consolation, the good spirit guides and counsels us" (SpEx No. 318).

"God alone can give consolation to the soul without any previous cause . . . that is, without any preceding perception or knowledge of any subject by which a soul might be led to such a consolation through its own acts of intellect and will" (SpEx No.320). "If a cause precedes, both the good angel and the evil spirit can give consolation to a soul, but for a quite different purpose. The good angel consoles for the progress of the soul, that it may advance and rise to what is more perfect. The evil spirit consoles for purposes that are the contrary, and that afterwards he [the evil spirit] might draw the soul to . . . perverse intentions and wickedness" (SpEx No. 331). "It is a mark of the evil spirit to assume the appearance of an angel of light" (SpEx No. 332).

---

**HERE IS A LEADERSHIP LESSON TO BE DERIVED FROM THE IGNATIAN DESCRIPTION OF "CONSOLATION":**

*An emotional environment of "peace and quiet," especially in the midst of great crisis and stress, is essential for effective leadership. Ignatius associates hope with consolation. Without hope in his or her heart, it is useless for a leader to try to lead.*

# TWELVE

## DESOLATION

*I call desolation what is entirely the opposite of what is de-scribed [above, as consolation]. [Desolation is] darkness of soul, turmoil of spirit, inclination to what is low and earthly, restless-ness rising from many disturbances and temptations which lead to want of faith, want of hope, want of love. The soul is wholly slothful, tepid, sad, and separated, as it were, from its Creator and Lord. For just as consolation is the opposite of desolation, so the thoughts that spring from consolation are the opposite of those that spring from desolation (SpEx No. 317).*

*In time of desolation we should never make any change, but re-main firm and constant in the resolution and decision which guided us the day before the desolation, or in the decision to which we adhered in the preceding consolation. For just as in consolation the good spirit guides and counsels us, so in deso-lation the evil spirit guides and counsels. Following his counsels we can never find the way to a right decision (SpEx No. 318).*

*Though in desolation we must never change our former reso-lutions, it will be very advantageous to intensify our activity against the desolation. We can insist more upon prayer, upon meditation, and on much examination of ourselves. We can make an effort in a suitable way to do some penance (SpEx No. 319).*

*When one is in desolation, he should be mindful that God has left him to his natural powers to resist the different agitations and temptations of the enemy in order to try him. He can resist with the help of God, which always remains, though he may not clearly perceive it (SpEx No. 320).*

*When one is in desolation, he should strive to persevere in patience (SpEx No. 321).*

The principal reasons why we suffer from desolation are three: (1) "we have been tepid and slothful or negligent in our exercises of piety;" (2) "God wishes to try us, to see how much we are worth and how much we will advance in His service and praise when left without the generous reward of consolations"; (3) "God wishes to give us a true knowledge and understanding of ourselves" (SpEx No. 322). Desolation means feeling disconsolate and empty.

HERE IS A LEADERSHIP LESSON TO BE DERIVED FROM THE IGNATIAN IDEA OF DESOLATION:

*Patience protects the self-aware leader from an unwise reversal of course when darkness sets in; the absence of hope, faith, and love signals the need to wait patiently for clarity and a certain stillness of soul before taking action.*

# THIRTEEN

# LOVE

> *Take, Lord, and receive all my liberty, my memory,*
> *my understanding, and my entire will, all that I have*
> *and possess. Thou hast given all to me. To Thee, O*
> *Lord, I return it. Dispose of it wholly according to*
> *Thy will. Give me Thy love and Thy grace, for this*
> *is sufficient for me* **(SpEx No. 234).**

St. Ignatius provides a famous pre-note to the "Contemplation to Attain the Love of God" (SpEx No. 230): "Before presenting this exercise it will be good to call attention to two points: The first is that love ought to manifest itself in deeds rather than in words. The second is that love consists in a mutual sharing of goods. For example, the lover gives and shares with the beloved what he possesses, or something of that which he has or is able to give; and vice versa, the beloved shares with the lover. . . . Thus one always gives to the other."

Ignatius then places the one making the Exercises "in the presence of God our Lord and of His angels and saints" (SpEx No. 232). Then he has the exercitant ask "for an intimate knowledge of the many blessings received, that filled with gratitude for all, I may in all things love and serve the Divine Majesty" (SpEx No. 233). Next, "I will ponder with great affection how much God our Lord has done for me, and how much he has given me of what He possesses, and finally, how much, as far as He can, the same Lord desires to give Himself to me according to His divine decrees. Then I will reflect upon myself, and consider, according to all reason and justice, what I ought to offer the Divine Majesty, that is, all I possess and myself with it. Thus, as one would do who is moved by great feeling, I will make this offering of myself (SpEx No. 234):

Next, Ignatius directs the retreatant "to reflect how God dwells in creatures: in the elements giving them existence, in the plants giving them life, in the animals conferring upon them sensation, in man bestowing understanding. He dwells in me and gives me being, life, sensation, intelligence, and makes a temple of me, besides having created me in the likeness and image of the Divine Majesty" (SpEx No. 235). This awareness prompts one to pray, in the words quoted above: "Take, Lord, and receive . . . ."

---

**THE LEADERSHIP LESSONS TO BE DRAWN FROM THESE CONSIDERATIONS ARE THESE:**

*Leadership is an act of love. Reminders of God's love are everywhere in creation. Leadership, as an exercise of love, is a privileged way to encounter the presence of God in both leader and led.*

# FOURTEEN

# LOVE WILL DECIDE EVERYTHING

> *Nothing is more practical than finding God, that is, than falling in love in a quite absolute, final way. What you are in love with, what seizes your imagination, will affect everything.*
> *It will decide what will get you out of bed in the morning,*
> *what you will do with your evenings,*
> *how you will spend your weekends,*
> *what you will read,*
> *who you know,*
> *what breaks your heart,*
> *and what amazes you with joy and gratitude.*
> *So fall in love, stay in love, and it will decide everything.*
>
> **—Pedro Arrupe, Superior General of the
> Society of Jesus, 1965–83**

Pedro Arrupe was a great Jesuit leader. Like St. Ignatius, he led from a desk in Rome, although modern means of travel enabled him to visit Jesuit works worldwide. This reflection of his is rooted in his own prayerful consideration over the years of the "Contemplation to Attain the Love of God," which was with him at the desk and in all his travels.

FROM THIS REFLECTION, SEVERAL IGNATIAN LEADERSHIP LESSONS FLOW:

*Love sets priorities. Without priorities, leadership energy is dissipated.*

*Pedro Arrupe suggests that if love sets the leadership agenda, it "will decide everything."*

# FIFTEEN

## LEADERSHIP QUALITIES OF A JESUIT GENERAL

In the *Constitutions of the Society of Jesus*, authored by Ignatius, the qualities to be found in a superior general are listed (*Constitutions*, Part IX, Chapter 2, Nos. 723–35). Among them are union with God in prayer; love of fellow Jesuits; humility; self control; magnanimity and fortitude of soul; understanding and judgment; discretion; being "vigilant and solicitous to undertake enterprises"; being energetic; "reputation, high esteem and whatever else aids toward prestige with those within and without [the Society]"; being "outstanding in every virtue."

"If any of these aforementioned qualities should be wanting, there should at least be no lack of great probity and of love for the Society, nor of good judgment accompanied by sound learning."

After outlining the ideals relating to the one who governs and the style of governance, the *Constitutions* state: "He will achieve this kind of government primarily by the influence and example of his life, by his charity and love of the Society, . . . by his prayer, . . . and by his sacrifices" (No. 790). It is also worth noting that Ignatius acknowledged the importance of prestige in support of effective leadership, while insisting that both good reputation and prestige be grounded in humility.

---

**HERE ARE THE LEADERSHIP LESSONS TO BE DRAWN FROM THESE CRITERIA:**

*There is no substitute for good character in a leader. Love of the organization and its members is essential, as are magnanimity of spirit and generosity of heart. Prestige and good reputation are not to be disdained by a leader, just contained within humility.*

---

# Sixteen

# Choice or "Election"

There is in the Spiritual Exercises an "Introduction to Making a Choice of a Way of Life" (No. 169), a section on "Matters about Which a Choice Should be Made" (Nos. 170–74), another section on "Three Times When a Correct and Good Choice of a Way of Life May be Made" (Nos. 175–77), and still another dealing with "Two Ways of Making a Choice of a Way of Life in the Third Time" [a time of tranquility] which includes the "First Way of Making a Good and Correct Choice of a Way of Life" (Nos. 178–83) and the "Second Way of Making a Correct and Good Choice of a Way of Life" (Nos. 184–88).

"There are things that fall under an unchangeable choice, such as the priesthood, marriage, etc. There are others with regard to which our choice may be changed, for example, to accept or relinquish a benefice, to receive or renounce temporal goods" (SpEx No. 171). Our leadership concern here is with choices that "may be changed."

The three times when a "correct and good" choice of a way of life may be made are these: (1) when God "so moves and attracts the will that a devout soul without hesitation, or the possibility of hesitation, follows what has been manifested to it" (SpEx No. 175); (2) when "much light and understanding are derived through experience of desolations and consolations and discernment of diverse spirits" (SpEx No. 176); and (3) in a "time of tranquility . . . a time when the soul is not agitated by different spirits, and has free and peaceful use of its natural powers" (SpEx No. 177).

Focusing now on making a "choice subject to change" and making it in a "time of tranquility," these guidelines (SpEx No. 179–82) are helpful: (1) It is necessary to keep as my aim the end for which I am created." (2) "I must be indifferent." (3) "I should be like a balance at equilibrium . . . ready to follow whatever I perceive is more for the glory and praise of God and the salvation of my soul." (4) After weighing the advantages and disadvantages, "I will consider which alternative appears more reasonable . . . and come to a decision in the matter under deliberation because of weightier motives presented to my reason, and not because of any sensual inclination." There are four additional rules (SpEx Nos.184–88): (1) "The love that moves . . . one to choose must descend from above, that is, from the love of God." (2) "I should represent to myself someone I have never seen or known, and whom I would like to see practice all perfection" and tell that person what is best to do and then do the same myself. (3) Next, "consider what . . . action I would wish to have followed in making the present choice if I were at the moment of death" and make my decision accordingly. (4) Finally, place myself in the "presence of my Judge on the last day, and reflect what decision in the present matter I would then wish to have made."

---

**HERE IS THE LEADERSHIP LESSON RELATED TO ALL OF THIS:**

*In a time of tranquility, the will of the leader can become aligned with the will of God. When that happens, good choices will be made.*

---

# SEVENTEEN

# ADMONITOR

> *"The Society should have with the superior general . . . some person who . . . [a]fter he has had recourse to God in prayer . . . [will] admonish the general about anything in him which he thinks will be more conducive to greater service and glory to God. The general in turn ought to be content with what is provided"* (**Constitutions of the Society of Jesus**, **Part IX, Chapter 4, No. 770).

The above excerpt from the *Constitutions* comes from the hand of Ignatius and refers to what he called the "provident care" that the Society should exercise in regard to the superior general. The caring function is called admonition; the person who exercises this care is called the admonitor. Note that the admonitor has no authority, but enjoys the confidence of the general. He has access to the general at any time. And note further that the general "ought to be content" to have an admonitor. The admonitor is appointed by the Congregation that elected the general.

The motivation for all of this is to assure that the Society's service to others is the best possible.

**HERE IS THE LEADERSHIP LESSON TO BE DERIVED
FROM THE EXISTENCE OF THIS FUNCTION:**

*Every leader should have someone who is willing and able to tell him, in confidentiality and with absolute freedom, the unvarnished truth. The organization suffers in a situation where "even your best friend won't tell you."*

# EIGHTEEN

## GLOBALIZATION

"The more universal the good is, the more it is divine."

> *"To be able to meet the spiritual needs of souls in many regions with greater facility and with greater security for those who go among them for this purpose, the superiors of the Society . . . will have authority to send any of the Society's members whomsoever to whatsoever place these superiors think it more expedient to send them" (Constitutions, No. 618). "To proceed more successfully in this sending of subjects to one place or another, one should keep the greater service of God and the more universal good as the norm to hold before his eyes as the norm to hold oneself on the right course" (Constitutions, No. 622a). "The more universal the good is, the more it is divine. Therefore preference ought to be given to those persons and places which, through their own improvement, become a cause which can spread the good accomplished to many others who are under their influence or take guidance from them" (Constitutions, No. 622d).*

The expression, "the more universal the good is, the more it is divine," (*quo universalius, eo divinius*) is a classic Ignatian principle. Ignatius, in incorporating this phrase into the Constitutions of the Society, gives further evidence of his global perspective, always seeking broader influence, a wider reach, the greater good, and, of course, the greater glory of God. He therefore takes a "whomsoever-whatsoever" approach to apostolic assignments, not in the sense that anyone can do anything anywhere, but in the more magnanimous outlook that no one should be held in one place when there is greater need and greater good to be achieved by this one in some other (often more distant) place.

---

**THE LEADERSHIP LESSON TO BE TAKEN FROM**
**"QUO UNIVERSALIUS, EO DIVINIUS" IS THIS:**

*Not only is the "big picture" important for effective leadership, casting the leadership net as widely as possible is characteristic of Ignatian leadership.*

# NINETEEN

# OUR WAY OF PROCEEDING

> *"Certain attitudes, values, and patterns of behavior join together to become what has been called the Jesuit way of proceeding. The characteristics of our way of proceeding were born in the life of St. Ignatius and shared by his first companions. Jerome Nadal writes that 'the form of the Society is in the life of Ignatius.' 'God set him up as a living example of our way of proceeding.'"*
>
> —Decree 26, 34th General Congregation of the
> Society of Jesus (1995).

The expression "our way of proceeding" was used by Ignatius in the Constitutions and elsewhere. The 34th General Congregation summarized this "way" by employing the following set of headings in its 26th Decree titled "Characteristics of our Way of Proceeding": (1) Deep Personal Love for Jesus Christ; (2) Contemplative in Action; (3) An Apostolic Body in the Church; (4) Solidarity with Those Most in Need; (5) Partnership with Others; (6) Called to Learned Ministry; (7) Men Sent, Always Available for New Missions; (8) Ever Searching for the *Magis*.

The "Conclusion" to Decree 26 reads: "Our way of proceeding is a way of challenge. But "this way of proceeding is the reason why every son of the Society will always act and react in a consistently Jesuit and

Ignatian way, even in the most unforeseen circumstances" (Pedro Arrupe, *Our Way of Proceeding*, n. 55, AR 17 (1979): 719).

---

**THE LEADERSHIP LESSON TO BE DRAWN FROM "OUR WAY OF PROCEEDING" IS CONTAINED IN THIS PRAYER OF PEDRO ARRUPE:**

*Lord, meditating on "our way of proceeding,"*
*I have discovered that the ideal of our way of*
*acting is your way of acting.*
*Give me that sensus Christi that I may feel*
*with your feelings, with*
*the sentiments of your heart, which basically are*
*love for your Father and*
*love for all men and women.*
*Teach me how to be compassionate to the suffering,*
*to the poor,*
*the blind, the lame, and the lepers.*
*Teach us your way so that it becomes our way today,*
*so that we may*
*come closer to the great ideal of St. Ignatius:*
*to be companions of Jesus,*
*collaborators in the work of redemption.*

# TWENTY

## THE MANNER IS ORDINARY

> *"For good reasons, having always in view God's greater service, the manner of living as to external things is ordinary . . . ."*
>
> **(St. Ignatius of Loyola, *Institute* (Rule) *of the Society of Jesus*, Chapter 1, No. 8).**

The full text of this rule goes on to specify that there are no regular penances or austerities required of Jesuits, as was typically the case in other religious orders. Fasts and penances could weaken a person and impede apostolic effectiveness. Moreover, it was the personal experience of Ignatius that certain austerities and penitential practices repelled others and hindered greater good. Jesuits, while living their vow of poverty, were to dress and follow a lifestyle comparable to diocesan priests.

"The manner is ordinary" translates practically into an absence of privilege and perquisites; it mandates the use of material things in a way that makes the Jesuit available as well as accountable to those he is there to serve. This famous phrase, "The Manner is Ordinary," was chosen by Jesuit Father John LaFarge as the title for his 1954 autobiography.

**HERE IS A LEADERSHIP LESSON TO BE DRAWN FROM THE IGNATIAN EXPRESSION "THE MANNER IS ORDINARY":**

*The purpose of leadership is service and they lead most effectively who refuse to let themselves enjoy a lifestyle that is too far removed in privilege and possessions from those they hope to serve.*

# TWENTY-ONE

# THIRD DEGREE OF HUMILITY

> *"The third Kind of Humility. This is the most perfect kind of humility. It consists in this. If we suppose the first and second kind attained, then whenever the praise and glory of God would be equally served, I desire and choose poverty with Christ poor, rather than riches, in order to imitate and be in reality more like Christ our Lord; I choose insults with Christ loaded with them, rather than honors; I desire to be accounted as worthless and a fool for Christ, rather than to be esteemed as wise and prudent in this world. So Christ was treated before me"* (SpEx No. 167).

There are, according to St. Ignatius, three levels of alignment of one's will with the will of God. The first is necessary for salvation. "I so subject and humble myself as to obey the law of God our Lord in all things" (SpEx No. 165). This level of humility is thus understood as obedience to God's will. The second kind or degree of humility means "that I neither desire nor am I inclined to have riches rather than poverty, to seek honor rather than dishonor, to desire a long life rather than a short life, provided only in either alternative I would promote equally the service of God our Lord and the salvation of my soul" (SpEx No. 166). This is what we've seen earlier in this book as "indifference"—humility thus understood eliminates one's own desire as finally decisive. The third or highest degree of

269

humility, outlined above, implies the desire to be like Christ who is poor, despised, and deemed foolish.

This third is a high level or degree of sanctity—a goal to be sought, a condition to be valued. Ignatius says that the one making the Exercises "should beg our Lord to deign to choose him [or her] for this kind of humility . . . provided equal praise and service be given to the Divine Majesty" (SpEx No. 168).

This is a way of promoting the imitation of Christ and saying simply that Christ is the norm.

---

**THIS IS THE LEADERSHIP LESSON TO BE DERIVED FROM A CONSIDERATION OF THE THIRD DEGREE OF HUMILITY:**

*In a secular setting completely unrelated to the context of Ignatian spirituality, namely, a back-office service company SEI Investments in Oak, Pennsylvania, the word* **humbition** *is held up for praise and imitation. "At SEI, the most effective leaders exude a blend of humility and ambition—humbition—that relies on the power of persuasion rather than formal authority"* **(See William C. Taylor and Polly LaBarre,** *Mavericks at Work,* **New York: Harper Paperback, 2008, p. 240).** *The Ignatian leadership principle that is relevant here is that humility, as demonstrated in the life of Christ, is a highly desirable leadership characteristic. Think of it as humbition.*

# BIBLIOGRAPHY

Alsop, Joseph. *FDR: 1882–1945*. New York: Random House Gramercy, 1982.

Ambrose, Stephen E. *The Supreme Commander: The War Years of General Dwight D. Eisenhower*. New York: Doubleday, 1970.

Badaracco, Joseph L., Jr. *Leading Quietly: An Unorthodox Guide to Doing the Right Thing*. Boston: Harvard Business School Press, 2002.

Barone, Orlando R. "A Voice Can Speak Volumes," *Philadelphia Inquirer* (March 1, 2009).

Bartlett, Thomas. "Phoenix Risen: How a History Professor Became the Pioneer of the For-Profit Revolution," *The Chronicle of Higher Education* (July 10, 2009): 1, A10–A13.

Benjamin, Martin. *Splitting the Difference: Compromise and Integrity in Ethics and Politics*. Lawrence: University Press of Kansas, 1990.

Bennis, Warren. *On Becoming a Leader*. New York: Basic Books, revised edition, 2003.

Blaisdell, Bob, ed. *The Wit and Wisdom of Abraham Lincoln*. Mineola, NY: Dover, 2005.

Bolt, Robert. *A Man for All Seasons*. New York: Random House, 1960.

Branch, Taylor. *Parting the Waters: America in the King Years 1954–63*. New York: Simon and Schuster, 1988.

Bryant, Adam. "The Divine, Too, Is in the Details," *New York Times* (June 21, 2009).
———. "In Praise of All That Grunt Work," *New York Times* (May 31, 2009).

———. "Think 'We' for Best Results," an interview with Nell Minor, *New York Times* (April 19, 2009).

Burns, James MacGregor. *Leadership*. New York: Harper & Row, 1978.

Campbell, Andrew, and Stuart Sinclair. "The Crisis: Mobilizing Boards for Change," *McKinsey Quarterly* (February 6, 2009).

Dalmases, Cándido de, S.J. *Ignatius of Loyola, Founder of the Jesuits*. St. Louis: Institute of Jesuit Sources, 1985.

Carlin, John. *Playing the Enemy: Nelson Mandela and the Game That Made a Nation*. New York: Penguin, 2008.

Carter, Stephen. *Integrity*. New York: Harper Perennial, 1996.

"The C.E.O., Now Playing on YouTube," *New York Times* (May 10, 2009)..

Churchill, John. "Liberal Arts for Leadership," *The Key Reporter* 74, no. 3 (Fall 2009).

Collins, James C. *Good to Great: Why Some Companies make the Leap and Others Don't*. New York: HarperCollins, 2001.

———, and Jerry I. Porras. *Built to Last: Successful Habits of Visionary Companies*. New York: HarperCollins, 1994.

Commager, Henry Steele. *The American Mind: An Interpretation of American Thought and Character since the 1880s*. New Haven, CT: Yale University Press, 1950.

Cooper, Morton. *Change Your Voice, Change Your Life: A Quick, Simple Plan for Finding and Using Your Natural, Dynamic Voice*. Los Angeles: Voice and Speech Company of America, 17th printing, 1999.

Covey, Stephen R. *The Seven Habits of Highly Effective People: Restoring the Character Ethic*. New York: Simon & Schuster, 1989.

Crittenden, Michael R. "Sheila Bair, Chairman, Federal Deposit Insurance Corp.," *Wall Street Journal* (November 10, 2008).

Dalmases, Cándido de, S.J. *Ignatius of Loyola, Founder of the Jesuits*, trans. Jerome Aixala. St. Louis: Institute of Jesuit Sources, 1985.

Downes, Lawrence E. "Still Singing," *New York Times* (May 5, 2009).

Easaran, Eknath. *Gandhi the Man: The Story of His Transformation*. Tomales, CA: Blue Mountain Press, 1997.

Eichel, Larry. "Next Up: Test of Obama as Leader," *Philadelphia Inquirer* (November 9, 2008).

"Eliza Doolittle Dept. Correcting Caroline," *New Yorker* (January 12, 2009): 18–19.

Emerson, Ralph Waldo. "Self-Reliance." Mount Vernon, NY: Peter Pauper Press, 1949.

"Ensemble Acting, in Business," *New York Times* (June 7, 2009).

"Feedback in Heaping Helpings," *New York Times* (March 29, 2009).

"For Homeland Security Nominee, Good Leadership Is in the Details," *New York Times* (January 15, 2009); online at w.nytimes.com/2009/01/15/us/politics/15napolitano.html.

"Four E's (a Jolly Good Fellow): Do the Democratic Presidential Candidates Have What It Takes to Lead?" *Wall Street Journal* (January 23, 2004).

Futrell, John C., S.J. *Making an Apostolic Community of Love*. St Louis: Institute of Jesuit Sources, 1970.

Gardner, Howard. *Leading Minds: An Anatomy of Leadership*. New York: Basic Books, 1995.

Gardner, John W. *On Leadership*. New York: Free Press, 1990.
————. *Self-Renewal*. New York: Harper Colophon, 1963.

Garten, Jeffrey E. *The Mind of the C.E.O.* New York: Perseus Basic, paperback, 2002.

"Generation S," *America* (March 2, 2009).

Goleman, Daniel, Richard Boyatzis, and Annie McKee. *Primal Leadership: Learning to Lead with Emotional Intelligence*. Boston: Harvard Business School Press, paperback, 2004.

Golin, Al. *Trust or Consequences: Build Trust Today or Lose Your Market Tomorrow*. New York: American Management Association, 2003.

Goodwin, Doris Kearns. *Team of Rivals: The Political Genius of Abraham Lincoln*. New York: Simon and Schuster, 2005.

Greenleaf, Robert. *Servant Leadership: A Journey into the Nature of Legitimate Power and Greatness*. Mahwah, NJ: Paulist Press, 25th anniversary edition, 2002.

Gupta, Rajat, and Jim Wendler. "Leading Change: An Interview with the CEO of P&G," *McKinsey Quarterly* (July 2005).

Halpern, Belle Linda, and Kathy Lubar. *Leadership Presence: Dramatic Techniques to Reach Out, Motivate, and Inspire*. New York: Gotham Books, 2004.

Haughney, Christine. "Fordham Seeks to Build on Manhattan Campus," *New York Times* (January 23, 2009).

Hauptman, Arthur M., "Strategic Responses to Financial Challenges," pamphlet published by the Association of Governing Boards of Universities and Colleges (1998).

Hayward, Steven F. *Churchill on Leadership: Executive Success in the Face of Adversity*. New York: Random House Gramercy, 2004.

Heifetz, Ronald. *Leadership Without Easy Answers*. Cambridge, MA: The Belknap Press of Harvard University Press, 1994.

————, and Marty Linsky. *Leadership on the Line: Staying Alive through the Dangers of Leading*. Boston: Harvard Business School Press, 2002.

————, Alexander Grashow, and Marty Linsky. *The Practice of Adaptive Leadership: Tools and Tactics for Changing Your Organization and the World*. Boston: Harvard Business School Press, 2009.

"He Was Promotable, After All," *New York Times* (May 3, 2009).

Herold, David M., and Donald B. Fedor. *Change the Way You Lead Change*. Stanford, CA: Stanford University Press, 2008.

Hesse, Hermann. *The Journey to the East*, trans. Hilda Rosner. New York: First Noonday, paperback, 1957.

Hughes, Emmett John. *Ordeal of Power*. New York: Atheneum, 1963.

Iacocca, Lee. *Where Have All the Leaders Gone?* New York: Scribner, 2007.

Ignatius of Loyola. *Autobiography: St. Ignatius' Own Story*, trans. W. J. Young, S.J. Chicago: Regnery, 1956.

"In a Word, He Wants Simplicity," *New York Times* (May 24, 2009).

"In Defense of Obamanomics," *Wall Street Journal* (March 9, 2009).

Junger, Sebastian. *The Perfect Storm: A True Story of Men against the Sea*. New York: Harper, 1997.

Kakutani, Michiko. "The Deciders and How They Decide," *New York Times* (May 8, 2009).

Kanter, Rosabeth Moss. *Confidence: How Winning Streaks and Losing Streaks Begin and End*. New York: Three Rivers Press, 2004.

Kantor, Jodi, and Javier C. Hernandez. "A Harvard Lightning Rod Finds Path to Renewal," *New York Times* (December 7, 2008).

Katzenbach, Nicholas deB. *Some of It Was Fun: Working with RFK and LBJ*. New York: Norton, 2008.

"The Keeper of That Tapping Pen," *New York Times* (March 22, 2009).

Keith, Kent M. *The Case for Servant Leadership*. Westfield, IN: Greenleaf Center for Servant Leadership, 2008.

Kellerman, Barbara. *Followership: How Followers Are Creating Change and Changing Leaders*. Boston: Harvard Business Press, 2008.

Kelly, Chris. "We Are in This Together," (Scranton) *Sunday Times* (September 28, 2008).

Kennedy, Robert G., Gary Atkinson, and Michael Naughton, eds. *The Dignity of Work: John Paul II Speaks to Managers and Workers*. Lanham, MD: University Press of America, 1994.

Kenniston, Kenneth. *Young Radicals: Notes on Committed Youth*. New York: Harcourt Brace, 1968.

"Knock-Knock: It's the C.E.O.," *New York Times* (April 12, 2009).

Koehler, Michael. *Coaching Character at Home: Strategies for Raising Responsible Teens*. Notre Dame, IN: Ave Maria, 2003.

Kotter, John P. *Leading Change*. Boston: Harvard Business School Press, 1996.

Kouzes, James M., and Barry Z. Posner. *The Leadership Challenge*. San Francisco: Jossey-Bass, fourth edition, 2007.

"Leadership Lessons from Abraham Lincoln: A Conversation with Historian Doris Kearns Goodwin," *Harvard Business Review* (April 2009): 43–47.

Lencioni, Peter. *Death by Meeting: A Leadership Fable*. San Francisco: Jossey-Bass, 2004.

Mark Leibovich. "Speaking Freely, Sometimes, Biden Finds Influential Role," *New York Times* (March 29, 2009).

Liedtka, Jeanne, Robert Rosen, and Robert Wiltbank. *The Catalyst: How You Can Become an Extraordinary Growth Leader*. New York: Crown Business, 2009.

Lodge, George C. *The New American Ideology*. New York: New York University Press, paperback, 1986.

Lonergan, Bernard. *Method in Theology*. St. Louis: Herder & Herder, 1972.

Lopez, Isabel O. "Becoming a Servant-Leader: The Personal Development Path," in Spears, ed., *Reflections on Leadership*.

Lowenstein, Roger. *Origins of the Crash: The Great Bubble and Its Undoing*. New York: Penguin, 2004.

Lowney, Chris. *Heroic Leadership: Best Practices from a 450-Year-Old Company that Changed the World*. Chicago: Loyola Press, 2003.

Luntz, Frank. "Words That Pack Power," *Business Week* (November 3, 2008).

Lynch, William F., S.J. *Images of Hope: Imagination as Healer of the Hopeless*. New York: Mentor–Omega, 1966.

Macht, Norman L. *Connie Mack and the Early Years of Baseball*. Lincoln: University of Nebraska Press, 2007.

Marshall, Edward M. *Transforming the Way We Work: The Power of the Collaborative Workplace*. New York: American Management Association, 1995.

McCullough, David. *Truman*. New York: Simon & Schuster, 1992.

Murray, Alan. "Indiscreet E-Mail Claims a Fresh Casualty," *Wall Street Journal* (March 9, 2005).

Nunberg, Geoffrey. "Initiating Mission-Critical Jargon Reduction," *New York Times* (August 3, 2003).

Parks, Sharon Daloz. *Leadership Can Be Taught: A Bold Approach for a Complex*. Boston: Harvard Business School Press, 2005.

Pearce, Craig L. "Follow the Leaders: You've created a team to solve a problem. Here's some advice: Don't put one person in Charge," *Wall Street Journal* (July 7, 2008).

"Perfect Storm Warning: Don't Take It as an Excuse," *Washington Post* (December 10, 2008).

"Q&A with Al Golin," *The Public Relations Strategist* (Fall 2003): 28–29.

Quain, Bill, Joseph J. Corabdi, and Jack Krutsick. *College Success for Less: Pay Less and Get More—The Insiders' Guide for Parents*. Ocean City, NJ: Wales, 2008.

Richin, Roberta. *Connecting Character to Conduct: Helping Students Do the Right Things*. Alexandria, VA: Association for Supervision and Curriculum Development, 2000.

Ricks, Tomas E. *Fiasco: The American Military Adventure in Iraq*. New York: Penguin, 2006.

Rodman, Peter W. *Presidential Command*, with introduction by Henry Kissinger. New York: Alfred A. Knopf, 2009.

Sampson, Anthony. *Mandela: The Authorized Biography*. New York: Alfred A. Knopf, 1999.

Senge, Peter M. *The Fifth Discipline*: *The Art and Practice of the Learning Organization*. Garden City, NY: Doubleday, paperback, 2006.

———. "Robert Greenleaf's Legacy: A New Foundation for Twenty-First Century Institutions," in Spears, ed., *Reflections on Leadership*, 229.

"Servants First: America's business and political titans face an alienated public. It's time for servant leadership," *Houston Chronicle* (December 13, 2008).

Shell, G. Richard, and Mario Moussa. *The Art of Woo: Using Strategic Persuasion to Sell Your Ideas*. New York: Penguin, 2007.

Simon, Arthur. *The Rising of Bread for the World: An Outcry of Citizens against Hunger*. Mahwah, NJ: Paulist Press, 2009.

Smith, R. Jeffrey, Michael D. Shear, and Walter Pincus. "In Obama's Inner Circle, Debate over Memos' Release Was Intense," *Washington Post* (April 24, 2009).

"So, You Want to Be an Entrepreneur," *Wall Street Journal* (February 23, 2009).

Sorensen, Theodore C. *Counselor: A Life at the Edge of History*. New York: Harper Collins, 2008.

Sosik, John, and Don Jung. *Full Range Leadership Development: Pathways for People, Profit and Planet*. New York: Psychology Press, 2010.

Spears, Larry C., ed. *Reflections on Leadership: How Robert K. Greenleaf's Theory of Servant Leadership Influenced Today's Top Management Thinkers*. New York: Wiley, 1995.

"Taking the Ted out of Turner Broadcasting," *Business Week* (May 4, 2009).

Taylor, William C., and Polly LaBarre. *Mavericks at Work: Why the Most Original Minds in Business Win*. New York: Harper Paperback, 2008.

Tichy, Noel M., and Warren G. Bennis. *Judgment: How Winning Leaders Make Great Calls*. New York: Portfolio, 2007.

"To Lead, Create a Shared Vision," *Harvard Business Review* (January 2009).

Vlasic, Bill. "G.M. Insider Wants to Show He's Tough Enough," *New York Times* (June 16, 2009).

Welch, Jack, with John A Byrne, *Jack: Straight from the Gut*. New York: Business Plus, 2001.

Wheatley, Margaret. *Finding Our Way: Leadership for an Uncertain Time*. San Francisco: Berrett-Koehler, 2005.

Weaver, Richard M. *Ideas Have Consequences*. Chicago: University of Chicago Press, 1948.

Wheatley, Margaret. *Leadership and the New Science: Discovering Order in a Chaotic World*. San Francisco: Berrett-Koehler, 1999.

White, Ronald C., Jr. *A. Lincoln: A Biography*. New York: Random House, 2009.

Wolffe, Richard. *Renegade: The Making of a President*. New York: Crown, 2009.

Zinsser, William. *On Writing Well*. New York: Harper Collins, 30th anniversary edition, 2006.

# INDEX

# ACKNOWLEDGMENTS

I've received encouragement and help along the way from many friends, notably my agent Michael Snell, who makes sure I stay connected to the front end of the "humbition" engine, mentioned early in this book, while he attends to the back end.

Helpful comments on this project in its various stages of syllabus, outline, essay, and manuscript came from Karin Botto, Elizabeth Doherty, Mike Farrell, John Fontana, Tom Healey, Bob Holliday, John DiIulio, Joe Kiernan, Lamar Reinsch, and Tom Smolich.

For the opportunity to write this book, I owe a special debt of thanks to Jesuit Father Timothy R. Lannon, president of St. Joseph's University in Philadelphia, who invited me to accept a professorship there and do research and teaching on the leadership theme. The time was right and the environment perfect.

My Jesuit friend Jim Connor, past president of the Jesuit Conference and former executive director of the Woodstock Theological Center, advanced this project in many ways, but particularly by collaborating with me in compiling the appendix presented under the title, "Principles of Ignatian Leadership." Identification, interpretation, and explanation of these core Ignatian values show how Ignatian spirituality and the Jesuit way of proceeding have made a unique contribution to the art and practice of leadership.

My thanks, finally, to Jeff Gainey, director of the University of Scranton Press, for his enthusiasm and encouragement, and for his attention to the many details involved in bringing this book into print. Expert copy-editing by John Hunckler avoided embarrassment for the author and provided smoother sailing for the reader.

# ABOUT THE AUTHOR

William J. Byron, S.J. is university professor of business and society at St. Joseph's University in Philadelphia. He is past president of the University of Scranton, The Catholic University of America, Loyola University of New Orleans, and St. Joseph's Preparatory School in Philadelphia. Author of fourteen books and editor of two, he taught economics and social ethics at Loyola University Maryland and Georgetown University. He holds a doctorate in economics from the University of Maryland.